Opera in Performance

Opera in Performance elucidates the performative dimension of contemporary opera productions.

What are the most striking and decisive moments in a performance? Why do we respond so strongly to stagings that transform familiar scenes, to performers' bodily presence, and to virtuosic voices as well as ill-disposed ones? Drawing on phenomenology and performance theory, Clemens Risi explains how these moments arise out of a dialogue between performers and the audience, representation and presence, the familiar and the new. He then applies these insights in critical descriptions of his own experiences of various singers, stagings, and performances at opera houses and festivals from across the German-speaking world over the last twenty years. As the first book to focus on what happens in performance as such, this study shifts our attention to moments that have eluded articulation and provides tools for describing our own experiences when we go to the opera.

This book will particularly interest scholars and students in theater and performance studies, musicology, and the humanities, and may also appeal to operagoers and theater professionals.

Clemens Risi is professor of theater studies at the Friedrich-Alexander-Universität Erlangen-Nürnberg.

Routledge Advances in Theatre & Performance Studies

This series is our home for cutting-edge, upper-level scholarly studies and edited collections. Considering theatre and performance alongside topics such as religion, politics, gender, race, ecology, and the avant-garde, titles are characterized by dynamic interventions into established subjects and innovative studies on emerging topics.

Dramaturgies of Interweaving
Engaging Audiences in an Entangled World
Edited by Erika Fischer-Lichte, Christel Weiler, Torsten Jost

Jerzy Grotowski and Ludwik Flaszen
Five Encounters with the Sages
By Juliusz Tyszka

American Cultures as Transnational Performance
Commons, Skills, Traces
Edited by Katrin Horn, Leopold Lippert, Ilka Saal, Pia Wiegmink

Performances that Change the Americas
Edited By Stuart Alexander Day

Barrie Kosky on the Contemporary Australian Stage
Affect, Post-Tragedy, Emergency
By Charlotte Farrell

Surviving Theatre
The Living Archive of Spectatorship
By Marco Pustianaz

Opera in Performance
Analyzing the Performative Dimension of Opera Productions
By Clemens Risi

Poetic Images, Presence, and the Theater of Kenotic Rituals
By Eniko Sepsi

Opera in Performance
Analyzing the Performative Dimension of Opera Productions

Clemens Risi

Translated by Anthony Mahler

LONDON AND NEW YORK

First published 2022
by Routledge
2 Park Square, Milton Park, Abingdon, Oxon OX14 4RN

and by Routledge
605 Third Avenue, New York, NY 10158

Routledge is an imprint of the Taylor & Francis Group, an informa business

© 2022 Clemens Risi

Translated by Anthony Mahler

Originally published: Theater der Zeit, Berlin 2017, www.theaterderzeit.de

The right of Clemens Risi to be identified as author of this work has been asserted by him in accordance with sections 77 and 78 of the Copyright, Designs and Patents Act 1988.

All rights reserved. No part of this book may be reprinted or reproduced or utilised in any form or by any electronic, mechanical, or other means, now known or hereafter invented, including photocopying and recording, or in any information storage or retrieval system, without permission in writing from the publishers.

Trademark notice: Product or corporate names may be trademarks or registered trademarks, and are used only for identification and explanation without intent to infringe.

British Library Cataloguing-in-Publication Data
A catalogue record for this book is available from the British Library

Library of Congress Cataloguing-in-Publication Data
Names: Risi, Clemens, author.
Title: Opera in performance : analyzing the performative dimension of opera productions / Clemens Risi.
Description: Abingdon, Oxon; New York : Routledge, 2021. | Includes bibliographical references and index.
Identifiers: LCCN 2021009452 (print) | LCCN 2021009453 (ebook) | ISBN 9780367645021 (hardback) | ISBN 9781003124863 (ebook)
Subjects: LCSH: Opera–21st century. | Opera–Production and direction–Germany–History–21st century. | Opera–Production and direction–Austria–History–21st century.
Classification: LCC ML1706 .R57 2021 (print) | LCC ML1706 (ebook) | DDC 792.509/05–dc23
LC record available at https://lccn.loc.gov/2021009452
LC ebook record available at https://lccn.loc.gov/2021009453

ISBN: 978-0-367-64502-1 (hbk)
ISBN: 978-0-367-64505-2 (pbk)
ISBN: 978-1-003-12486-3 (ebk)

DOI: 10.4324/9781003124863

Typeset in Times New Roman
by SPi Technologies India Pvt Ltd (Straive)

Contents

List of illustrations vi
Acknowledgments x

Introduction: Opera and the performative 1

PART I
Theoretical foundations 19

1 Beyond interpretation 21
2 Beyond semiotics: The interplay of representation and presence 43
3 Theories of performance and the performative 50
4 The entanglement of the senses: Premises from perception theory 60

PART II
Analytical approaches 69

5 Symbioses and contestations: The interaction of auditory and visual elements 71
6 The interplay of representation and presence in performance 90
7 The voice and the body in opera performances 110
8 Rhythm and experiences of time in opera 125
9 The future of opera? On the mediated experience and distribution of opera performances 148

Conclusion 162

List of performances discussed 165
Bibliography 168
Index 183

List of illustrations

Figures

0.1 *Die Entführung aus dem Serail*, staging by Calixto Bieito, Maria Bengtsson as Konstanze, Guntbert Warns as Bassa Selim, Jens Larsen as Osmin, extra, Komische Oper Berlin, 2004. Photo courtesy of Monika Rittershaus. 2
0.2 *Die Fledermaus*, staging by Hans Neuenfels, David Moss as Prince Orlofsky, Salzburg Festival, 2001. Photo courtesy of Mara Eggert and the Deutsches Theatermuseum, Munich. 3
0.3 *Radamisto*, staging by Sigrid T'Hooft, Delphine Galou as Zenobia, Berit Barfred Jansen as Fraarte, Händel-Festspiele Karlsruhe, Badisches Staatstheater Karlsruhe, 2009. Photo courtesy of Jacqueline Krause-Burberg. 7
1.1 *Don Giovanni*, staging by Calixto Bieito, Francesca Scaini as Donna Anna, José Montero as Don Ottavio, Staatsoper Hannover, 2002. Photo courtesy of A. T. Schaefer. 25
1.2 *Die Entführung aus dem Serail*, staging by Calixto Bieito, Maria Bengtsson as Konstanze, Guntbert Warns as Bassa Selim, Komische Oper Berlin, 2004. Photo courtesy of Monika Rittershaus. 28
5.1 *Le nozze di Figaro*, staging by Claus Guth, Salzburg Festival, 2006. Photo courtesy of Monika Rittershaus. 75
5.2 *Lohengrin*, staging by Peter Konwitschny, Thomas Moser as Lohengrin, Eva Marton as Ortrud, Inga Nielsen as Elsa, Hans-Joachim Ketelsen as Telramund, chorus, Staatsoper Hamburg, 1998. Photo courtesy of Jörg Landsberg. 75
5.3 *Lohengrin*, staging by Peter Konwitschny, Emily Magee as Elsa, Gran Teatre del Liceu, Barcelona, 2006. Screenshot from the DVD recording. © 2007 by Fundació del Gran Teatre del Liceu and EuroArts. 76
5.4 *Lohengrin*, staging by Peter Konwitschny, Luana DeVol as Ortrud, Gran Teatre del Liceu, Barcelona, 2006. Screenshot from the DVD recording. © 2007 by Fundació del Gran Teatre del Liceu and EuroArts. 78

List of illustrations vii

5.5 *Tannhäuser*, staging by Sebastian Baumgarten, Bayreuth Festival, 2011. Photo courtesy of the Bayreuth Festival and Enrico Nawrath. 79
5.6 *Tannhäuser*, staging by Sebastian Baumgarten, Lars Cleveman as Tannhäuser, Bayreuth Festival, 2011. Photo courtesy of the Bayreuth Festival and Enrico Nawrath. 80
5.7 *Don Carlo*, staging and dramaturgy by Jossi Wieler and Sergio Morabito, Vladimir Kuzmenko as Don Carlo, Motti Kastón as Posa, Staatsoper Stuttgart, 2001. Photo courtesy of A. T. Schaefer. 81
5.8 *Il trovatore*, staging by Balász Kovalik, Mikolaj Zalasinski as Luna, Staatstheater Nürnberg, 2012. Photo courtesy of Ludwig Olah and Staatstheater Nürnberg. 82
5.9 *Le nozze di Figaro*, staging by Christoph Marthaler, Jürg Kienberger as recitativist, Salzburg Festival, 2001. Photo courtesy of Ruth Walz. 85
6.1 *Nabucco*, staging by Hans Neuenfels, Susan Neves as Abigaille, chorus, Deutsche Oper Berlin, 2000. Photo courtesy of Detlef Kurth. 91
6.2 *Don Carlo*, staging and dramaturgy by Jossi Wieler and Sergio Morabito, Motti Kastón as Posa, Tichina Vaughn as Eboli, Staatsoper Stuttgart, 2001. Photo courtesy of A. T. Schaefer. 92
6.3 *Nabucco*, staging by Hans Neuenfels, Susan Neves as Abigaille, Alexander Heidenreich as Frank Frühkirch, Deutsche Oper Berlin, 2000. Photo courtesy of Detlef Kurth. 97
6.4 *Lohengrin*, staging by Peter Konwitschny, Emily Magee as Elsa, Luana DeVol as Ortrud, chorus, Gran Teatre del Liceu Barcelona, 2006. Screenshot from the DVD recording. © 2007 by Fundació del Gran Teatre del Liceu and EuroArts. 101
6.5 *Lohengrin*, staging by Kasper Holten, Klaus Florian Vogt as Lohengrin, Ricarda Merbeth as Elsa, Deutsche Oper Berlin, 2012. Photo courtesy of Marcus Lieberenz. 102
6.6 *Lohengrin*, staging by Kasper Holten, Klaus Florian Vogt as Lohengrin, chorus, Deutsche Oper Berlin, 2012. Photo courtesy of Marcus Lieberenz. 103
6.7 *Die Meistersinger von Nürnberg*, staging by Katharina Wagner, Franz Hawlata as Hans Sachs, extras, Bayreuth Festival, 2007. Photo courtesy of the Bayreuth Festival and Jochen Quast. 105
6.8 *Die Meistersinger von Nürnberg*, staging by Katharina Wagner, Franz Hawlata as Hans Sachs, extras, Bayreuth Festival, 2007. Photo courtesy of the Bayreuth Festival and Jörg Schulze. 106
6.9 *Die Meistersinger von Nürnberg*, staging by Katharina Wagner, Franz Hawlata as Hans Sachs, Bayreuth Festival, 2007. Photo courtesy of the Bayreuth Festival and Enrico Nawrath. 107
7.1 *Oberto*, staging by Pier'Alli, Francesca Sassu as Leonora, Giovanni Battista Parodi as Oberto, Teatro Verdi Busseto, 2007. Photo courtesy of Roberto Ricci and the Teatro Regio di Parma. 112

viii *List of illustrations*

7.2 *Médée*, staging and set design by Ursel Herrmann and Karl-Ernst Herrmann, Iano Tamar as Médée, Deutsche Oper Berlin, 2002. Photo courtesy of Bernd Uhlig. 118

8.1 *Die Walküre*, staging by Patrice Chéreau, Peter Hofmann as Siegmund, Jeannine Altmeyer as Sieglinde, Bayreuth Festival, 1980. Photo courtesy of Wilhelm Rauh and the Nationalarchiv der Richard-Wagner-Stiftung, Bayreuth, Zustiftung Wolfgang Wagner. 129

8.2 *Tristan und Isolde*, staging by Heiner Müller, Siegfried Jerusalem as Tristan, Waltraud Meier as Isolde, Bayreuth Festival, 1999. Photo courtesy of the Bayreuth Festival and Anne Kirchbach. 130

8.3 *Katja Kabanowa*, staging by Michael Thalheimer, Stephen Rügamer as Boris, Melanie Diener as Katja, Staatsoper Berlin, 2005. Photo courtesy of Monika Rittershaus. 132

8.4 *Jenůfa*, staging by Christof Loy, Jennifer Larmore as the Kostelnička, Deutsche Oper Berlin, 2012. Photo courtesy of Monika Rittershaus. 133

8.5 *Jenůfa*, staging by Christof Loy, Will Hartmann as Laca, Jennifer Larmore as the Kostelnička, Michaela Kaune as Jenůfa, Deutsche Oper Berlin, 2012. Photo courtesy of Monika Rittershaus. 136

8.6 *Don Giovanni*, staging by Calixto Bieito, Francesca Scaini as Donna Anna, Gary Magee as Don Giovanni, Staatsoper Hannover, 2002. Photo courtesy of A. T. Schaefer. 140

8.7 *Idomeneo*, staging by Hans Neuenfels, Charles Workman as Idomeneo, Deutsche Oper Berlin, 2003. Photo courtesy of Mara Eggert. 144

9.1 Screenshot showing user comments on YouTube in response to a clip of Edita Gruberová performing the final aria in Donizetti's *Lucrezia Borgia* at the Gran Teatre del Liceu, Barcelona, 2008; clip from *Die Kunst des Belcanto*, directed by Claus Wischmann and Stefan Pannen (ZDF 2008); https://www.youtube.com/all_comments?v=fFOEISUIXeM, accessed 3 June 2011, no longer available. 150

9.2 Screenshot showing user comments on YouTube in response to a clip of Edita Gruberová performing the final aria in Donizetti's *Lucrezia Borgia* at the Gran Teatre del Liceu, Barcelona, 2008; clip from *Die Kunst des Belcanto*; https://www.youtube.com/watch?v=DeJzZ0lUnIo, accessed 2 October 2013, user comment has since been removed. 151

9.3 Screenshot showing the number of views on YouTube of "Opera en el Mercado," a video recording of an opera flash mob performing parts of Verdi's *La traviata* at the Mercado Central in Valencia on 13 November 2009, https://www.youtube.com/watch?v=Ds8ryWd5aFw, accessed 18 November 2020. 155

List of illustrations   ix

9.4 Screenshot showing the number of views on YouTube of "Christmas Food Court Flash Mob, Hallelujah Chorus – Must See!," a video recording of a flash mob performing the "Hallelujah" chorus from Handel's *Messiah* in the food court of a mall in Niagara Falls on 13 November 2010, https://www.youtube.com/watch?v=SXh7JR9oKVE, accessed 18 November 2020.   156

Musical examples

1.1 Johann Strauss, *Die Fledermaus: Operette in 3 Akten*, RV 503, libretto by Richard Genée, ed. Michael Rot, vol. 3 of *Neue Johann Strauss Gesamtausgabe*, ser. 1, group 2 (Vienna: Strauss Edition, 1999), 207–8. Reproduced by the kind permission of Schott Music, Mainz.   22
1.2 Strauss, *Die Fledermaus*, 211.   24
1.3 Wolfgang Amadeus Mozart, *Entführung aus dem Serail*, K. 384, ed. Gerhard Croll, vol. 12 of *Neue Ausgabe sämtlicher Werke*, ser. 2, *Bühnenwerke*, group 5, *Opern und Singspiele* (Kassel: Bärenreiter, 1982), 129–30. Reproduced by the permission of Bärenreiter-Verlag, Kassel.   26
5.1 Wolfgang Amadeus Mozart, *Le nozze di Figaro*, K. 492, ed. Ludwig Finscher, vols. 16.1–2 of *Neue Ausgabe sämtlicher Werke*, ser. 2, *Bühnenwerke*, group 5, *Opern und Singspiele* (Kassel: Bärenreiter, 1973), 526–27. Reproduced by the permission of Bärenreiter-Verlag, Kassel.   73
8.1 Leoš Janáček, *Jenůfa: Její pastorkyňa (Ihre Ziehtochter)*, trans. Max Brod, piano score (Vienna: Universal-Edition, 1917), 176–77. © by Universal Edition, Vienna, UE 13932 (previously UE 5821).   135

Acknowledgments

This book and the thoughts presented in it are largely due to the inspiring atmosphere at the Freie Universität Berlin's collaborative research center "Performing Cultures," of which I had the privilege to be a member. First and foremost, I would like to thank Erika Fischer-Lichte for her support as well as Christa Brüstle and Jens Roselt, whom I had the opportunity to work with for many years. I would also like to thank David J. Levin and Albrecht Riethmüller for promoting my work and ideas in multiple respects.

My thanks go to the publishers, opera houses, and photographers that generously provided me with documentary material on the performances; to Anthony Mahler for the brilliant translation; to Routledge and Laura Hussey for including my book in their series; to Laura Kersten for help in proofreading the final manuscript; and to the Friedrich-Alexander-Universität Erlangen-Nürnberg, the Universitätsbund, and the Dr. Alice Rössler-Stiftung for supporting the translation financially. I am very grateful to my family for all the different ways they provide support. Without Bettina, this book would not exist; I owe her all my gratitude.

Introduction
Opera and the performative

> The operatic stage must challenge the spectator in such a way that he sits on the very edge of his seat and from there risks, wide awake and with critical pleasure, privately engaging with what is offered, with every aria, with every fugue, and with every movement.
>
> –Hans Neuenfels[1]

Komische Oper Berlin, June 2004. The public dress rehearsal of Calixto Bieito's staging of Wolfgang Amadeus Mozart's *Die Entführung aus dem Serail* was being performed in front of a full house, Kirill Petrenko conducting.[2] During Konstanze's aria "Martern aller Arten" (Tortures most surely await),[3] in which she steadfastly resists Bassa Selim's demands that she love him, the singer Maria Bengtsson as Konstanze was bound to a chair and, like us, had to watch as a prostitute, played by an extra, was tortured with a knife to the point of unconsciousness by the pimp Osmin (Jens Larsen) and was then desecrated and slaughtered (see Figure 0.1).

In the middle of the vocally most demanding passage of the aria,[4] the audience broke out in an uproar. Boos, whistles, loud calls like "Stop!" or "Mozart would turn in his grave!" increased to the point that for a while the noise level in the auditorium noticeably exceeded that on the stage and in the orchestra pit.

Bieito's staging of Mozart's *Entführung aus dem Serail* made us ask what terms like "Serail" (seraglio), "Haremsmäuse" (harem-mice),[5] or "Martern aller Arten" (Tortures most surely await) mean for us and how the oppression of women and violence against them can be conveyed today. The chosen setting was a brothel; the sexual and violent practices shown were—as one could read in the press—widespread in the scene. One didn't have to wait for long for the predictable reactions. In addition to the audience's response at the dress rehearsal, there was an immediate uproar among the circle of sponsors and friends of the Komische Oper Berlin and extended debates at performance talks, in university seminars, and, of course, in the press, from quality feature articles to the tabloids. On 22 June 2004, the *BZ*, the Berlin paper with the largest circulation, devoted its entire front page ("Sex Scandal

DOI: 10.4324/9781003124863-1

2 *Introduction*

Figure 0.1 Die Entführung aus dem Serail, staging by Calixto Bieito, Maria Bengtsson as Konstanze, Guntbert Warns as Bassa Selim, Jens Larsen as Osmin, extra, Komische Oper Berlin, 2004.

Photo courtesy of Monika Rittershaus.

at the Komische Oper—And What's More, Our Taxes Are Paying for It!") and two more pages in the middle section to the production.[6]

Scene change: Salzburg Festival, summer 2001, Felsenreitschule. Johann Strauss's operetta *Die Fledermaus* was playing, directed by Hans Neuenfels and conducted by Marc Minkowski. A television team at the premiere of the festival captured the audience's reactions: "It's hard for an Austrian to watch." "It is disrespectful to the audience and our foreign guests. I feel ashamed for those who created it. Disgusting!" "This is shit! This should be banned, you understand? Everybody should go to the fucking jail, including Gérard Mortier, the idiot!" "I booed, I also cried because that is all my youth, that is my entire childhood. I heard all of that on New Year's Eve. So I think it is really sad that Austria has gone so downhill that we put up with such things."[7]

What had happened? Gérard Mortier, the artistic director of the festival since 1991, had dared to alienate his audience once again and even more radically in his last year with his choice of stage director and with that director's view on one of the most beloved pieces of the repertoire. Particularly controversial was the appearance of the famous vocalist and percussionist David Moss in the role of Prince Orlofsky, a role that usually belongs as a trousers role to the classic repertoire of mezzo-sopranos and altos. Especially Moss's first appearance with the couplet "Ich lade gern mir Gäste ein" (I like to invite guests) aroused loudly voiced displeasure from most of the festival visitors—and at the same time it motivated the DVD company Arthaus to concentrate their advertising strategy entirely on Moss (see Figure 0.2).[8]

David Moss was wearing a dressing gown and striped pajamas with his shirt unbuttoned such that one could see his naked upper body; his hair was done in Rasta style. But his vocal performance is what particularly attracted everyone's attention. What Moss did *not* offer was the usual and expected bel canto ideal of a "beautiful or brilliant voice characterized by a wide-ranging, full, warm, soft, and dazzling sound with a regular vibrato," which is produced by "a low position of the larynx, an expanded vocal tract, and an optimal balance of expiratory pressure and laryngeal function"[9]—an ideal that, for example, the mezzo-soprano Brigitte Fassbaender has inscribed into the memories of many operagoers and that is always present as a sonorous

Figure 0.2 Die Fledermaus, staging by Hans Neuenfels, David Moss as Prince Orlofsky, Salzburg Festival, 2001.

Photo courtesy of Mara Eggert and the Deutsches Theatermuseum, Munich.

expectation. Moss opposed this firmly established vocal code with a palette of expressions intensified using a wireless microphone, which particularly irritated many audience members and collided with their expectations. This palette included bass, full, and breathy tones; the voice flipping over into a falsetto; wheezing, croaking, and sighing noises; and imprecise intonation. To top it all off, Moss's Orlofsky also snorted a line of cocaine between single phrases—a distressing image whose duration interfered with the musical continuity of the progression of stanzas and prioritized plot over music.

What unites these two events is a bundle of seemingly typical operatic performance practices that have been spreading for the last few decades, particularly in the German-speaking world.[10] They are quite often referred to with the concept of *Regietheater* (director's theater)—a concept that is often criticized in the same breath due to its lack of conceptual precision, a concept that is, in any case, itself intensely disputed.[11]

The performances are usually announced as productions of traditional material and function in particular through the idea and practice of the repertory system.[12] Regietheater thus essentially has to do with well-known works in which creative authorship is ascribed to the composer on the one hand and the director on the other. These works create an expectation for both recognition and surprise through deviation. (World premieres of new compositions and the unearthing of forgotten works are not the focus of these performance practices.)

Such stagings particularly attend to the relationship of auditory and visual elements, that is, to the question of how the musical and scenic levels interact. This attention to the interplay of listening and viewing particularly applies to the performers and singers since the body is given just as much weight as the voice, both in the staging and in the audience's perception.

The deviations of what one experiences from what many expect in the performance of a well-known work of the canonical repertoire quite often culminate in irritation about whether the experience of the staging can be called an interpretation of a well-known work at all or whether it is instead something entirely different. The premieres of such Regietheater productions are often (but not always) accompanied by vociferous audience reactions, ranging from simultaneous approval and dislike to protests, scandals, and walkouts.

Hardly any other form of theater can trigger such vehement reactions—in both positive and negative forms—as performances of the operatic repertoire. From fans' declarations of love to furious and loud protests and uproars, opera currently invites perhaps the most diverse and extreme forms of expression in the performative interaction between the stage and the audience. It is this interrelationship of performers and audience in the singular performative event of opera—for which the interplay of bodies, voices, time, and perception are determinate—that the following reflections are devoted to.

At least since the debates about Wieland Wagner's Bayreuth productions of *Die Meistersinger von Nürnberg* in 1956 and 1963—and in particular since the arrival of Regietheater in opera (beginning in the 1970s with directors like Ruth Berghaus, Patrice Chéreau, Götz Friedrich, Joachim Herz, Harry Kupfer, and Hans Neuenfels)—the question of the possibilities, limits, and necessities of stage directing in opera has been a topic of discussion. This is the question of the much-cited connection of "work and reproduction,"[13] the question of the supposed dichotomy of substance and change, of preserving a "work's substance"[14] and changing it through alterations.

When the discussion is about what approach is "right," one can observe a real fight between preservationists and reformers. On the side of the preservationists rages the fear of destruction. They speak of "operatic theater" as a "construction site for dismantling the texts,"[15] of an "incapacitation and degradation of the texts" that leads to the "incapacitation of the spectator," and of the "stranglehold of alleged interpreters who degrade the work into a basis for their own way of dealing with reality."[16] With regard to the staging practices at the Bayreuth Festival, some speak of a "workshop for producing tools that do not lead to permanent renewal but to the destruction of the inventory" and of "tortured, abused, disheveled, jumbled, degraded works," of works that should, some hope, "finally" come to "rest" through the closure of such workshops.[17] What is the threat here? What is it that is allegedly abused and destroyed? With an object like music theater, which actually only finds its purpose in the fleeting and multimedial form of a one-time theatrical event, diagnoses like those cited are extremely difficult to verify. This is because an opera staging, and this is one of the starting theses of this study, transforms a template or material into a new medium, since the score and libretto do not provide any bodies, voices, or movements. Each performance leads to a meeting of the most dissimilar events—to a conjuncture of more or less foreseeable, planned actions (shaped by the stage design, costumes, and choreography) and entirely unforeseeable events like the particular presence or state of a singer, performer, or conductor on a certain day and the inexhaustible reservoir of associations, expectations, and current states in the audience. Transforming the material (that is, the score) into another material (namely, the performance) inevitably changes it. And every era, every generation, continually redefines the freedoms and limits to these changes. Performance—in contrast to reading or academically engaging with texts, for instance—also means leaving something behind; it means setting aside the world of printed traces on the page of the book or score and the imaginations connected to it and negating, after a certain point, the reality of what is written so as to devote oneself to the reality of the living moment in scenic realization, to creating a new reality.

Today operatic performance practices seem to be moving in three directions. First, there are attempts to expose texts to new frictions by combining them with other material. For example, a few years ago in an interview with Barbara Beyer, the director Sebastian Baumgarten expressed a desire to be able to work with fragments in opera: "I would be more interested in treating extracts of Verdi, Mozart, Bach, or Wagner, in working with fragments. In an extract

6 *Introduction*

or an enlargement, I am still able to describe something precisely, I can still delve into it."[18] Such a technique has been increasingly practiced in recent years under the term *creations*, which—going back to an idea of the artistic director Gérard Mortier's—has been particularly employed at festivals like the Ruhrtriennale. It has to do with hybrid forms that arise in interstices between theater and opera and that grant music a conspicuous place. These hybrids do not, however, worry about borders between genres or feel beholden to the unity of a score or the like; instead, they freely compile fragments from very different contexts. Such "creations" by, for example, Christoph Marthaler (*The Unanswered Question*, Theater Basel, 1997) or Alain Platel (*Wolf oder wie Mozart auf den Hund kam*, Ruhrtriennale, 2003) can truly be described as reviving historical practices of performance and staging, such as pasticcio (collecting individual arias or entire acts from different works into a new constellation), or very generally as reintroducing traditions of interpolated arias, abbreviations, arrangements, and so on—practices that went out of fashion with the strengthening of the concept of the work in the nineteenth century.

Second, demands for *Werktreue* (faithfulness to a work and text), which were thought to have been overcome, still stubbornly persist among both those who experience and those who produce operas. One continually hears from opponents of the trend in Regietheater to revamp operas: Why can't one make the scenery as it was in the time when the music being performed originated, that is, as it was in the eighteenth or nineteenth century? It is, of course, possible to apply the knowledge we have about historical performances—as is done, for example, in the performances supervised and produced by the Centre de musique baroque de Versailles or in Sigrid T'Hooft's powerful stagings, which have been performed with great success (like Handel's *Radamisto* at the 2009 Händel-Festspiele in Karlsruhe; see Figure 0.3).

Yet as informative and aesthetically fascinating as this extension of experiments with historically informed performance practices to the scenery may be, neither the experiences nor the effects from that time can be reconstructed in today's utterly different performance and viewing conditions. In this regard, René Jacobs once rightly argued that to achieve the historical viewing conditions of the baroque, there couldn't be any electric lighting or a single restroom in the theater.[19] In addition, past audiences had a familiarity with the specific meanings of particular gestures that singers made on stage—a familiarity that has now been lost.[20] Historical gestures can be studied and reproduced, but they will always be a construction and never a reconstruction since the effect is a priori a different one based on our lack of understanding. Immediacy and familiarity with the language of gestures and movement can be achieved if current, familiar, and also thoroughly everyday gestures are employed—a means of (often modernizing) Regietheater. When one is confronted with repertoires of historical gestures, their foreignness comes to light, as does the fact that they have lost the clear legibility they possessed in their historical epoch. With the recognition of this foreignness, the staging practices of historically informed performance practices prove to be no more legitimate as methods of performance than other staging

Figure 0.3 *Radamisto*, staging by Sigrid T'Hooft, Delphine Galou as Zenobia, Berit Barfred Jansen as Fraarte, Händel-Festspiele Karlsruhe, Badisches Staatstheater Karlsruhe, 2009.

Photo courtesy of Jacqueline Krause-Burberg.

practices that work with choreographic language or stylized formalizations they develop themselves.

Viewed in this way, "historically informed" means acknowledging that one cannot reconstruct history because one cannot reproduce all the same conditions (we are different, we hear differently, we experience differently). But it also means accepting that among the infinitely many imaginable performance realities for a certain musical-dramatic template, there isn't *one* that is fundamentally better than the others. And finally, being "historically informed" should entail recognizing that the tradition of handling the material at hand in a free, varying, improvisational, and experimental way is much longer than the tradition of clinging to existing conventions. If we start with such a desire to experiment, it becomes clear that historically informed performance practices actually do have potential beyond the niches of special historical festivals. This desire to experiment pushes the door wide open to the present, making today's visual vocabulary and repertoires of movement available to opera.

The performance practices that are especially widespread in the German-speaking world and that can be subsumed under the keyword *Regietheater in opera* move between the named trends of fragmentation and the recompilation of material on the one hand and the demands for historical performance practices in the sense of a supposedly realizable *Werktreue* on the other. This trend maintains an opera's musical dramaturgy while at the same time

8 *Introduction*

radically questioning, reexamining, and recontextualizing the transmitted and ascertainable strata of meaning in the available texts (libretto, score, discourse on the staging history). Tangibly changing the shape of the score in its musical dramaturgy (such as its sequence and completeness) still represents a taboo in this operatic performance practice. Alterations to the musical succession and dramaturgy (such as the interruptions in Peter Konwitschny's Berlin production of *Don Giovanni* in 2003 or his Hamburg production of *Die Meistersinger* in 2002) that go beyond historically conventional deletions or careful reinstrumentalizations of, for example, continuo instruments are radical exceptions.

Regietheater's primarily intellectual engagement with new readings and meanings has increasingly brought the "other" side of experiencing opera performances to light again: the experience of moments that cannot be described as the representation *of something* but rather as moments that primarily trigger intense, bodily reactions, moments that are frequently characterized by irritation, intensity, the suspension of understanding meaning, the coming to consciousness of perception, and conscious experiences of time. I am referring here to the interrelation of representation and presence, of sense and sensuality, at work in every opera performance; this interrelation determines the perceptual process that characterizes each individual performance.[21] In this relation, representation and presence are not at all mutually exclusive. On the contrary, sense and sensuality reciprocally determine one another. Moments of presence are responsible for endowing a scene with a specific meaning, and a process of understanding meaning must precede the suspension of understanding it. As Hans-Thies Lehmann would formulate it: perceiving singing actors on the operatic stage alternates between believing what they portray (representation) and admiring their autodeixis (the act of performers presenting themselves in their qualities).[22]

If the performative dimension of opera is to move into the center of this study, then it must address the question of how to grasp this dimension theoretically and analytically. Scholarship on opera and music theater, which is traditionally (and internationally) almost exclusively at home in musicology, primarily understands itself as a history of composition and librettos and usually attends particularly to the score in its analysis. In contrast, the question of an adequate analytical approach to the performative dimension of music theater has largely remained ignored, although one can find recent initial attempts to investigate it in both theater studies and musicology. Here I would like to name the exemplary work of Carolyn Abbate, Robert Braunmüller, Joy Calico, Linda and Michael Hutcheon, Gundula Kreuzer, David J. Levin, Christopher Morris, Stephan Mösch, Gerd Rienäcker, Mark Schachtsiek, Jürgen Schläder, Mary Ann Smart, and Robert Sollich.[23] Each in their own way, they have all allowed the performative events of opera productions to clearly inspire their thinking. My own thinking on the performative dimension owes a lot to their work. But their studies tend to focus more on how stagings transform the templates and less on the performative event as such. They usually do not vigorously engage with the performative dimension.

In musicology, two directions have become established in the recent scholarship: "music as performance"[24] and interpretation research.[25] Insights from them have also been productive for my reflections, even though the exponents of "music as performance" have so far largely left out opera as a field of investigation. As for interpretation research, I will later explain in detail how many of these studies tend to establish or begin with a hierarchy between score and performance[26]—a hierarchy that codifies the score as the starting point and goal for analyzing interpretations or performances.

In contrast to this position, and by expanding on and broadening the positions named above, this study is devoted to establishing a new understanding of the relationship of text and performance, to shifting the focus. Instead of speaking of a performance as an interpretation of the score, I argue that the score is to be understood as one of many different materials[27] for producing a performance. This shift in focus directs our attention to the elements and events of a performance that cannot be found in the score but determine the effect and perception of a performance just as much as, if not more than, the template materials such as the script or the score. What I mean are the concrete sounds of individual voices, the concrete movements of individual bodies, communication that always occurs in new and different ways, and the dialogue between the performers and the audience. This opens our eyes to what is unique about performance, to what differentiates it from texts and other artifacts: namely, that it only exists in the moment, in the time of its appearance, and in the bodily copresence and interaction of performers and audience members.

This study proposes that we analyze opera performances by starting with and focusing on their performative dimension. The study is devoted to transferring the concept of performance as event to opera by building on and developing current scholarship on performance theory,[28] theories of the performative,[29] and perception theory, especially in phenomenology.[30] The study's approach is based on the observation that only categories from the post-1960s performative turn in the arts—the concentration on materiality, the emphasis on sensual and not meaningful moments, and the focus on the eventness of performance—can describe certain moments that occur in opera performances.

This study understands itself as a plea to transfer our (often latent) awareness of the relevance of opera's performative dimension into a form of academic engagement that considers how all the elements that constitute performance are perceived. What I am proposing is a new orientation or realignment for analyzing opera that addresses concrete examples and focuses on the interaction of auditory and visual elements,[31] the interplay of representation and presence,[32] the relation of voice and body,[33] the experience of temporality and rhythm,[34] and the question of the possibility of mediatizing opera in performance.[35]

My use of both the concept of staging or production and that of performance is justified by the heterogenous situation sketched above, in which the focus in the opera business is still predominantly on the (musical) work and in so-called Regietheater, on the director's position as the authorial agent as well as on playing with expectations and on the intricate entanglement of representation and moments of presence. While the concept of staging directs attention to the (plannable) process of transforming preexisting material into the here and now of scenic realization, the perspective of performance takes into account precisely this here and now without looking back at what precedes the performance. Where the study refers to the discourse of operatic performance and attends to the question of framing the expectations that result from the concept of the operatic repertoire, it also sometimes operates with the concept of staging. But it programmatically does not discuss staging in the sense of a global structure of work transformation, that is, of a work viewed as a totality; instead, it focuses on single moments or sequences that are conspicuous in a performance.

The study does not intend to investigate stagings of operas by a particular composer (for example, by Mozart or Verdi or Wagner) or from a particular epoch (for example, from the baroque or the nineteenth century). It is not about, for instance, identifying a particular style in stagings of Mozart, Verdi, or Wagner. Bieito's and Neuenfels's stagings of Verdi are too different from one another to do so (as are the Bieito's and Neuenfels's stagings of Mozart). And while the similarity of Bieito's stagings of Mozart and Verdi on the one hand or of Neuenfels's on the other could tempt one to look for particular staging styles with regard to a director instead of with regard to a composer, the question of a director's personal style is also inadequate, since, first, directors are influenced by trends that connect them to stagings by other directors and, second, opera performances can, of course, in their specific effect never be completely reduced to a director's personality. There is the tendency in the discourse about stagings and performances to identify them with the name of the director, but in addition to the conceptual work of the directorial team, many other factors decisively contribute to creating a performance—in particular, the performers and singers with their own particular ideas and the audience with entirely different ideas and expectations. This study thus examines the relationship of the materials employed in performances independently of a particular composer or director. It is about elements and categories of performance that result from the interaction of different materials and how the audience experiences them. But one could indeed also find certain isolated commonalities in a director's staging style, and I will also go into how stagings react in their scenic decisions to certain musical or musical-dramaturgical features of the staged work or to a specific compositional style.

When, for example, I attend to Bieito's staging of Mozart's *Entführung aus dem Serail*, I am not primarily concerned with Mozart's opera and also not with the scenic potential in the materials that can be renewed or implemented or realized by a staging in the sense of interpretation. And I am also not primarily concerned with appreciating a director's signature style. Instead, the study emphasizes the mode of realization, which is medially different from that of the templates. The metonymic shift in "Bieito's *Entführung*" (Bieito as a metonymy for everyone who contributed to the performance) thus marks the creation of something new, which only has to do with the templates to the extent that they enter into the performance as material.

That the music—as it is given in the score—is normally performed in its entirety and in its given order is, on the one hand, a concession to the claim, still valid in opera, of the unity of the work's substance (spoken theater has been profoundly altering templates for many years). But on the other hand, it determines the frame: a frame that in its familiarity evokes specific expectations, triggers specific memories, and thereby first sets in motion the play of friction between the familiar and what deviates from it. By at least adopting a well-known structure (music and plot), this frame creates tension with the performance. This tension could not arise if unfamiliar material (that is, new musical material) were employed, and it would also be less if the performance did not cling to a firm musical structure. In this context, the special perceptual situation in "creations" becomes clear: here, well-known excerpts evoke the addressed frame and trigger for one moment an island of familiarity, perhaps with a trace of melancholy: Where is the opera in its entirety? Where is the rest of the familiar Verdi or Mozart music? One effect of these "creations" is the continual evocation of these absences of music. Here too, tension, which in this case is the effect of absence, would not be able to appear without the otherwise practiced adherence to entirety.

This investigation furthermore does not intend to judge which staging is right or wrong or what a staging "may" or "may not" do. Instead, the focus is on the question of why and how a certain performance was able to affect the audience in a certain way. When the media or an audience judges a performance, they very often refer to how close or distant it is from a well-known template as a criterion. What this normally evaluates, however, are effects that arise in the performance on the basis of all the employed materials—so the evaluative categories should actually be acquired from performative reality. But since people evaluating an opera usually do not possess any categories for performative reality, the positive effect of a performative constellation is merely explained by saying that the staging stayed true to the score at its base, while a negative effect is attributed to the claim that the staging was not adequate to the score. Concretely, this means that when a performance was not gripping or when a performer was dull or when the interaction of plot, text, music, and image did not amaze or move or something like that, then people do not normally look for performative flaws but rather for infidelity toward what is commonly understood as the work. In this infidelity, they also often see the reason for the inadequacy of the performance.

This principle also functions in reverse: a director can move very far from an allegedly secure understanding of the work, yet if the results of the performance are compelling, then many people will be of the opinion that the performance was so good because the staging did justice to the work. And again they do not look at the performative qualities of the performance;

instead, they simply compare it with the templates. The distance from the templates can be equally great in both positive and negative cases, but in both, people will explain success or failure by how close or distant the performance is in relation to the templates. What is more, the criteria for judging a performance as "close" or "distant" are normally acquired from personal experience—for example, from someone's own first experience with a particular opera—but are used as objective criteria. The call for *Werktreue* and the search for levels of meaning in the work thus evade the necessity of explaining the performative. A lack of categories to do so leads to this interpretive state of emergency.

Finally, the present study is also not about giving an overview of the fundamental tendencies in current operatic staging practices, as, for example, Jürgen Schläder and Stephan Mösch have at least begun to do in their essays "Strategien der Opern-Bilder" (Strategies of operatic imagery) and "Störung, Verstörung, Zerstörung: Regietheater als Rezeptionsproblem" (Disturbance, distress, destruction: Regietheater as a problem of reception); it is rather a systematic investigation into the categories (that is, into the interaction of auditory and visual elements, the interplay of representation and presence, the relation of voice and body, and the experience of temporality and rhythm) that are relevant to experiencing opera in its performative dimension—no matter which type of staging practice is at issue.[36] The thesis is, in any case, that different operatic staging practices or aesthetics of staging make different demands on and challenges to perception. This means that the particular relationship of the categories that I claim are relevant to all opera performances should allow us to draw conclusions about different staging aesthetics since the particular relationship is a result of each different aesthetic. To systematize this and, if possible, to convert it into a typology must, however, be left to future investigations. This study endeavors to sound out the range and limits of perspectives in theater studies and musicology so as to be able to attend to the specific features of performances in opera. The primary question is to what extent the perspectives shaped by theories of performance, performativity, and phenomenology can contribute to more precisely understanding, describing, and explaining the processes and conditions of performance and perception that are specific to opera performances.

My thoughts on contemporary opera performances are primarily devoted to productions since the 1970s, that is, since the spread of Regietheater in opera, with a focus on performances from the last fifteen to twenty years of repertoire classics by Cherubini, Donizetti, Handel, Janáček, Massenet, Mozart, Puccini, Johann Strauss, Verdi, and Wagner in stagings by Sebastian Baumgarten, Calixto Bieito, Thomas Bischoff, Patrice Chéreau, Claus Guth, Ursel and Karl-Ernst Herrmann, Kasper Holten, Peter Konwitschny, Balázs Kovalik, Christof Loy, Christoph Marthaler, Heiner Müller, Peter Mussbach, Hans Neuenfels, Michael Thalheimer, Katharina Wagner, Karsten Wiegand, and the director duo Jossi Wieler and Sergio Morabito.

The stagings have been performed at festivals and opera houses such as the Bayreuth Festival, the Deutsche Oper Berlin, the Komische Oper Berlin, the Staatsoper Berlin, the Staatsoper Hamburg, the Staatsoper Hannover, the Staatstheater Nürnberg, the Salzburg Festival, and the Staatsoper Stuttgart. In addition, I examine the performances of individual singers like Cecilia Bartoli, Maria Bengtsson, Edita Gruberová, David Moss, and Anna Netrebko. With a few exceptions, I experienced all the performances I discuss live. The book combines and integrates a series of preliminary publications that have appeared in different places, in earlier versions, and in different contexts; it fits them together, however, into this larger theoretical framework for the first time.[37]

The investigations are about finding a way to analyze, diagnose, and describe the complexity of opera's performative dimension. Chapter 5 discusses different relationships in the interaction of auditory and visual elements. It is concerned with cases in which the integration of sound and image is determined by the music—that is, with when the staging reacts to certain particularities of the musical composition—but also with cases of the reverse, in which the interaction is perceived as if the musical shape resulted from the staging. Chapter 6 particularly attends to the relationship of the significative and material qualities of performance, that is, the duality of every body and every voice on stage. The effect of this duality is that as a member of the audience, I perceive at every moment both the fictive body of the character and the concrete body of the performer, and as a listener, I hear in every moment both the fictive voice of the character and the concrete, individual voice of the singer. Chapter 7 maintains the focus of Chapter 6 as here too voice and body are at the center of observation, but now in their relation to one another. It investigates how the bodily movements of singers interact with their voices and how the voices and bodies of audience members interact with those of performers. Chapter 8 treats the central question of temporal relationships in performance—that is, the potential of every single performance to create its own new temporalities—and discusses the hypothesis that a performance can transform objective, measurable time into its own entirely different felt time. Finally, Chapter 9 poses the question of whether and to what extent the particularities ascertained for live opera performances can be transferred into a mediatized format or can even be intensified in mediatized forms.

My interest is thus in opera *in performance*, understood as a dialogue of stage and audience, as an active relationship between spectators or listeners and performers on stage. The focus of attention is on what plays out between the participants of an opera performance, where *participants* means both the performers and the audience. How can what happens in the moment of a performance be described and explained? What are the important, striking, decisive moments when an opera is performed? And what about them can be described and formulated better than has been the case so far through a focus on the performative with the approaches provided by performance theory and theories of the performative?

14 *Introduction*

Notes

1. Klaus Umbach, "'Oper muß wieder anstrengend werden': Regisseur Hans Neuenfels über Probleme und Skandale des Musiktheaters," *Der Spiegel*, 15 November 1982, 249.
2. The premiere was on 20 June 2004. I attended the dress rehearsal on 18 June 2004 and a performance on 10 December 2004.
3. English translation from J. D. McClatchy, trans., *Seven Mozart Librettos* (New York: W. W. Norton, 2011), 199.
4. Wolfgang Amadeus Mozart, *Die Entführung aus dem Serail*, K. 384, ed. Gerhard Croll, vol. 12 of *Neue Ausgabe sämtlicher Werke*, ser. 2, *Bühnenwerke*, group 5, *Opern und Singspiele* (Kassel: Bärenreiter, 1982), 214–15.
5. McClatchy, *Seven Mozart Librettos*, 251.
6. "Sex-Skandal an Komischer Oper – Und dafür gibt's auch noch Steuergelder!," *BZ*, 22 June 2004: 1, 14–15.
7. *titel-thesen-temperamente*, aired 19 August 2001, on ARD.
8. I attended the performance at the Salzburg Festival on 22 August 2001. See Johann Strauss, *Die Fledermaus*, staging by Hans Neuenfels, Marc Minkowski conducting, recorded at the Salzburg Festival 2001 (Leipzig: Arthaus 2003), DVD.
9. Theda Weber-Lucks, "Vokale Performancekunst: Zur Verknüpfung von Stimme, Körper, Emotion – Meredith Monk und Diamanda Galas," *Positionen: Beiträge zur Neuen Musik* 40 (1999): 28.
10. Even though Johann Strauss's *Die Fledermaus* is an operetta according to the conditions of its creation and to historical genre classifications, today this work is part of the operatic repertoire with regard to its performance practices. Hans Neuenfels's Salzburg production was thus based, in particular in its performative dimension and the dynamics of its reception, on the same conditions as the stagings and performances of operas that this study otherwise treats exclusively.
11. On the debate over the concept of *Regietheater*, see, among others Wolfgang Ullrich, "'Die Kunst ist Ausdruck ihrer Zeit': Genese und Problematik eines Topos der Kunsttheorie," in *Angst vor der Zerstörung: Der Meister Künste zwischen Archiv und Erneuerung*, ed. Robert Sollich, Clemens Risi, Sebastian Reus, and Stephan Jöris (Berlin: Theater der Zeit, 2008), 233–46; and Stephan Mösch, "Geistes Gegenwart? Überlegungen zur Ästhetik des Regietheaters in der Oper," in *Mitten im Leben: Musiktheater von der Oper zur Everyday Performance*, ed. Anno Mungen (Würzburg: Königshausen and Neumann, 2011), 85–103.
12. Canonization processes have recently become a focus in the humanities, especially in literary studies. The concepts of a repertoire classic and a classic staging are to be understood in the sense of their significant roles within the canon and not at all as belonging to an epoch.
13. See, for example, Sigrid Wiesmann, ed., *Werk und Wiedergabe: Musiktheater exemplarisch interpretiert* (Bayreuth: Mühl'scher Universitätsverlag Bayreuth Werner Fehr, 1980).
14. On the problematization of the concept of the work (in opera), see, for example, Lydia Goehr, *The Imaginary Museum of Musical Works: An Essay in the Philosophy of Music* (Oxford: Oxford University Press, 1992); Horst Weber, ed., *Oper und Werktreue* (Stuttgart: J. B. Metzler, 1994).
15. Laurenz Lütteken, "Wider den Zeitgeist der Beliebigkeit: Ein Plädoyer für die Freiheit des Textes und die Grenzen der Interpretation," *wagnerspectrum* 2 (2005): 24.
16. Lütteken, 24.
17. Lütteken, 28.
18. Sebastian Baumgarten, "Aus dem Geist der Musik heraus das Heutige denken," in: *Warum Oper? Gespräche mit Opernregisseuren*, ed. Barbara Beyer (Berlin: Alexander, 2005), 49.

Introduction 15

19 René Jacobs, "Händel-Aufführung heute: Instrumente und Gesang in Oper und Oratorium," (lecture, "Alte Musik – live" series, Musikinstrumenten-Museum Berlin, 8 June 2008).
20 The strictly regulated gesture practices in theater corresponded to ceremonial practices outside of theater, such as at official court events, which were often just as regulated.
21 On this, see especially Chapters 2 and 6.
22 See Hans-Thies Lehmann, "Die Gegenwart des Theaters," in *Transformationen: Theater der neunziger Jahre*, ed. Erika Fischer-Lichte, Doris Kolesch, and Christel Weiler (Berlin: Theater der Zeit, 1999), 17.
23 Carolyn Abbate, *In Search of Opera* (Princeton: Princeton University Press, 2001); Abbate, "Music—Drastic or Gnostic?," *Critical Inquiry* 30, no. 3 (Spring 2004): 505–36; Robert Braunmüller, *Oper als Drama: Das realistische Musiktheater Walter Felsensteins* (Tübingen: Max Niemeyer, 2002); Braunmüller, "Auf dem Marsch durch die Institutionen: Götz Friedrichs Bayreuther *Tannhäuser* von 1972," in *Realistisches Musiktheater: Walter Felsenstein; Geschichte, Erben, Gegenpositionen*, ed. Werner Hintze, Clemens Risi, and Robert Sollich (Berlin: Theater der Zeit, 2008), 65–72; Joy H. Calico, *Brecht at the Opera* (Berkeley: University of California Press, 2008); Linda Hutcheon and Michael Hutcheon, *Opera: Desire, Disease and Death* (Lincoln: University of Nebraska Press, 1996); Gundula Kreuzer, "Authentizität, Visualisierung, Bewahrung: Das reisende 'Wagner-Theater' und die Konservierbarkeit von Inszenierungen," in Sollich, Risi, Reus, and Jöris, *Angst vor der Zerstörung*, 139–60; Kreuzer, "Voices from Beyond: Verdi's *Don Carlos* and the Modern Stage," *Cambridge Opera Journal* 18, no. 2 (July 2006): 151–79; Kreuzer, "*Wagner-Dampf*: Steam in *Der Ring des Nibelungen* and Operatic Production," *Opera Quarterly* 27, no. 2–3 (Spring/Summer 2011): 179–219; David J. Levin, "Reading a Staging/Staging a Reading," *Cambridge Opera Journal* 9, no. 1 (March 1997): 47–71; Levin: "Response to James Treadwell," *Cambridge Opera Journal* 10 (1998): 307–11; Levin, *Unsettling Opera: Staging Mozart, Wagner, and Zemlinsky* (Chicago: University of Chicago Press, 2007); Levin, "*Die Meistersinger von Nürnberg*: Drastisch oder gnostisch?," in Sollich, Risi, Reus, and Jöris, *Angst vor der Zerstörung*, 260–71; Levin, "The Mise-en-scène of Mediation: Wagner's *Götterdämmerung* (Stuttgart Opera, Peter Konwitschny, 2000–2005)," *Opera Quarterly* 27, no. 2–3 (Spring/Summer 2011): 219–34; Christopher Morris, "Digital Diva: Opera on Video," *Opera Quarterly* 26, no. 1 (Winter 2010): 96–119; Morris, "Wagnervideo," *Opera Quarterly* 27, no. 2–3 (Spring/Summer 2011): 235–55; Stephan Mösch, "Störung, Verstörung, Zerstörung: Regietheater als Rezeptionsproblem," in Sollich, Risi, Reus, and Jöris, *Angst vor der Zerstörung*, 216–32; Mösch, "Geistes Gegenwart?"; Gerd Rienäcker, "Begegnungen mit Felsensteins Musiktheater," in Hintze, Risi, and Sollich, *Realistisches Musiktheater*, 35–48; Mark Schachtsiek, "'Missachtung von Form ist Verlust an Sinn': Von Ruth Berghaus' besonderem Umgang mit der Kunstform Oper," in Hintze, Risi, and Sollich, *Realistisches Musiktheater*, 188–202; Jürgen Schläder, "Strategien der Opern-Bilder: Überlegungen zur Typologie der Klassikerinszenierungen im musikalischen Theater," in *Ästhetik der Inszenierung: Dimensionen eines künstlerischen, kulturellen und gesellschaftlichen Phänomens*, ed. Josef Früchtl and Jörg Zimmermann (Frankfurt am Main: Suhrkamp, 2001), 183–97; Schläder, "Kontinuität fragmentarischer Bildwelten: Postmoderne Verfahren im Stuttgarter Ring von 1999/2000," in *OperMachtTheaterBilder: Neue Wirklichkeiten des Regietheaters*, ed. Schläder (Leipzig: Henschel, 2006), 191–218; Mary Ann Smart, *Mimomania: Music and Gesture in Nineteenth-Century Opera* (Berkeley: University of California Press, 2004); Smart, "Resisting Rossini or Marlon Brando Plays Figaro," *Opera Quarterly* 27, no. 2–3 (Spring/Summer 2011): 153–78; Sollich, Risi, Reus, and Jöris, *Angst vor der Zerstörung*; Robert Sollich, "Staging Wagner – and Its History: *Die Meistersinger von Nürnberg* on a

16 *Introduction*

Contemporary Stage," *Wagner Journal* 3, no. 1 (2009): 5–13; Sollich, "Die verkehrte Welt ist die bessere Welt: Peter Konwitschnys Musiktheater zwischen den Traditionen," in Hintze, Risi, and Sollich, *Realistisches Musiktheater*, 203–21.

24 Nicholas Cook, "Analysing Performance and Performing Analysis," in *Rethinking Music*, ed. Cook and Mark Everist, rev. ed. (Oxford: Oxford University Press, 2001), 239–61; Cook, "Between Process and Product: Music and/as Performance," *Music Theory Online* 7, no. 2 (April 2001), http://www.mtosmt.org/issues/mto.01.7.2/mto.01.7.2.cook.html; Christa Brüstle, "Performance/Performativität in der neuen Musik," in *Theorien des Performativen*, ed. Erika Fischer-Lichte and Christoph Wulf, special issue, *Paragrana: Internationale Zeitschrift für Historische Anthropologie* 10, no. 1 (2001): 271–83; Christa Brüstle, "Klang als performative Prägung von Räumlichkeiten," in *Kommunikation – Gedächtnis – Raum: Kulturwissenschaften nach dem "Spatial Turn,"* ed. Moritz Csáky and Christoph Leitgeb (Bielefeld: Transcript, 2009), 113–29.

25 See, for example, Hermann Danuser, "Zur Aktualität musikalischer Interpretationstheorie," *Musiktheorie* 11, no. 1 (1996): 39–51; Hermann Gottschewski, *Die Interpretation als Kunstwerk: Musikalische Zeitgestaltung und ihre Analyse am Beispiel von Welte-Mignon-Klavieraufnahmen aus dem Jahre 1905* (Laaber: Laaber-Verlag, 1993); Hans-Joachim Hinrichsen, "Musikwissenschaft: Musik – Interpretation – Wissenschaft," *Archiv für Musikwissenschaft* 57, no. 1 (2000): 78–90; Albrecht Riethmüller, "Interpretation in der Musik," in *Interpretation*, ed. Gerhard Funke, Riethmüller, and Otto Zwierlein (Stuttgart: Franz Steiner, 1998), 17–30. On this, see Chapter 1.

26 See Chapter 1.
27 On the concept of material, also see Chapter 1.
28 See Chapters 2 and 3.
29 See Chapter 3.
30 See Chapter 4.
31 See Chapter 5.
32 See Chapter 6.
33 See Chapter 7.
34 See Chapter 8.
35 See Chapter 9.
36 My decision not to respond to the (per se utopic but nevertheless perhaps increasing) demand for an exhaustive or at least representative typology of current operatic staging practices also means that a whole series of important and much discussed opera directors—such as David Alden, Tatjana Gürbaca, Stefan Herheim, and Dmitri Tcherniakov—do not appear at all in this study.
37 Clemens Risi, "Von (den) Sinnen in der Oper: Überlegungen zur Aufführungsanalyse im Musiktheater," in *Theater als Paradigma der Moderne? Positionen zwischen historischer Avantgarde und Medienzeitalter*, ed. Christopher Balme, Erika Fischer-Lichte, and Stephan Grätzel (Tübingen: A. Francke, 2003), 353–63; Risi, "The Performativity of Operatic Performances as Academic Provocation: Response to David J. Levin," in *Verdi 2001: Atti del Convegno internazionale; Proceedings of the International Conference; Parma – New York – New Haven; 24 January – 1 February 2001*, vol. 2, ed. Fabrizio Della Seta, Roberta Montemorra Marvin, and Marco Marica (Florence: Leo S. Olschki, 2003), 489–96; Risi, "Sinn und Sinnlichkeit in der Oper: Zu Hans Neuenfels' *Idomeneo* an der Deutschen Oper Berlin," *Theater der Zeit* 58, no. 6 (2003): 38–39; Risi, "Am Puls der Sinne: Der Rhythmus einer Opernaufführung zwischen Repräsentation und Präsenz – zu Mozart-Inszenierungen von Calixto Bieito und Thomas Bischoff," in *TheorieTheaterPraxis*, ed. Hajo Kurzenberger and Annemarie Matzke (Berlin: Theater der Zeit, 2004), 117–27; Risi, "Rhythmen der Aufführung: Rhythmus-Kollisionen bei Steve Reich und Heiner Goebbels," in *Kunst der Aufführung – Aufführung der Kunst*, ed. Erika Fischer-Lichte, Risi, and Jens Roselt (Berlin:

Theater der Zeit, 2004), 165–77; Risi, "Die bewegende Sängerin: Zu stimmlichen und körperlichen Austausch-Prozessen in Opernaufführungen," in *Klang und Bewegung: Beiträge zu einer Grundkonstellation*, ed. Christa Brüstle and Albrecht Riethmüller (Aachen: Shaker, 2004), 135–43; Risi, "'Keinen Wagner-Kult mehr. Sondern Theater, Theater, Theater': *Der Ring des Nibelungen* und das Regietheater," in *Von der Zukunft einer unmöglichen Kunst: 21 Perspektiven zum Musiktheater*, ed. Bettina Knauer and Peter Krause (Bielefeld: Aisthesis, 2006), 139–47; Risi, "Hören und Gehört werden als körperlicher Akt: Zur feedback-Schleife in der Oper und der Erotik der Sängerstimme," in *Wege der Wahrnehmung: Authentizität, Reflexivität und Aufmerksamkeit im zeitgenössischen Theater*, ed. Erika Fischer-Lichte, Barbara Gronau, Sabine Schouten, and Christel Weiler (Berlin: Theater der Zeit, 2006), 98–113; Risi, "'Die andere Zeit': Zur Zeiterfahrung und Performativität von Opernaufführungen," in *Musik und kulturelle Identität: Bericht über den XIII. Internationalen Kongress der Gesellschaft für Musikforschung Weimar 2004*, ed. Detlef Altenburg and Rainer Bayreuther, vol. 3 (Kassel: Bärenreiter, 2012), 463–69; Christa Brüstle and Risi, "Aufführungsanalyse und -interpretation: Positionen und Fragen der 'Performance Studies' aus musik- und theaterwissenschaftlicher Sicht," in *Werk-Welten: Perspektiven der Interpretationsgeschichte*, ed. Andreas Ballstaedt and Hans-Joachim Hinrichsen (Schliengen: Argus, 2008), 108–32; Risi, "'Martern aller Arten': Calixto Bieitos Suche nach der Wahrheit des Musiktheaters," in Hintze, Risi, and Sollich, *Realistisches Musiktheater*, 132–47; Risi, "David Moss in Salzburg, oder: Die Aufführung als Provokation einer Musiktheaterwissenschaft," in *Strahlkräfte: Festschrift für Erika Fischer-Lichte*, ed. Christel Weiler, Jens Roselt, and Risi (Berlin: Theater der Zeit, 2008), 54–65; Risi, "Mozart-Musiktheater: Wege des Performativen," in *Wege zur Klassik*, ed. Dagmar Hoffmann-Axthelm, special issue, *Basler Jahrbuch für historische Musikpraxis* 30 (2006): 137–48; Risi, "Die neuen *Meistersinger* und die Angst vor der Zerstörung," in Sollich, Risi, Reus, and Jöris, *Angst vor der Zerstörung*, 272–79; Risi, "Opern-Gesten: Zur Aufführungspraxis der Oper des 19. Jahrhunderts in historischer und aktueller Perspektive," in *Gesten: Inszenierung, Aufführung, Praxis*, ed. Christoph Wulf and Erika Fischer-Lichte (Munich: Wilhelm Fink, 2010), 154–62; Risi, "Arbeit an der Oper als Arbeit am Mythos: Medea und die Präsenz des Mythos bei Iano Tamar und Maria Callas," in *Medeamorphosen: Die Künste und der Mythos*, ed. Nike Bätzner, Matthias Dreyer, Erika Fischer-Lichte, and Astrid Silvia Schönhagen (Munich: Wilhelm Fink, 2010), 34–43; Risi, "*Lohengrin* im Klassenzimmer und die Lust der Inszenierung an der Musik," *Rampenlicht: Oper Leipzig* 3/4 (2010): 14–15; Risi, "Die Posen der Diva: Inszenierung und Wahrnehmung der Außergewöhnlichen heute: Anna Netrebko 'gegen' Edita Gruberova," in *Diva: Die Inszenierung der übermenschlichen Frau; Interdisziplinäre Untersuchungen zu einem kulturellen Phänomen des 19. und 20. Jahrhunderts*, ed. Rebecca Grotjahn, Dörte Schmidt, and Thomas Seedorf (Schliengen: Argus, 2011), 195–206; Risi, "The Diva's Fans: Opera and Bodily Participation," in *On Participation and Synchronisation*, ed. Kai van Eikels, Bettina Brandl-Risi, and Ric Allsopp, special issue, *Performance Research* 16, no. 3 (2011): 49–54; Risi, "Das Surplus der Performance oder der 'Beziehungszauber' der Aufführung: Dahlhaus' *Figaro*-Analysen im Lichte aktueller Inszenierungen," in *Carl Dahlhaus und die Musikwissenschaft: Werk, Wirkung, Aktualität*, ed. Hermann Danuser, Peter Gülke, and Norbert Miller (Schliengen: Argus, 2011), 142–47; Risi, "Opera in Performance: In Search of New Analytical Approaches," *Opera Quarterly* 27, no. 2–3 (Spring/Summer 2011): 283–95; Risi, "Bühne als Labor: Die Bayreuther Festspiele im 21. Jahrhundert," in *Richard Wagner: Persönlichkeit, Werk und Wirkung*, ed. Helmut Loos (Markkleeberg: Sax, 2013), 327–34; Risi, "Barockoper heute: Ein Versuch über den Begriff der historisch informierten Aufführungspraxis," in *Musiktheater im Fokus*, ed. Sieghart Döhring and Stefanie Rauch (Sinzig:

Studiopunkt, 2014), 387–94; Risi, "Verdi und Wagner auf dem Theater," in *Verdi und Wagner: Kulturen der Oper*, ed. Arnold Jacobshagen (Cologne: Böhlau, 2014), 321–34; Risi, "Die Stimme in der Oper zwischen Mittel des Ausdrucks und leiblicher Affizierung," in *Die Zukunft der Oper: Zwischen Hermeneutik und Performativität*, ed. Barbara Beyer, Susanne Kogler, and Roman Lemberg (Berlin: Theater der Zeit, 2014), 267–75.

Part I
Theoretical foundations

1 Beyond interpretation

When scholars discuss opera performances, then it is usually within the paradigm of interpretation.[1] In music, *interpretation* does not primarily refer—as it does in textual or visual studies—to explanatory exegesis of a text or image in another text but rather to the translation of a written score into sound. Based on this premise, interpretation research and interpretation theory focus on the relation between the template and its realization as the central object of investigation; the interpretative history and performative tradition of the work also always play a role.[2]

In this sense, one could say that the performances described in the introduction—Maria Bengtsson's as Konstanze and David Moss's as Orlofsky—are, like many other performances before them, interpretations of Wolfgang Amadeus Mozart's or Johann Strauss's scores. And, in fact, one can gain valuable insights into a performance from analyzing how it engaged with the template and with the history of performances of that template.

Moss's flipping of his voice, for example, can be seen in a tradition of all the Orlofsky singers who have used flipping their voices as a symptom of the character's drunk state, and in a certain sense, the notation even invites the performer to do this through high G♭s and A♭s that break out of the melodic line and also break a contralto's customary tessitura (see Example 1.1, mm. 7, 11, 12, 14, 16, 18).[3] With grumbling in the bass regions, Moss invoked another performance tradition as well, namely, the reveling and roaring in the deepest register that star mezzos and contraltos such as Brigitte Fassbaender have been fond of practicing (see Example 1.1, mm. 20–25).[4]

But perhaps the most impressive sequence came after Orlofsky snorted coke and before the beginning of the second stanza when the vocal experimenter David Moss presented all his extraordinary capabilities. This sequence too can be understood as engaging with virtuosic practices: with adorning a cadence before the conclusion of a solo number, or here before the da capo. To do so, Moss used exactly the point where the score indicates a general pause (see Example 1.2, m. 49).[5]

One can also formulate profitable insights into the Berlin *Entführung aus dem Serail* from the perspective of interpretation. Calixto Bieito aspires to mediate historical material for today's audiences, and he claims that his works

DOI: 10.4324/9781003124863-3

22 Theoretical foundations

Example 1.1 Johann Strauss, *Die Fledermaus: Operette in 3 Akten*, RV 503, libretto by Richard Genée, ed. Michael Rot, vol. 3 of *Neue Johann Strauss Gesamtausgabe*, ser. 1, group 2 (Vienna: Strauss Edition, 1999), 207–8.

Reproduced by the kind permission of Schott Music, Mainz.

Beyond interpretation 23

Example 1.1 (Continued)

24 *Theoretical foundations*

Example 1.2 Strauss, *Die Fledermaus*, 211.

are able to relate opera to real life. In his case, it is always about radically questioning a template with regard to its relevance today. For example, the character Osmin lists a considerable repertoire of atrocities humans can commit against one another: "Erst geköpft, dann gehangen, / Dann gespießt auf heißen Stangen, / Dann verbrannt, dann gebunden / Und getaucht, zuletzt geschunden" (First beheaded, then hung like a hound, / What's left can be put on a skewer. / Then burned, and bound, and drowned— / A thoroughly dead wrongdoer!).[6] Such fantasies can be easily translated into acts of sex and violence, and that is what the staging does.

A relation like that of template and interpretation, which I have so far pursued on the level of vocal interpretation or on the level of the interpretation of text and plot, also exists on the level of auditory and visual elements. Primarily of interest here are endeavors to scenically substantiate formal and structural features in the musical sequence.[7] This is how Peter Sellars[8] and Calixto Bieito[9] both posed, in their respective stagings of Mozart's *Don Giovanni*, the question of how the change in affect and tempo from larghetto to allegretto moderato can be legitimized in Donna Anna's aria "Non mi dir" (Never say) in act 2.[10] Both found an answer in ways of stimulating Donna Anna's body. In Peter Sellars's 1987 staging, which played in Spanish Harlem, her body was stimulated by drugs. Here Donna Anna was addicted and shot up between parts of her aria. Her vision of a better and pain-free future—"forse un giorno il cielo ancora / sentirà pietà di me" (Heaven soon will bring relief. / It must take pity on me)[11]—thus became understandable as a very concrete vision under the influence of a mind-expanding drug. In Bieito's staging, her body was stimulated by sexual acts that Don Ottavio performed on her (see Figure 1.1). The change of tempo in the aria was legitimized by a change in the scenic rhythm and vice versa.[12]

Bieito's version of Konstanze's aria "Ach ich liebte, war so glücklich" (Oh, I was in love, so filled with joy)[13] also undertook a scenic legitimation of a musical structure through stimulating her body; here it was not, however, the change of tempo from adagio to allegro but rather the question of how the endless,

Figure 1.1 *Don Giovanni*, staging by Calixto Bieito, Francesca Scaini as Donna Anna, José Montero as Don Ottavio, Staatsoper Hannover, 2002.

Photo courtesy of A. T. Schaefer.

26 *Theoretical foundations*

enormously demanding coloraturas in the third octave, could be scenically or emotionally substantiated. In the staging, Bassa had tied Konstanze onto a sort of dog leash with a collar and pulled on it during the first string of coloratura (see Example 1.3, mm. 101–3). Konstanze was trying to fight this strangling

Example 1.3 Wolfgang Amadeus Mozart, *Entführung aus dem Serail*, K. 384, ed. Gerhard Croll, vol. 12 of *Neue Ausgabe sämtlicher Werke*, ser. 2, *Bühnenwerke*, group 5, *Opern und Singspiele* (Kassel: Bärenreiter, 1982), 129–30.

Reproduced by the permission of Bärenreiter-Verlag, Kassel.

Beyond interpretation 27

Example 1.3 (Continued)

choker around her neck with her hands. Bassa then took off one of her shoes and guided her foot to his mouth; he washed her hair and rubbed over her now half-naked body with a towel; with the last string of coloratura, Bassa finally reached into her underpants and groped her (see Figure 1.2). Thus, in the way they were executed, Konstanze's coloraturas and high notes appeared as reactions to the acts performed upon her—as expressions of pain (and ecstasy?); the performers' actions and affects became the catalysts for her musical expression.

28 *Theoretical foundations*

Figure 1.2 Die Entführung aus dem Serail, staging by Calixto Bieito, Maria Bengtsson as Konstanze, Guntbert Warns as Bassa Selim, Komische Oper Berlin, 2004.
Photo courtesy of Monika Rittershaus.

The scene of Konstanze's aria "Martern aller Arten" (Tortures most surely await),[14] which I described in the introduction, can also be read in Bieito's staging as an interpretation in the hermeneutic sense: the stubborn Konstanze was shown what happens to stubborn women in an overly explicit way. The tormentors' actions can also be construed as a violent compensation for their impotence in view of Konstanze's steadfastness.

The focus on how a performance deals with a template is particularly profitable when it has to do, as in these cases, with performances of repertoire classics.

Interpretation in musicology

Performing historical texts (as is the case with productions of historical repertoire classics) makes interpretation and thinking about interpretation necessary. On the genesis of the concept of interpretation, Hermann Danuser writes:

> Interpretation ... arose ... when in the course of historicism in the eighteenth and especially in the nineteenth centuries, understanding musical works and their texts became a problem that could not be immediately "solved" and translated into a currently relevant meaning.[15]

The following fundamental supposition is important to understanding Danuser's concept of interpretation:

> The musical text, the web of relations of meaning written down by a composer, cannot be understood ... in itself. In whatever way it is manifested, ... the written text is never complete in the sense that the transmitted information could be converted unambiguously into a particular sonic realization.[16]

Thus, the written text cannot be consulted alone as the criterion for evaluating an interpretation. Danuser therefore builds on this supposition with the idea, or vision, of a complex cohesion based on a logic that is to be reenacted in the interpretation:

> As a condition of interpretation, [we can] name the vision of a complex "cohesion" of single factors, elements, sections, and movements of a musical work. From this it follows that the interpretative activity—insofar as it is performative—cannot be viewed in isolation from the musical logic .... In order to captivate their listeners, interpretive artists have to shape the sonic process of the musical sequence as convincingly as possible, and this also means doing so in a way that is logically consistent and surprising.[17]

But who defines the term *logically consistent*? Danuser suggests that this is established by the "text," understood as the "cohesion of a semantic framework, a web of individual elements."[18] At the same time, however, he shows—as quoted above—that a text is never "complete in the sense that the transmitted information could be converted unambiguously into a particular sonic realization." The second term Danuser names is *surprising*. It refers to the necessary openness of an interpretation: "The interpretation of a work [may] be approached, even and in particular with regard to its sonic realization, as something open."[19] At the same time, the term *surprising* makes clear that this openness has to play out within a defined, known context, because to be able to surprise, the interpretation, or performance, has to play out within the framework of something that is somehow familiar. Interpretation thus moves between some kind of set limit ("logically consistent") and a necessary openness or freedom ("surprising"). Perhaps the combination can be thought of in such a way that the limits, or frameworks, on which interpretations are measured are always newly and individually set, constructed, and formed by interpreters or audience members. In any case, the active negotiation of the limit is necessary for setting in motion the process of surprise described above, a surprise that is only visible or hearable as a surprise within certain limits. In this, it is also important to recognize that the limits, or frameworks, are not given, are not fixed, are not set in advance, but are rather newly defined and constructed in every moment of interpretation, in every performance, on the basis of individuals' respective predispositions, of their respective knowledge about the work being performed.

In the case of a performance of a historical repertoire classic, the relation to the text at its base always plays an important role, and it does so both in the staging process and in the perception of the performance, since the audience also always refers to their own knowledge of the template. In view of this, Hermann Gottschewski offers a productive approach. It proceeds from the following observation: "The interpreter does not [let] the interpretative structure arise out of nothing but rather [builds it] up on the basis of the structure of the composition."[20] Gottschewski advances a more radical position than Danuser since he ascribes to the interpreter full responsibility for the experience of art that takes place in the performance:

> How much do we have Beethoven to thank for the experience of art we have at an interpretation of a Beethoven piano sonata by a great pianist and how much the interpreter? When interpreters appear on stage, consciously performing the art of interpretation, I lean toward pronouncing that they have full power over their creation.[21]

From this position, it is only a small step to my privileging of performance and understanding of the score as material for producing a performance (and not as the starting point or goal of an interpretation or of an analysis of an interpretation as Danuser proposes). If one follows Gottschewski, then the search for criteria to analyze an interpretation leads to the assertion that these criteria must be suited to analyzing performances and not to analyzing compositions or structures.

Approaches based on interpretation theory from musicology and arguments based on performance theory from theater studies come very close together and share similar premises on the question of the relevance of the audience. In the case of live interpretation, the audience plays just as decisive of a role in the discourse on interpretation as it does in performance theory. On this, Danuser writes:

> In addition to its uniqueness, ... it is, above all, the communicative aspect that differentiates live interpretation from not-live interpretation. At a live interpretation in a concert hall, a communication, a reciprocal reaction, a rhetorical response of the interpreter to the listeners can—indeed, must—come into play instead of a solipsistic sonic representation of a textual work .... The best concert player ... [is the interpreter] who can specifically shape the course of a work in a lively interplay with the audience—adapting to the

conditions of the space's acoustics, the instruments, the warmth in the hall, etc., etc., even to the audience's power of comprehension and their individual reactions.[22]

Danuser's formulation of "lively interplay" brings into view the reciprocally influencing processes between performers and audience that Erika Fischer-Lichte has described in performance theory as a feedback loop.[23]

Another important premise of Regietheater as it is understood in this study—namely, as a necessary revamping of historical material—also finds a parallel in Danuser's interpretive approach when he speaks of the necessity to "contextualize" an interpretation: "With this, I understand the processes that take place or that are staged as securing a reference point for understanding a musical interpretation in the present."[24] Adapting to today's horizon of understanding is an aspect that Wolfgang Ullrich underscores with regard to Regietheater, and he finds its origin already in Hegel. According to Ullrich, Hegel's *Vorlesungen über die Ästhetik* (*Aesthetics: Lectures on Fine Art*), which are based on transcriptions of multiple lecture classes from the 1820s in Berlin, "thought, probably for the first time in a specific and differentiated way, about the challenge entailed in staging an already older artwork—a play or an opera—anew."[25] According to Hegel:

> Therefore, if foreign [that is, especially old] dramatic works are staged, every people has the right to ask for remodellings. Even the most excellent piece *requires* remodelling from this point of view. It could of course be said that what is really excellent must be excellent for all time, but the work of art has also a temporal, perishable side, and this it is which requires alteration. For the beautiful appears for others, and those for whom it has been brought into appearance must be able to be at home in this external side of its appearance.[26]

In this sense, one could also understand Danuser's plea for the dependence of interpretation on context and the resulting obligation to change and innovation:

> From the fact … that the dependence of interpretation, both performative and hermeneutic-critical, on context cannot be lifted, I derive the interpreter's duty to reflect continually on the context current for us so as to obtain from it the possibilities of change and innovation.[27]

Looking back at Hegel and at Ullrich's reading of Hegel, one could even take this passage further and think of it as a plea for the necessity of Regietheater's revampings of operas.

The extent to which methods of composition analysis are based on interpretations and dimensions of performance is demonstrated by Hans-Joachim Hinrichsen's studies on Hans von Bülow's Beethoven interpretations (in

Hinrichsen's words, his "practical interpretation" as a conductor of Beethoven's orchestral works) and on Hugo Riemann's musicological analyses. We have Hinrichsen's perspective to thank for the both surprising and convincing insight that allegedly text- and work-centered musicological analyses of compositions depend to a large extent on particular experiences of sonic realizations, that is, on specific and time-bound interpretations. Hinrichsen's thesis is that Riemann, as a student of Bülow's, developed his theory based on Bülow's practical interpretations but later kept secret the source of his theory (that is, praxis):

> Academic engagements with music depend to an extent on sonic reality (just as they have an effect back on it), an extent that they often only limitedly convey .... In truth, supposedly impartial, objective description is not based on evidence of the analyzed structure but rather—as can be recognized today—on experience with the characteristic interpretive style of one's own time .... An academic analysis of a score never penetrates to "the work itself" but rather to its categorial representation in the circle of score and sonic realization and so too of practical and theoretical interpretation.[28]

The relevance of sonic reality as the basis for thinking and writing about music is also emphasized in Carolyn Abbate's essay "Music—Drastic or Gnostic?" In this essay, Abbate subjects her own discipline of musicology to the self-critical diagnosis that it has always exclusively understood itself as a hermeneutic discipline and has thereby lost sight of its actual object, the sound of sensually experienceable music.[29] Instead of thematizing the dimension of experience while listening, musicological analyses place, as a rule, more value and focus on discovering hidden layers of meaning in the score, although it is usually the experience of listening and not the written score—that is, listening to music—that drew the analysts to the object in the first place.

Opera in performance and the concept of the work

The predominant focus on scores and not on sonic reality is largely based on an understanding of what is the actual object of investigation. This raises the question of to what extent and on what level this object can be addressed as an "artwork" in its traditional (or newly defined) attributes. The concept of the artwork evokes a long and intense debate in the academic disciplines concerned with art. When it turns to the performative arts—like music and theater—the already very complicated discussion of the concept of the work becomes even more unwieldy. One cannot ignore the persistent presence of this debate—especially as part of the continually expressed demands for *Werktreue* (faithfulness to a work)—nor can the discussion be brought to a simple solution. Instead, I will argue for an expanded understanding of the work with reference to positions advanced by Albrecht Wellmer, Anselm Gerhard, and Erika Fischer-Lichte.

Beyond interpretation   33

The philosopher Albrecht Wellmer, who also engaged extensively with questions of art, in particular of the performative arts, observes with regard to the problem of our understanding of the work:

> Works [have] their being only in the historical process of their realization, interpretation, and reception .... To answer the question of how and where works "are," one always also has to think of realization (performance), interpretation, and reception as this "how" and "where." The being of works is thoroughly historical and not detachable from the "how" and "where" of their realization and experience. Even if artworks' mode of being cannot be determined by their empirically traceable effects, the empirical evidence of their effects and the history of their reception become part of the form in which each work has come down to us.[30]

The highly problematic concept of *Werktreue* is still—and especially in debates about current stagings of well-known works from the operatic repertoire—endemic in letters from audience members, in Internet forums, and in blogs as a seal of approval and as a demand, even if the impossibility of such a concept has been proved multiple times in theater studies and now also in in opera scholarship. The musicologist Anselm Gerhard puts it thus:

> The question must be allowed as to how "faithfulness," "authenticity," can be possible in a medium based on an ontological process of transformation .... It doesn't matter how you look at it, the ... concept of "Werktreue" not only lacks differentiation but also every possibility of doing justice to the tricky contradictions and aporias of a culture defined by historicism, a culture that insists above all on transforming past "works" into the present of a stage performance today.[31]

The position in theater studies, which Gerhard also refers to, has been pointedly formulated by Erika Fischer-Lichte: "The concept of 'Werktreue' cannot ... be used as an objectively descriptive concept. It is instead a subjective, normative, evaluative concept."[32]

On the side of artistic practice, Peter Konwitschny expressed a very similar view in a conversation with Barbara Beyer:

> We only have the scores as a template. The score is the skeleton; actual theater begins with living people; for a certain time, they lend their lives to the work, bringing the skeleton to life for three hours .... It is not our task to produce plays as the authors envisioned; how would that even work? Our task is to pose certain important questions in such a way that they are discussed. The plays are the material for doing so; they are not an end in themselves .... We cannot produce theater as it was done one hundred or two hundred years ago. The notes are the material, and our present penetrates into it; that is unavoidable. In ten years, different

people with different experiences will work in theater. And their view, their interpretation of a piece will inevitably be different from ours. A novel that one reads at twenty and then again twenty years later also becomes a new book. This understanding has to be more widespread and obvious, including among critics.[33]

This should not mean calling into question or eliminating music theater's textuality or relation to a work in its entirety. The goal is to refer to the performance of music as a cultural practice that has just as much claim to academic reflection as the music fixed in the score has always had in musicology. For the performative practices of opera, the persistent relevance of the concept of the work in music is precisely what makes stagings and performances that bring tension into ossified expectations so exciting. Only in deviating from a supposedly stable origin does such a performance prove to be powerful. The starting material (the score, the libretto, the discourse about a particular opera, knowledge about it in the world) and the expectations of audience members belong just as much to this origin. Everything should be taken into account. Just the focus of how we approach opera and opera in performance should change. Performance should not be viewed as another piece of the puzzle in understanding the score better, but rather, the other way around, the widespread knowledge about a template and the general fact of previous knowledge should be considered in analyzing the cultural practice of performance.[34] For what always fascinates in such performances is precisely the experience of difference—the tension that sets in between the template one believes to be familiar and the experienced reality of the performance—and how this tension is experienced by audience members.[35]

Opera in performance as work on myth

In a conversation with Barbara Beyer, the director Jossi Wieler and the dramaturg Sergio Morabito, who as a duo have staged numerous operas, had a revealing disagreement on exactly this point. For future work on opera, Jossi Wieler demands something that has long been common practice in theater:

> What was unthinkable in theater twenty, thirty years ago—using an *Emilia Galotti* as material or Ibsen's *The Lady from the Sea*—is now self-understood and should also be possible in music theater .... One would have to deal with a piece as with a world premiere, and in addition to opera dramaturgs, one would need the conductor to be a collaborator who would virtually compose the work anew. I do believe that one can decompose opera, but that does not mean one must.[36]

In opposition, Sergio Morabito objects:

> I have a problem with such an approach .... The nature of our task demands something that is actually not compatible with our thinking,

feeling, and understanding today, namely, bringing back to life an operatic score written for a certain historical form of theater that no longer exists—and that is where the actual challenge of directing opera lies, precisely here is where the experiment, the wager of our work, begins .... It is really about what resists [our understanding], what cannot be understood, what is irretrievably foreign to our theater today, and it would be disastrous to simply take out these irritations.[37]

Perhaps a reference to a different concept than that of the work could make clearer what constitutes the tense relation between a template one believes to be familiar and a current performance. Here a certain conception of *myth* as it has appeared in theories by Hans Blumenberg and Claude Lévi-Strauss, among others, appears promising. Starting with their conceptions of myth, I want to claim that engaging with operas from past epochs can be understood as "work on myth."

In his 1955 essay "The Structural Study of Myths," the anthropologist Claude Lévi-Strauss states:

> A myth always refers to events alleged to have taken place in time: before the world was created, or during its first stages—anyway, long ago. But what gives the myth an operative value is that the specific pattern described is everlasting; it explains the present and the past as well as the future.[38]

The myth draws some of its appeal and dissemination from, among other things, always narrating something from the past, from referring to something in the past, and so from producing a structure of repetition that at the same time, however, helps to order the present, to structure, and to outline options for action in the future. But what particularly interests me in Lévi-Strauss's conception of myth is the insight that among the numerous versions of a myth, there cannot be any authentic one, that they are all to be viewed as equal. With his theory, Lévi-Strauss overcomes the "problem which has been so far one of the main obstacles to the progress of mythological studies, namely, the quest for the *true* version, or the *earlier* one,"[39] and instead proposes that "we define the myth as consisting of all its versions."[40] He continues: "If a myth is made up of all its variants, structural analysis should take all of them into account .... There is no one true version of which all the others are but copies or distortions. Every version belongs to the myth."[41] In his book *Work on Myth*, Hans Blumenberg describes this relation in a similar way:

> Myth has always already passed over into the process of reception, and it remains in that process no matter what violence is applied in order to break its bonds and to establish its final form. If it is present to us only in the forms of its reception, there is no privilege of certain versions as more original or more final .... Freud and Sophocles would

then have to be regarded equally as "sources" in relation to the Oedipus material. All variants could lay claim to the same mythological seriousness.[42]

Expressed pointedly: "The reception of the sources produces the sources of reception."[43] The fascinating thing about myth is its incompleteness, its interminability—the possibility and necessity of continuing to write the myth with each work, of writing it anew, of writing it again. Each version perpetuates the myth and yet participates in the great entirety of the myth.[44]

Now, to what extent is this model relevant for defining opera from the perspective of its performance? First, the penchant of theaters, conductors, directors, and dramaturgs to keep on engaging with well-known material and operas as well as the audience's desire to keep on experiencing such long-familiar material and operas are motivated by a temporality of the templates that is similar to that of myth. When opera productions work with historical material (that is, well-known pieces, texts, scores), the material is always looked at from a new perspective and perpetuated using modern means. The model can thus explain why composers keep on devoting themselves to old material (that is, myths and stories) and why opera houses, conductors, and directors keep engaging with old operas (that is, the variants of the myths already formed in texts and notes).

But a second possibility of the analogy is, in my opinion, even more fascinating. It has to do with the relation of score and performance in opera. In my view, transferring the conception of myth can support the argument that there cannot be a definitive, sole form of an opera as a work, that instead an opera only exists in the abundance of its various performances. I am thus interested in renouncing the possibility of being able to find something like the essence of a work in a performance or staging. Every performance of an opera engages with the materials, by which I mean the concrete textual and musical material, the voices and bodies on stage, and the accumulated knowledge about the template and past performances (that is, the performance history[45]). In the language of myth theory, the employed materials would always be further, equal versions.

When a director or a theater tackles an opera, they are never engaging with the work of a certain composer but rather usually with the imagined core of a theme—"imagined" because a thematic core actually first becomes visible through the layering of different versions or pages. In reading "work on opera" as "work on myth," concrete libretti, scores, and also various stagings and performances can be understood as "versions." This makes clear how different musical settings of the same material and different stagings of the same opera play a significant role in producing an opera and in its perception by audience members (as the horizon of their knowledge). It becomes clear that the goal of a performance does not primarily consist in ensuring a better understanding of an opera or the preservation of a tradition; instead, it is always about new attempts to attain an outlook on the world and on one's self through engaging with the material.

In the transfer to opera, the incompleteness and interminability of myth thus mean that just as each version of a myth continues to compose the myth, each staging or performance also continues to compose the opera. For analysis, this entails the task of unearthing, describing, and interpreting bundles of relations so as to reveal—with a simultaneous historical consciousness—the current relevance of works.

Beyond hierarchies: The concept of material

Why is the analogy to the concept of myth better suited than an approach with the concept of interpretation? With regard to Regietheater stagings that revamp operas, one often hears not only from the audience but also in the press: "But one can't do it *that* way." What is rejected is precisely the tension, the friction that forms between the template, the supposedly well-known intentions of its authors, and its realization. Even among audience members from the fields of professional criticism and academia, who are actually favorably disposed toward Regietheater, one hears the reproach that a staging really strayed too far from the template. In my view, two contradictions can be found here. First, by applying the interpretation paradigm to the cases of David Moss's and Maria Bengtsson's performances, I showed that these radical stagings came close to their templates with respect to the text and the music, and that they can in this sense be understood as interpretations. Second—a theoretically much more significant problem—how can one conceptualize at all something like wanting to come close to a template that originated under entirely different cultural, social, and aesthetic conditions? We obviously cannot go back and leave behind the experiences of seeing and hearing that we've had as witnesses of the twentieth and twenty-first centuries. No one can readjust their eyes and ears for the eighteenth century or for any time other than their own. The key methodological problem is, in my opinion, that with the concept of interpretation, one buys into precisely this predicament of wanting to get closer to a template that one cannot treat in any other way than in a creative dialogue. The concept of interpretation implies, at least in the generally accepted understanding, a tendency toward establishing a hierarchy between the score and the performance—a hierarchy that ascribes a more important role to the score than to the performance and that codifies the score as the starting point and goal of analyzing interpretations or performances, since, according to this idea, a performance represents only one of the potentially infinite number of possibilities for realizing the score. At the same time, this implies that the score already contains all the *possible* performative realities. This excludes certain performative realities, namely, those that cannot be obtained from reading and analyzing the score according to the rules of translation established by the so-called historically oriented practice of performance. It is thus a normative position. And for that reason, this understanding blocks our view of many existing performative realities and of performance elements that a priori cannot be part of a medium operating with textual signs like a score, such as the concrete sounds of voices or bodies that fill a space with their materiality and so on.

Hans Heinrich Eggebrecht opposes this limitation of the concept of interpretation when he writes: "The quality of i[nterpretation] was considered to be dependent on the degree of convergence with what was intended in the composition. But the pursuit of the true i[nterpretation] is foiled by the individual and historical subjectivity of the interpreter."[46] Nevertheless, one still encounters a certain ambiguity in musicological discussions about the concept of interpretation, for example, when Danuser writes, as mentioned above, about the "whole artistic responsibility"[47] of the interpreter "to captivate his listeners"[48] and about how the score "is not a criterion that permits one to determine what is right or wrong,"[49] yet in the same breath assumes that only a "logically consistent"[50] realization can captivate the listeners and that a "presentation of complex music cannot succeed without analytically penetrating the score, without which the connections, differences, and functions of the parts of the musical form will remain unclear."[51] As stated above, a tendency to establish a hierarchy between the score and the performance becomes manifest after all,[52] and it codifies the score as the starting point and goal of analyzing interpretations or performances.

One can free oneself from this theoretical and aesthetic dilemma if one shifts one's focus in observing the relationship between score and performance, between the textual template and the music-theatrical realization, and leaves behind the supposed necessity of reducing a staging to how accurately it deals with the template. Influenced in particular by the performative turn in the humanities but also following positions in musicology—such as that of Nicholas Cook, who demands, under the heading "music as performance,"[53] a "stronger consideration of the body and corporeality whether with regard to the production of sound, the movements of bodies, gestures, and so on or in view of listeners' or the audience's 'bodily responsivity'"[54]—this study views and illuminates the relationship between score and performance from a somewhat different perspective. What happens if instead of speaking of a performance as an interpretation of a score, we speak of a score as one of multiple materials for producing a performance? From this perspective, the score may remain one of the privileged materials—also from the production team's perspective—just not the starting point and goal for analyzing the performance. When I speak of *material* here, I am not referring to one of the specific concepts that has been developed in the scholarship and theories on material (for example, Adorno's or Butler's) but rather to a use of the word that marks, in the sense of material for playing with and using, the difference to the status of the text in the process of analysis. The concept should show that the text is not more but also not less than one material among others (voices, bodies, costumes, movements, etc.) for producing a performance. This conception assumes that the decisive components for judging a performance are then not the text or the relationship between performance and text but rather the many different relationships that a performance can newly create between the different materials.[55]

This shift in focus opens our eyes, on the one hand, to all the elements of performance that cannot be traced back so easily or even at all to a textual form of the score, such as the particular voices and bodies of the singers and performers, and, on the other, to what is unique about performance and distinguishes it from texts and other artifacts: that it exists only in the moment, in the time of its appearance. That is the focus in this study: understanding performance as a living, one-time, and currently relevant event that also obeys rules of the present moment and engages with very different present and historical materials: present materials such as voices, bodies, movements, images; historical materials such as a score by Mozart, Verdi, Wagner, or another composer and a textual template, a libretto. It is about the live presence of theater, which takes place precisely and only in the simultaneous corporeal presence of performers and audience members; about the unpredictable dimensions of performance, the feedback loop between the stage and the auditorium.[56]

It is necessary to change the perspective because what happened on the performative level at, for example, the Komische Oper Berlin during the dress rehearsal of Konstanze's aria was, in my opinion, much more exciting than what a hermeneutic interpretation could bring to light. What one could see there, in all its graphic nature, subjected our bodies and perceptual apparatuses to a liminal experience. The "Martern" aria is one of the vocal high points of every *Entführung*, especially with such an exquisite Konstanze as Maria Bengtsson's. An audience that has been feverishly awaiting this aria for perhaps the whole evening would never disturb this number with so much as a cough, let alone actively intervene in it through heckling, unless something extraordinary had happened to the audience's sensory perception. Against this backdrop, the protests can be understood as physically necessary defense reactions against an assault on their own bodies and sensory perception. If it hadn't been a corporeally necessary and urgent reaction, then hardly anyone would have protested right in the middle of this aria.

By taking the template seriously (for many, too seriously), Bieito's *Entführung* violated the limits of many audience members' sense of decency and taboo, and very explicitly made liminal experiences possible that allowed the opera to become a currently relevant medium. These liminal experiences and violations of limits triggered very concrete physical reactions and actions, such as leaving the auditorium, slamming doors, and heckling. What happened here should be described as a degree of involvement that became manifest in concrete, active participation. But the assault on our visual perception had yet another consequence: the interaction and reciprocal intensification of visual and auditory perception made it appear as if the rococo powder that had been sitting like mildew on our reception of Konstanze's aria was being stirred up and blown away, revealing the liminal vocal and acoustic experience that this aria actually represents. This can also be understood as an engagement with the minimization of the abysses that this opera treats or with some of the audience's suppression of these abysses.

And the singing? And Maria Bengtsson? She sang for her life, for her survival, not only in the role of Konstanze in the face of the tortures she endures, which were presented in total clarity, but also as a singer in the face of an

40 *Theoretical foundations*

unbridled audience that was drowning her out. With all the vehemence at her disposal, she resisted the floods of disapproval coming from her audience. In my memory, the effect of her aria was a double one: her singing became even more intense and urgent than it already was, and at the same time, it conveyed a fragility or need for protection. Both together—caused in particular by the audience's intervening—made this moment painful, intense, demanding on all the senses, overdemanding, overpowering.

What could be experienced here is what is the case for every performance from a performative perspective, namely, the active participation of the audience and their interrelation with the performers and processes on stage. This does not mean that the characteristic interaction for performances always has to be expressed in such extremes, in such vociferous expressions as protests. Other symptoms of interaction include tense, silent concentration; loud applause and ovations that are perhaps nowhere so vehement as in opera; as well as a lack of concentration, boredom, and apathy—activities and passivities that are felt by performers and so influence the course of the performance. In the dress rehearsal of the "Martern" scene from *Die Entführung aus dem Serail*, the interaction occurred very concretely as an interplay between the stage (singing, action), the audience (protests, heckling, averting one's gaze), and again the stage (even more intense singing). Here something happened that is referred to in performance theory, following Erika Fischer-Lichte, as "autopoietic feedback loops,"[57] which take place precisely and only in the simultaneous bodily presence of performers and audience members and constitute the unpredictable dimension of performance. One can't grasp this with theories of interpretation. It calls for expanding the perspective to theories that are devoted to performance as an event sui generis.

Notes

1 For a detailed look at the multifaceted history and use of the term *interpretation*, see Riethmüller, "Interpretation in der Musik."
2 See Hans Heinrich Eggebrecht, "Interpretation," in *Riemann Musik Lexikon*, updated 13th ed., ed. Wolfgang Ruf in collaboration with Annette van Dyck-Hemming, vol. 2 (Mainz: Schott, 2012), 449–50.
3 Johann Strauss, *Die Fledermaus: Operette in 3 Akten*, RV 503, libretto by Richard Genée, ed. Michael Rot, vol. 3 of *Neue Johann Strauss Gesamtausgabe*, ser. 1, group 2 (Vienna: Strauss Edition, 1999), 207–8, mm. 7, 11, 12, 14, 16, 18.
4 Strauss, 208, mm. 20–25.
5 Strauss, 211, m. 49.
6 Mozart, *Entführung*, 85–86; McClatchy, *Seven Mozart Librettos*, 157.
7 On this, see Chapter 5.
8 The premiere was at the Monadnock Music Festival in Manchester, New Hampshire, in 1980, with revivals at the PepsiCo Summerfare in Purchase, New York, in 1987 and at the Vienna Festival in 1989 with a video recording (London: Decca, 1991).
9 English National Opera, London, 2001; Staatsoper Hannover, 2002.
10 See Wolfgang Amadeus Mozart, *Il dissoluto punito ossia il Don Giovanni*, K. 527, ed. Wolfgang Plath and Wolfgang Rehm, vol. 17 of *Neue Ausgabe sämtlicher Werke*, ser. 2, *Bühnenwerke*, group 5, *Opern und Singspiele* (Kassel: Bärenreiter, 1968), 388.

11 Mozart, *Don Giovanni*, 384–92, no. 23; McClatchy, *Seven Mozart Librettos*, 649.
12 See Jürgen Schläder's similar argumentation on Peter Sellars's 1987 production in "Strategien der Opern-Bilder," 194–95.
13 Mozart, *Entführung*, 119–31; McClatchy, *Seven Mozart Librettos*, 169.
14 McClatchy, *Seven Mozart Librettos*, 199.
15 Danuser, "Aktualität musikalischer Interpretationstheorie," 40.
16 Danuser, 40.
17 Danuser, 41.
18 Danuser, 41.
19 Danuser, 41.
20 Hermann Gottschewski, "Interpretation als Struktur," in *Musik als Text: Bericht über den internationalen Kongress der Gesellschaft für Musikforschung, Freiburg im Breisgau, 1993*, ed. Hermann Danuser and Tobias Plebuch, vol. 2 (Kassel: Bärenreiter, 1998), 156.
21 Gottschewski, 156.
22 Danuser, "Aktualität musikalischer Interpretationstheorie," 44.
23 See Chapter 3.
24 Danuser, "Aktualität musikalischer Interpretationstheorie," 47.
25 Ullrich, "Die Kunst ist Ausdruck ihrer Zeit," 233.
26 Georg Wilhelm Friedrich Hegel, *Aesthetics: Lectures on Fine Art*, trans. T. M. Knox, vol. 1 (Oxford: Oxford University Press, 1975), 277.
27 Danuser, "Aktualität musikalischer Interpretationstheorie," 49.
28 Hinrichsen, "Musikwissenschaft," 88–89.
29 Abbate, "Drastic or Gnostic?"
30 Albrecht Wellmer, "Werke und ihre Wirkungen: Kein Beitrag zur Rezeptionstheorie des Musiktheaters," in *Zukunftsbilder: Richard Wagners Revolution und ihre Folgen in Kunst und Politik*, ed. Hermann Danuser and Herfried Münkler (Schliengen: Argus, 2002), 261.
31 Anselm Gerhard, "Was ist Werktreue? Ein Phantombegriff und die Sehnsucht nach 'Authentischem,'" in *Werktreue: Was ist Werk, was Treue?*, ed. Gerhard Brunner and Sarah Zalfen (Vienna: Böhlau, 2011), 20, 23.
32 Erika Fischer-Lichte, "Was ist eine 'werkgetreue' Inszenierung? Überlegungen zum Prozess der Transformation eines Dramas in eine Aufführung," in *Das Drama und seine Inszenierung: Vorträge des internationalen literatur- und theatersemiotischen Kolloquiums, Frankfurt am Main, 1983*, ed. Fischer-Lichte with assistance from Christel Weiler and Klaus Schwind (Tübingen: Max Niemeyer, 1985), 46. See also Christopher Balme, "Werktreue: Aufstieg und Niedergang eines fundamentalistischen Begriffs," in *Regietheater! Wie sich über Inszenierungen streiten lässt*, ed. Ortrud Gutjahr (Würzburg: Königshausen and Neumann, 2008), 43–50.
33 Peter Konwitschny, "Wir bauen die Katastrophen nach," in Beyer, *Warum Oper?*, 26, 28, 36.
34 In his writings, the musicologist Nicholas Cook pursues a similar objective, without, however, considering the special performative conditions of the operatic repertoire. See Cook, "Process and Product."
35 On this, see also Cook, "Process and Product," para. 11.
36 Jossi Wieler and Sergio Morabito, "Es gibt keine richtige Interpretation," in Beyer, *Warum Oper?*, 65.
37 Wieler and Morabito, 65–66.
38 Claude Lévi-Strauss, "The Structural Study of Myth," *Journal of American Folklore* 68, no. 270 (1955): 430.
39 Lévi-Strauss, 435.
40 Lévi-Strauss, 435.
41 Lévi-Strauss, 435–36.
42 Hans Blumenberg, *Work on Myth*, trans. Robert M. Wallace (Cambridge: MIT Press, 1985), 270–71.

42 *Theoretical foundations*

43 Blumenberg, 299.
44 "Thus, myth grows spiral-wise until the intellectual impulse which has orginated it is exhausted. Its growth is a continuous process whereas its structure remains discontinuous." Lévi-Strauss, "Structural Study of Myth," 443.
45 On the reception of sources and the sources of reception, see again Blumenberg, *Work on Myth*, 299.
46 Eggebrecht, "Interpretation," 449.
47 Danuser, "Aktualität musikalischer Interpretationstheorie," 42.
48 Danuser, 41.
49 Danuser, 42.
50 Danuser, 41.
51 Danuser, 46.
52 This hierarchy of the score over the performance can be traced back historically to the adamant view of a composer aesthetics that was decisively influential in music at the end of the nineteenth century and, especially, in the first half of the twentieth century. See Danuser, 41–42.
53 Cook, "Process and Product."
54 Brüstle and Risi, "Aufführungsanalyse und -interpretation," 115. There Brüstle and I argue that the "score is ... viewed as a script, as a set of instructions, a kind of choreography of social interactions (a model that Cook adopted from the writings of, among others, the American scholar of theater studies Richard Schechner)" (116). See, for example, Richard Schechner, "Drama, Script, Theatre, and Performance," *Drama Review* 17, no. 3 (September 1973): 5–36. See also Bernhard Waldenfels, "Responsivity of the Body: Traces of the Other in Merleau-Ponty's Theory of Body and Flesh," in *Interrogating Ethics: Embodying the Good in Merleau-Ponty*, ed. James Hatley, Janice McLane, and Christian Diehm (Pittsburgh: Duquesne University Press, 2006), 91–106; Christian Kaden, Jan Brachmann, and Detlef Giese, "Zeichen," in *Die Musik in Geschichte und Gegenwart: Allgemeine Enzyklopädie der Musik begründet von Friedrich Blume*, 2nd rev. ed., ed. Ludwig Finscher, *Sachteil*, vol. 9 (Kassel: Bärenreiter, 1998), col. 2163: "Where it [music] does not see its essence in the congealed state of the 'product' or 'work' but rather in living action, in flowing energeia, there it ties its sound back to the producer, the musician, the sender—and anchors it in his corporeality. In this sense, it is not in the middle, between people, literally as a medium; it clings to people, is part of them, is their part."
55 On the concept of material and its manifestations in the different arts, see, for example, Reinhard Kapp, "Noch einmal: Tendenz des Materials," in *Musik*, ed. Kapp, Notizbuch 5/6 (Berlin: Medusa, 1982), 253–81; Andreas Haus, Franck Hofmann, and Änne Söll, eds., *Material im Prozess: Strategien ästhetischer Produktivität* (Berlin: Reimer, 2000); Sigrid G. Köhler, Jan Christian Metzler, and Martina Wagner-Egelhaaf, eds., *Prima Materia: Beiträge zur transdisziplinären Materialitätsdebatte* (Königstein im Taunus: Ulrike Helmer, 2004).
56 On this, see Chapter 3.
57 Erika Fischer-Lichte, *The Transformative Power of Performance: A New Aesthetics*, trans. Saskya Iris Jain (Abingdon: Routledge, 2008), 38–40.

2 Beyond semiotics

The interplay of representation and presence

Since its beginnings as an academic discipline, theater studies has investigated the characteristics that make theatrical performance unique. After the early and now discarded paradigm of reconstructing performances,[1] semiotic analysis became the main theoretical approach for engaging with the specific nature of performance, and it remained so for a long time. Following the theorem "culture as text," it understands a performance as a systematically structured, legible text. One of the great accomplishments of theater semiotics is how it systematically classifies the elements involved in the theatrical process as a precondition for discussing and writing about fleeting theatrical events. Initially assembled by Tadeusz Kowzan in 1968 and systematically presented by Erika Fischer-Lichte in 1983, this systematic classification consists in fourteen categories or—speaking semiotically—sign systems: words, intonation, mimicry, gestures, actors' movements in the space of the stage, characterization, hairstyle, costumes, props, decoration, lighting, music, sound effects, and the conception of space.[2]

The first step in semiotic analysis is segmentation, division into the smallest meaningful units (single gestures, single steps, single light changes, etc.). The performance is transcribed and dissected into single moments,[3] with the goal of being able to name the signs and sign combinations involved in the performance at every moment. Every single sign is conferred a meaning in the process of semiosis. This production of meaning can be observed in three dimensions: in the syntactic dimension (the relation of signs to other signs, for example, of a table to a chair or of a gesture to another gesture), in the semantic dimension (the relation of signs to their possible meanings, for example, of a hand gesture to its possible meaning as a wave goodbye), and in the pragmatic dimension (the relation of signs to their users, that is, to the audience members, for example, a gesture that means something different for each person). We can explain the three dimensions using the example of David Moss's singing, which is very unique in the context of operatic singing by trained singers. In the syntactic dimension, one can describe the contrast between the opera voices projecting beautiful sounds and David Moss's bass, scratchy, falsetto, and unclean tones amplified by a microphone. In the semantic dimension, one can understand opera voices as representing bel

DOI: 10.4324/9781003124863-4

44 Theoretical foundations

canto style or classical singing, which is synonymous with something like the norm (or default) of singing in the context of classical operetta and so does not allow any insights with regard to the inner state of characters; one can describe David Moss's singing, by contrast, with the keywords avant garde or contemporary music, and on the basis of this quality, one can understand him as representing a musical foreign body and the role of an eccentric. The pragmatic dimension raises the question as to what the respective style of singing can mean for particular listeners depending on their individual preferences. If one prefers the classical style of singing, then one will characterize David Moss's style as inappropriate or inadequate; but if one prefers a contemporary style and tends to distance oneself from the classical style of singing, then one will read operatic voices as outdated but still fitting. Proceeding from the sign systems of music and paralinguistic signs, both positions will lead to understanding David Moss's Orlofsky as representing an eccentric.

From the abundance of semiosis result different combinations and accumulations of meanings, for example, on the level of a character or also on the level of sign systems over the course of an entire performance, which can convey the overall meaning of a performance. Here the dramatic text at its basis can also play a role: that is, meanings are ascribed to the linguistic signs on the level of the characters, and they can then be compared with the meanings attached to the performance. But since this process is always a matter of transformations and translations, the concept of *Werktreue* also cannot come into play in performance analysis from this perspective, since it is not the work that becomes manifest in performance but rather only translations from texts into other materialities.[4] For these translations, there cannot be any absolute rules (only historically bound and conventional ones), since voices, bodies, movements, and scenic realizations do not appear in the dramatic text or score, only textualized linguistic signs and musical notations do, which are translated into other materialities according to particular principles that change depending on the time and prevailing aesthetic.

If one applies the semiotic approach to Hans Neuenfels's staging of *Die Fledermaus*, then one can read it as representing the Austrian Empire as a declining monarchy, which serves as a corrupt, hypocritical, decadent, xenophobic basis for fascist upstarts to rise to power. Some of the audience members' aggressive comments in response to David Moss's performance can be read in retrospect like a protest against this interpretation of Austrian (and as such, some of the audience members' own) history. In this context, David Moss as Prince Orlofsky represents the incarnation of decadence. He stands for a hedonistic generation that wants to forget everything, that shows no interest in public welfare or in the rules, whether they are social customs, a dress code, or the rules of a genre of art. With regard to proper artistic expression in operetta—that is, to singing—this generation, with their egoistic focus on their own pleasure, believes in "chacun à son gout." But does this adequately acknowledge, explain, and analyze the scandal and offense that David Moss's appearance triggered and the appeal he exerted?

It is the fate of prominent and widespread methods to be criticized, at times by their own creators.[5] The metaphor of "theater as text" has proven to be too rigid, too static, and too self-contained. Treating performance by viewing it as a text is limited to the interpretation of meaning; it is blind to eventness. In addition, individual processes of reception are not adequately taken into account in attempts to segment and transcribe performances; at most, they are inscribed in the subjectively biased segmentation and formulation of the transcripts and then have to be extracted again from them. This is, incidentally, the main criticism of Patrice Pavis's questionnaire for analyzing performances, which many scholars in theater studies have drawn on;[6] when one writes about an experience of a performance with keyword answers to a questionnaire, one risks losing the traces of subjective experience.[7]

Furthermore, the fourteen classical categories that underlie theater semiotics do not capture decisive factors of performance like rhythm, temporal extension, and the experience of continuity and discontinuity.[8] Yet precisely these points play an important role when one considers the specific characteristics of music theater and opera. Experiences of time and rhythm are shaped by the music or related to it in a very significant way. This observation reflects the fact that the approaches available for performance analysis in theater studies do not sufficiently address music for the purposes of analyzing music theater. Particularly since music is a sign system that demands much more attention in opera than in spoken theater, the difficulty of determining the meaning of individual signs particularly applies to musical signs. With the exception of language, sign systems do not have any clearly fixed denotations, which is particularly the case for musical signs.[9]

But the main criticism of semiotic performance analysis concerns how it reduces the theatrical process to a function of creating meaning, limiting it to a process of signification. Allow me to elucidate this with the two fundamentally important elements of body and voice. In semiotic performance analysis, performers' bodies are reduced to their function as signs for the body of a *character*, and their voices are understood to be the expressive capacity of a *character*. But what is not seen and not heard is the body as a sensual, phenomenal reality and the voice as a corporeally affective event.

Thus, this approach suppresses precisely those moments that elude being functionalized as signs—moments that cannot be described as the representation or embodiment *of something*; moments that rather primarily trigger intense experiences and bodily reactions. To account for this dimension, we must adopt different approaches. Hans-Thies Lehmann's proposed approach of an art of not-understanding (*Nicht-Verstehen*) can be seen as a helpful first step.[10] With reference to Susan Sontag's famous essay "Against Interpretation" and the "erotics of art"[11] she calls for, Lehmann describes a tendency in postdramatic theater in which *experience* takes evident priority over understanding meaning. The examples Lehmann names demonstrate that an extremely intensified presence of the body—its materiality and sexuality, including breathing, sweat, pain, strain, and the sheer physical being of performers—pushes its way to the fore over understanding or interpretation through "affects of attraction and repulsion."[12] Does this not bring us closer to Maria Bengtsson and David Moss as events?

With Maria Bengtsson's and David Moss's performances, one experiences the crisis of no longer being able to locate the theatrical frame that clearly separates the fictive and real theatrical worlds, a frame that is necessary for interpreting a performance. The tension of their performances is caused—one could say—by the indistinguishability of fiction and reality, by how the corporeality of the performers spills out beyond their roles. Is that the rebellious Konstanze fighting for her life? Is that Orlofsky groaning, panting, and wheezing? Or is it rather David Moss as David Moss who captivates me with all the virtuosity of his vocal expression and experimental pleasure? And is it not actually the revered singer Maria Bengtsson who is singing for her "survival" in the middle of an angry mob?

Becoming sensitive to the significative and nonsignificative character of elements of performance—to the play of representation and presence, which can be put into a familiar series of similarly conceived dichotomies—appears to be particularly important to experiencing opera performances.[13] In her engagement with the dimensions of the voice from the perspective of the philosophy of language, Sybille Krämer has called attention to how one can find the dynamic that unfolds in Nietzsche's writings between the art-theoretical categories of the Apollonian and the Dionysian—between, on the one hand, moderation and reason and, on the other, immoderate excess and the negation of distance—in different terminologies but with a very similar conception in Julia Kristeva, Roland Barthes, and Paul Zumthor:

> It is about the difference between the "symbolic" and the "semiotic" in Julia Kristeva, between "pheno-song" and "geno-song" in Roland Barthes, and Paul Zumthor's differentiation between the "text" and the "work." All three pairs of concepts—this is my hypothesis—can be read as versions of what Nietzsche means with the difference between tonal language and gestural language, between the Dionysian and the Apollonian.[14]

In going through these three theoretical edifices, Krämer finds it important that with all due respect for dichotomies and binary concepts, one side can never be thought without the other; that the two poles enter into a reciprocal relation of interdependence with one another.

With *representation*, the concept I use in this study, I refer to the dimension in which meanings are conferred on a staging, in which levels and layers of meaning are evoked in audience members. Every element is thus seen as a sign that means something; every element refers to something else. Every movement of a singer is read with regard to the movement of a character; every vocal expression with regard to the emotional state of a character.

With *presence*, by contrast, I want to address the dimension of perception that is not about the representation or portrayal of something; instead, every element (a movement, a tone) first of all only refers to itself. The signifying function appears to be suspended; instead, the quality, intensity, energy, and effect of an element is in the foreground of perception. A movement, a voice is perceived for itself. Such experiences can then also lead to associations that go in wild, disordered, and chaotic directions, associations that can be very distant from the plausible ascriptions of meaning in the context of the overall meaning of a performance (memories of other voices from other performances, everyday experiences, etc.). It is thus in the first place about intense experiences, bodily reactions, and certainly also irritating moments—about what, in Hans Ulrich Gumbrecht's words, "meaning cannot convey"[15] or about what Carolyn Abbate refers to as "drastic knowledge" in contrast to "gnostic knowledge."[16]

In her essay "Music—Drastic or Gnostic?," which I already mentioned in the last chapter, Abbate argues for focusing on the dimension of experience in music and opera. At the end of the essay, Abbate describes an autobiographical experience. She reports how she felt at a performance of Richard Wagner's *Die Meistersinger von Nürnberg* at the Metropolitan Opera in New York when Ben Heppner's voice spectacularly failed him in the role of Stolzing:

> He cracked on the high Gs and As while singing the first strophe in the first verse in the preliminary versions of the Prize Song, and at that point I made a quick calculation that he had five more strophes in two full verses in the preliminary version, and nine strophes in three verses in the final version in the last scene, in short lots more high Gs and As not even counting the act 3 quintet. This was when my eyes closed in despair .... Heppner would go on singing knowing what lay ahead. Now the other performers seemed ... still to inhabit their roles in Wagner's jolly Nuremberg, while Heppner became a unique human being in a singular place and time, falling from the high wire again and again.[17]

With her knowledge of the many high As that were still to be sung, Abbate empathized and suffered with the singer instead of with his role. The performance thereby acquired its unique, unrepeatable quality and conveyed—as she formulates it—a new kind of knowledge, a "drastic knowledge."[18]

> I was transfixed not by Wagner's opera but by Heppner's heroism, and what was important was not the apperception of concealed meaning through hermeneutic alchemy ... but the singular demonstration of moral courage, which, indeed, produces knowledge of something fundamentally different and of a fundamentally different kind. Perhaps one could call it drastic knowledge.[19]

I want to understand the experience of presence in performance as "drastic knowledge." What I mean is the intermittent radicalization of theatrical means in performance, that is, the concentration on materiality and processuality and disregard for the dimension of meaning—a concentration on moments to which one cannot immediately or cannot at all ascribe a specific meaning. These are moments when the combination of currently employed materials, which only exist in this process, and the effects of those materials are all that is relevant (bodies, voices, rhythms, sounds, and tones).

Again in this case, I don't mean to say that a performance only consists or could only consist of such moments. Rather, an interplay of representation and presence constitutes a performance. Thus, for example, in Neuenfels's *Fledermaus*, interpreting the meaning of the staging stood in the foreground for large stretches of the performance. Before Moss's entrance as Orlofsky, I was overcome by boredom with the dominance of interpreting meaning. With the Moss shock, a maelstrom began that swept me along and at the same time repelled me; in addition to the irritating nature of his body and voice, the return of interpretation—Orlofsky as a crack junkie—was soon also responsible for this. The vocally experimental sequence that Moss inserted between the two stanzas of his entrance couplet, which I discussed in the introduction, could also be perceived in this sense as a representation of the character's emotional state (the junkie's excess), while at the same time we experienced Moss in all his virtuosic self-referentiality.

The experience of such extraordinary moments cannot be generated by production strategies; that is, they cannot be ascribed to the plannable calculus of a production, and they cannot be sufficiently grasped from the perspective of interpretation research or through semiotic analysis. Only a theoretical position that decidedly places the complexity of the events of a performance under the auspices of the performative can develop a descriptive vocabulary and analytical toolbox for how opera negotiates performance.

Notes

1 See Guido Hiß, "Zur Aufführungsanalyse," in *Theaterwissenschaft heute: Eine Einführung*, ed. Renate Möhrmann (Berlin: Dietrich Reimer, 1990), 56–80.
2 See Erika Fischer-Lichte, *The Semiotics of Theater*, trans. Jeremy Gaines and Doris L. Jones (Bloomington: Indiana University Press, 1992), 260n2; and Hans-Thies Lehmann, "Die Inszenierung: Probleme ihrer Analyse," *Zeitschrift für Semiotik* 11, no. 1 (1989): 33. Fischer-Lichte added the conception of space as the fourteenth sign system to Kowzan's model.
3 On transcribed scores, see Hiß, "Zur Aufführungsanalyse," 74.
4 See Fischer-Lichte, *Semiotics of Theater*, 206.
5 See, for example, Erika Fischer-Lichte, *Ästhetische Erfahrung: Das Semiotische und das Performative* (Tübingen: A. Francke, 2001), 245–46.
6 Patrice Pavis, *Semiotik der Theaterrezeption* (Tübingen: Gunter Narr, 1988), 100–107.
7 Because complete sentences offer more possibilities for analyzing and reflecting on one's own attitude, composing a report on a performance has proven to be a better starting point both for working with students in seminars and for my own work.
8 Lehmann, "Inszenierung," 33.

9 Erika Fischer-Lichte, *Ästhetische Erfahrung*, 255–56. On this, see also Kaden, Brachmann, and Giese, "Zeichen."
10 On this and the following, see Hans-Thies Lehmann, "Über die Wünschbarkeit einer Kunst des Nichtverstehens," *Merkur*, May 1994, 426–31.
11 Susan Sontag, "Against Interpretation," in *Essays of the 1960s and 70s*, ed. David Rieff (New York: Library of America, 2013), 20.
12 Lehmann, "Kunst des Nichtverstehens," 428.
13 The understanding of representation I formulate here follows, among others, Carolyn Abbate, Erika Fischer-Lichte, Hans Ulrich Gumbrecht, and Sybille Krämer. See Abbate, "Drastic or Gnostic?"; Fischer-Lichte, *Transformative Power of Performance*; Hans Ulrich Gumbrecht, *Production of Presence: What Meaning Cannot Convey* (Stanford: Stanford University Press, 2004); Sybille Krämer, "Negative Semiologie der Stimme," in *Medien/Stimmen*, ed. Cornelia Epping-Jäger and Erika Linz (Cologne: DuMont, 2003), 65–84.
14 Krämer, "Negative Semiologie," 77.
15 Gumbrecht, *Production of Presence*.
16 Abbate, "Drastic or Gnostic?"
17 Abbate, 535.
18 Abbate, 535.
19 Abbate, 535.

3 Theories of performance and the performative

As shown in Chapter 2, the theorem "culture as text" or "theater as text" that underlies semiotically oriented performance analysis has proved to be too rigid. To do justice to the eventness of theatrical performance, an alternative point of reference is required.

> Up into the late 1980s, an understanding of culture expressed in the explanatory metaphor "culture as text" was predominant in cultural studies …. In the 1990s, a change of the scholarly perspective was in store. Then the largely overlooked performative traits of culture came into view; such traits establish an independent—practical—way of referring to worlds that already exist or are held to be possible, and they lend the resulting cultural actions and events a specific reality character that is not captured by the traditional text model. The metaphor of "culture as performance" began its ascent.[1]

The diagnosis of a performative turn both in culture and in cultural studies became the basis for manifold reflections on the potential of the concept of performativity as an explanatory model for a new understanding of culture. The credit for having made this perspective productive for theater studies is due in particular to Erika Fischer-Lichte and Jens Roselt. With its focus on corporeality, tonality, and vocality, the performance theory that Fischer-Lichte decisively initiated is devoted to the specific mediality of performance, that is, to the specific processes of perception and exchange that take place in a performance between the performers and audience members. In their essay "Attraktion des Augenblicks – Aufführung, Performance, performativ und Performativität als theaterwissenschaftliche Begriffe" (The attraction of the moment: Performance, performative, and performativity as concepts in theater studies), Fischer-Lichte and Roselt draw attention to how one can already identify a theory of performativity avant la lettre in the writings of Max Herrmann, one of the founding fathers of the discipline of theater studies.[2]

Fischer-Lichte's development of a new concept of performance as the basis for analyzing and understanding performances in her *Ästhetik des*

DOI: 10.4324/9781003124863-5

Performativen (*The Transformative Power of Performance*) is a central theoretical foundation for my reflections on the performative and perceptual dimensions of opera productions. Performance theory claims to apply to performances of all kinds. This study intends to examine how this approach can be made productive for performances of opera productions. To do so, it also has to clarify whether the specific materiality of opera in performance and its conditions of performance require an expansion or partial revision of this concept. A primary question is whether and to what extent the view inspired by the theories of the performative can help us grasp, describe, and explain more precisely the processes and conditions of performance, experience, and perception specific to opera performances.

Performance theory

How can theater studies define performance according to the premises of the performative turn, and what are the consequences? Fischer-Lichte proposes the following definition:

> Performance refers to an event that emerges from the confrontation and interaction of two groups of people who gather at a place at the same time so as to live through a situation together in bodily copresence where they act, in part in turns, as actors and spectators. What appears in a performance becomes manifest here and now, and is experienced in a particular way as present. A performance does not convey meanings already given somewhere else but rather produces new meanings that can be constituted by the individual participants in the course of the performance.[3]

Already in the first sentence, Fischer-Lichte names what is understood in performance theory as the specific mediality of performance. Outlining the particular medial constellation of a performance can make clear what differentiates and distinguishes performance in contrast to other medial forms of expression, such as texts, images, films, and other artifacts: namely, that it only exists in the moment, in the time of its appearance, and only in the bodily copresence and interaction of performers and audience members. An essential feature of this autopoietic feedback loop is that not only do performers affect spectators and listeners, but also the other way around. Certain rules may—depending on the rehearsals and staging strategies—govern a performance. But how a concrete performance, with its intensity, effect, and energetic force, actually takes place can only be predetermined to a limited degree if at all; instead, it depends on the unique, unrepeatable interaction between performers and audience members that occurs only in each unique constellation. If one understands performance in this way, then it becomes clear how much each person in the audience is jointly responsible for the event and effect of a performance. Roselt summarizes the core of performance theory in his *Phänomenologie des Theaters* (Phenomenology of theater) as follows:

In a performance, something happens between the stage and the audience that cannot be exclusively attributed to a staging, an expressive intention, or an aesthetic calculation; nor is it a purely subjective affair of each individual participant.[4]

A performance is thus "not merely the realization of a program"; rather, "in performing, something [can] happen between all the participants that goes beyond or infiltrates this program."[5] Roselt is referring to precisely this fact when he says "that something takes place in theater."[6] The precondition for this understanding of performance as an event is the "simultaneous presence of actors and spectators at a particular time and place."[7] Its phenomenological form is thus radically different from the alleged stability of the work: a performance, according to Roselt, "only exists in the moment of its concrete execution in front of spectators."[8] Roselt thereby underscores the fact that aspects of performative events cannot be reduced to intentional acts and cannot be planned; in this, Roselt refers to the positions of Martin Seel and Dieter Mersch. Seel writes:

> Not only every performance but every stage presentation entails that something happens in the presence of an audience that cannot be ascribed to the intentions involved. For the performers' actions essentially consist—like the staging they are indebted to—in letting something happen.[9]

Mersch formulates it thus: "The event, despite being something made, is not, however, something makeable. Planned, it is nevertheless not something plannable; constructed, it is, however, not something constructible."[10]

To clearly accentuate and precisely grasp the concept of performance, it is important and necessary—as Mersch's reflections about intentionality and planning clearly point out—to differentiate it from the concept of staging. Roselt elaborates the definition of the term *staging* as follows:

> A staging encompasses all the scenic elements and their arrangements, that is, actors, dramas, light, costumes, directorial insights, movements, and so on .... The course of a staging follows a plan and has a structure. Its dramaturgy is rehearsed and based on commitments and agreements between those involved.[11]

Fischer-Lichte defines *staging* in a very similar way. To specify it, she contrasts the concept of staging with that of performance in the same sentence:

> Thus I shall define staging as the process of planning (including chance operations and emergent phenomena in rehearsal), testing, and determining strategies which aim at bringing forth the performance's materiality. On the one hand, these strategies create presence and physicality; on the other, they allow for open, experimental and ludic spaces for unplanned and un-staged behavior, actions, and events.[12]

A significant difference between the concepts of staging and performance becomes clear in the question of a possible repetition. Roselt points out that a staging is "designed for repeatability":

> One can ... imagine the hypothetical that a spectator undertakes an experiment as the test subject and goes to the theater on all five evenings of *Ritter, Dene, Voss*. This spectator would witness one staging but five different performances, because he and Ilse Ritter, Kirsten Dene, and Gert Voss would be dealing with a different audience on each evening.[13]

But the difference is not only based on how a different composition of audience members gathers for the performance of the staging on each evening, "also the test subject himself is, as an individual spectator, different on each evening":

> What differentiates him today from himself yesterday is precisely the experience of yesterday's performance .... On each evening, he undergoes different transformations, directs his attention to different things, thinks different thoughts. These changes cannot be planned for him or for the actors.[14]

Thus, Roselt argues, "everything that happens in a performance [is] part of the performance; not only what happens on the stage but also what happens in the audience."[15] It is precisely this uniqueness and unpredictability of the composition of participants, their perceptual disposition, and their resulting different reactions to the actualization of the staging that is different at every performance and that allows a performance to become a singular, unrepeatable event.

Yet another feature responsible for the event-like character of a performance consists in the unpredictable meeting of independent and autonomous performers—both on the stage and in the auditorium. Roselt elaborates this again with reference to Seel:

> [It] should in no way be claimed that the interaction between the stage and the audience has to take place as an interference or as an explicit alteration to the staging. It is rather decisive that each performance is characterized by the possibility of this form of transgression. This potential is a decisive feature of the theatrical event, regardless of whether and how actors and spectators use it. With Seel, one can speak here of a "latent state" that makes the present experienceable in a particular way: "In contrast to the established praxis, the potentiality of the present announces its return in the event."[16]

In *The Transformative Power of Performance*, Fischer-Lichte proposes a new perspective on cultural processes that describes their dynamics and explains the effectiveness of those dynamics; such dynamics can be found in all cultural processes, that is, also in traditional theater and so too in performances of the traditional opera repertoire. This perspective hones our attention to processes that are extremely powerful (bodies, voices, rhythms, affects) but often overlooked or forgotten due to how we privilege the layers of meaning. Once we are aware of these processes, it becomes clear how relevant such factors are to the effectiveness and success of a performance.[17]

According to Fischer-Lichte, a performance is capable of effecting a status change. Spectators become actors and actors become spectators. In performances, one has experiences that differ strongly from everyday experiences and approach the experiential possibilities of rituals. This perspective is helpful for describing the particular intensity of experiences that theatrical performances make possible. Furthermore, as Fischer-Lichte argues, performances lastingly irritate or even suspend the familiar and habituated perceptual perspective that clearly separates subject and object. On the level of the relation of subject and object, performance unsettles the traditional relation of performer and audience (who is looking at and listening to whom?), and it also poses the fundamental question of where is the "work" that is to be watched or listened to, the "work" that could be abstracted from the performed actions? On the level of the relation of signifier and signified, one observes a clear shift toward emphasizing materiality, a predominance of the signifier over the signified, since what was usually overlooked becomes visible and stands in the foreground. Finally, Fischer-Lichte stresses awareness for the passing of time and for experiencing temporality as a feature of a situation of intensive perception.

Theories of the performative and opera in performance

Important theoretical catalysts and inspirations for the performative turn in culture and cultural studies include the theories of J. L. Austin and Judith Butler. As Fischer-Lichte summarizes, in his 1955 Williams James Lectures at Harvard, *How to Do Things with Words*, Austin "made a revolutionary discovery in language philosophy: linguistic utterances not only serve to make statements but they also perform actions, thus distinguishing constative from performative utterances."[18] A sentence therefore does not just say something but rather creates a reality, as at the christening of a ship or in the pronouncement of wedding vows.[19] Austin himself explicitly excluded the theatrical "as if" situation from his definition of successful speech acts, but in doing so he overlooked that new realities are also created in such situations with regard to how these speech acts affect audience members.

In transferring Austin's reflections to gender theory, Judith Butler has already brought Austin's approach into the context of performance theory (Butler speaks of the "dramatic"). For Butler, actions function to create identity. In her 1988 essay "Performative Acts and Gender Constitution," she demonstrates that "gender is ... an identity instituted through a *stylized repetition of acts*."[20] This means that there are not any fixed, stable identities that could be expressed by acts. Bodily actions that could be called performative do not make manifest any antecedently existing identity; instead, they newly create identities as their meaning. Identities form through actions; they are not predetermined.

If one transfers Austin's and Butler's positions to the conditions of the performance events of music theater, then one can postulate the following: gestures and vocal expressions do not only mean something, they do not only refer to something that they want to say, and they are also not secondary expressions of an antecedent work; rather they themselves effect something, trigger something, produce a new reality in the moment they are performed. An opera performance can also be viewed from this perspective: every action in the performance does not only refer to something previously recorded in music-theater notation but rather creates something new. A gesture or vocal expression on the stage does not always refer to the action of a presented dramatic role but rather occasionally refers only to itself as a performed action, as the gesture of a person on a stage.

Butler's diagnosis of gender performance as the "stylized repetition of acts" is particularly promising for contemplating opera performances. With attention to the processes of formalization and stylization in performances that are constantly repeated anew, one can explain how the interminable repetition of the repertoire still entails a certain degree of formal variability—a variability that is markedly limited by the integrity of the score and the expectations of the audience.

The linguists Ekkehard König and Ulrike Bohle have tried to systematize the different uses of the concept of the performative as it had developed in the work of different disciplines at the Berlin collaborative research center on "Performing Cultures." For an outsider's view on how this concept is used in theater studies, it is worth looking at König and Bohle's systematization in multiple regards. They write:

> From the perspective of theater studies, the performative can be equated with the essential traits of a performance, its particular materiality (spatiality, corporeality, voices, etc.) and aestheticity (event character), and this is when one abstracts performances from their relations to texts .... In the ascription of meaning, the focus is on what is produced as an effect on the individual spectator, that is, on what is more or less the perlocutionary in the sense of speech-act theory.[21]

But with reference to the textual template (and not only "when one abstracts performances from their relations to texts"), König and Bohle also provide an extremely productive idea for how to conceive and describe the specifically performative aspect of an opera performance:

> In institutional contexts in particular, the relevant performative utterances are prefabricated, entirely learned and recalled, unchangeable phrases. As a result, their use necessarily has, as with all larger prefabricated units (proverbs, idioms, quotes, phraseologisms, etc.), the character of repetition and recitation.[22]

56 *Theoretical foundations*

For the present context—the performative dimension of opera—the relation of a performance to its template (such as a score and other textual bases) as well as to performance conventions (such as a style of singing) is of decisive significance. In this context, the concept of the performative should serve to specify all the processes that take place in perceiving a unique and fleeting performance of a familiar template. König and Bohle point out that the uniqueness and unpredictability that characterize the performative can also particularly take place against the backdrop of a repeated template. And this repetition is then the precondition for being able to perceive that uniqueness, that unpredictability, at all—deviation in repetition, deviation from the template one believed to be familiar.

This perspective establishes a relation to a position of the literary scholar Paul Zumthor's, who formulates a few fundamental observations on the relation of text and spoken discourse in his essay "Body and Performance." These observations can be promisingly transferred to the focus on the performative dimension of opera. Zumthor writes:

> Speaking is not simply the executor of the linguistic system. It not only fails to confirm the system's precepts completely but, in its physicality, often contradicts these, to our surprise and pleasure.[23]

In the act of speaking, the *how* of saying exceeds *what* is said. As an action, speaking exceeds the guidelines of the linguistic system, changes them, and even contradicts them. This idea of a relation between guideline or template and act or realization in voiced language appears to be an extremely productive model for opera in performance, which is to be understood as the speech act of opera. Since Zumthor supplies his observation with the evaluative additions "to our surprise and pleasure," the potential the model possesses for conceiving the performative dimension of opera becomes even clearer: it consists in identifying the appeal of repeatedly realizing familiar templates—that is, the appeal of repeatedly staging and performing the classics of the opera repertoire—as an effect that can be explained with performance theory. Regarding friction between the performance and the familiar, the degree to which Zumthor's conception coincides with my own is also evident in the following remark on the "voice" and the "text intended for oral delivery":

> The effect ... is all the stronger, the better the voice sounds. In the intermediate spaces of the linguistic system, the desire to free oneself from its limits and to lose oneself in the wealth of its pure immediacy manifests itself. Perhaps the force of this desire is strengthened when the text intended for oral delivery naturally finds itself in the collective memory. Such a text is not isolated or disconnected from plot references but is destined, like the physical games in which it takes part, for play. Thus it offers, like any play, pleasure that comes from repetition and similarity.[24]

Hearing the voice makes possible an experience of pure presence that bursts open the limits of the linguistic system—and it does this all the more since the texts the voice realizes and exceeds are anchored in the collective memory, just as the operas treated here in performances and stagings are anchored in the collective memory as familiar repertoire classics. The fact that Zumthor's interest in medieval textual and performance practices does not mean "works" produced for textual fixation (that is, "literature" in the modern sense) draws an explicit connection—despite the supposed discrepancy in how performance practices in opera are related to a score (and that means a text)—to the conception of performance advanced here as taking place in the present. Familiar works invite us to play, to stage, to perform. And precisely through repetition and the invitation to witness similarities and deviations, playing with opera in performance produces pleasure. As if Zumthor himself had already had opera in performance in view and in his ear, he formulates the following about the event of the voice that merges with the bodies of the participants in the transgression and transformation of an existing situation: "Having become music, the poetic voice raises itself from the undifferentiated flow of noises and words. It becomes an event."[25] The intimate entwinement of voice and gesture is central to this since the "voice is functionally linked to gesture."[26] Zumthor points out that the "spoken word" does not live, "like the written, simply in a verbal context": "It necessarily belongs in the course of an existential situation that changes it in some way and whose totality is brought into play by the bodies of the participants."[27]

Zumthor's essay is entitled "Body and Performance," and so it falls in line with various efforts to explain the concepts of performance and the performative. Without explicitly naming Zumthor's position, but certainly reflecting it, Sybille Krämer and Marco Stahlhut claim that "a unified conception of the cultural processes that various theorists have called *performative* is out of the question."[28] But they still identify a "point of intersection common to all of them or a common basic intention in the use of the vocabulary of the performative. This can be described—condensed into a phrase—with 'constructed and not given'; or also [with] 'actions ('acts') and no identity.'"[29]

This outlines a conception of the performative that can be characterized as "strong," following Krämer and Stahlhut's differentiation between "weak," "strong," and "radical" performance concepts. By a "weak" performance concept, Krämer and Stahlhut understand the following: "We do not only speak about the world but also do something within the world by speaking."[30] Viewed in this way, performance refers "very generally" to "the action and use dimension of speech." The "strong" concept relevant to this study goes beyond that: "A 'performative' utterance is one that also executes what it signifies."[31] A performative utterance operates beyond the customary difference between "word and thing," the "means of representation and the represented." "Under certain conditions, words can become actions. Worldly states are not only represented through language but rather constructed and changed."[32] From such a perspective of performance theory, one can differentiate with regard to texts "between 'saying' and 'showing,' between 'what'

58 *Theoretical foundations*

and 'how'": "Where such a 'double exposure' is possible, a 'performative reading' of a text can question or critically comment on what is asserted in the 'constative reading' of the text."[33]

Krämer and Stahlhut summarize what can be understood with a performative orientation as follows: "Methodologically, the significance of a performative orientation consists in revising the conceptual relation between model and performance, pattern and use, or rule and application." It thus has to do with "no longer focusing on the aspect of form over performance but rather on performance over form."[34] This raises the question: "What is it then in performance that exceeds the model, in the application of a rule that modifies the rule, in short, in the repetition that at the same time changes what is repeated?"[35]

The performance of an opera does not only present that opera and our knowledge about it; rather, it also definitively and lastingly constitutes and changes our understanding of the opera.

Notes

1 Erika Fischer-Lichte, "Performativität/performativ," in *Metzler Lexikon Theatertheorie*, ed. Fischer-Lichte, Doris Kolesch, and Matthias Warstat, 2nd ed. (Stuttgart: J. B. Metzler, 2014), 253.
2 Erika Fischer-Lichte and Jens Roselt, "Attraktion des Augenblicks – Aufführung, Performance, performativ und Performativität als theaterwissenschaftliche Begriffe," in Fischer-Lichte and Wulf, *Theorien des Performativen*, 237–54.
3 Erika Fischer-Lichte, "Aufführung," in Fischer-Lichte, Kolesch, and Warstat, *Metzler Lexikon Theatertheorie*, 15–16.
4 Jens Roselt, *Phänomenologie des Theaters* (Munich: Wilhelm Fink, 2008), 46.
5 Roselt, 47.
6 Roselt, 47.
7 Roselt, 47.
8 Roselt, 47.
9 Martin Seel, "Ereignis: Eine kleine Phänomenologie," in *Ereignis: Eine fundamentale Kategorie der Zeiterfahrung; Anspruch und Aporien*, ed. Nikolaus Müller-Schöll (Bielefeld: Transcript, 2003), 40.
10 Dieter Mersch, *Ereignis und Aura: Untersuchungen zu einer Ästhetik des Performativen* (Frankfurt am Main: Suhrkamp, 2002), 234.
11 Roselt, *Phänomenologie des Theaters*, 52–53.
12 Fischer-Lichte, *Transformative Power of Performance*, 188.
13 Roselt, *Phänomenologie des Theaters*, 55.
14 Roselt, 56.
15 Roselt, 56.
16 Roselt, 58. For the quote from Seel, see Seel, "Ereignis," 38.
17 Fischer-Lichte developed the initial premises of her concept of performance through a discussion and theoretical systematization of a performance by Marina Abramović (*Lips of Thomas*, Innsbruck 1975). See Fischer-Lichte, *Transformative Power of Performance*, 11–23.
18 Fischer-Lichte, *Transformative Power of Performance*, 24.
19 On this, see J. L. Austin, *How to Do Things with Words*, ed. J. O. Urmson and Marina Sbisà, 2nd ed. (Cambridge: Harvard University Press, 1975). On Austin's differentiation of illocutionary, locutionary, and perlocutionary acts, see Ekkehard König and Ulrike Bohle, "Zum Begriff des Performativen in der

Sprachwissenschaft," in Fischer-Lichte and Wulf, *Theorien des Performativen*, 15: "After Austin introduces and explains the differentiation between 'performative utterances' and 'constative utterances' in the first part of his lectures, this opposition is then questioned in the further course of the lectures and finally abandoned .... This differentiation is replaced by the differentiation between different acts (speech acts) that are performed through every kind of utterance. In addition to the essentially interactive dimension of an utterance, the illocutionary act, which can be identified through verbs like *promise, request, ask, guarantee, question, claim, propose*, and so on, Austin further differentiates locutionary acts (the production of sounds, reference to the world, expressions of content, etc.) and perlocutionary acts (attaining effects on the addressee)." Also see Sybille Krämer and Marco Stahlhut, "Das 'Performative' als Thema der Sprach- und Kulturphilosophie," in Fischer-Lichte and Wulf, *Theorien des Performativen*, 37: "*That* we say something, the locutionary act makes sure of that; what we do *by* saying something, that is what the illocutionary act is about; what we want to effect on our listener *through* saying something is the task of the perlocutionary act."

20 Judith Butler, "Performative Acts and Gender Constitution: An Essay in Phenomenology and Feminist Theory," *Theatre Journal* 40, no. 4 (December 1988): 519.
21 König and Bohle, "Begriff des Performativen," 23.
22 König and Bohle, 21.
23 Paul Zumthor, "Body and Performance," in *Materialities of Communication*, ed. Hans Ulrich Gumbrecht and K. Ludwig Pfeiffer, trans. William Whobrey (Stanford: Stanford University Press, 1994), 222; translation modified.
24 Zumthor, 223; translation modified.
25 Zumthor, 224.
26 Zumthor, 224.
27 Zumthor, 224–25.
28 Krämer and Stahlhut, "Das 'Performative,'" 45.
29 Krämer and Stahlhut, 45.
30 Krämer and Stahlhut, 55.
31 Krämer and Stahlhut, 55.
32 Krämer and Stahlhut, 55.
33 Krämer and Stahlhut, 56.
34 Krämer and Stahlhut, 56.
35 Krämer and Stahlhut, 57.

4 The entanglement of the senses
Premises from perception theory

If a performance is defined as a process that takes place through the actions of performers and audience members, then all the participants of a performance (that is, also the audience members) are, first of all, equally responsible for realizing it; second, it becomes clear that what matters is the individual experiences of each and every person; these experiences must be taken seriously as parts of the performance and are not dependent on the intentions of the work or the author and cannot be attributed to them. This means that no event can be described independently from subjective corporeal experience. For that reason, the present study relies on, in addition to performance theory, phenomenological investigations on the dissolution of the subject–object dichotomy (Husserl, Merleau-Ponty, Roselt, Waldenfels), that is, on studies on subjective corporeal experience as well as on investigations from perceptual psychology and physiology (Behne, Brandstätter, Emrich) as a central point of reference for finding possible ways to describe the conditions under which the performative process takes place.

On the particular necessity of integrating the audience in phenomenological theories of performance, Jens Roselt writes in his *Phänomenologie des Theaters*: "A theory of performance that wants to do justice to the distinctive temporal and spatial features of theater [must] always integrate the audience in its reflections." As he makes clear, this "does not have to do with an audience as perhaps conceived by those responsible for and involved in a performance."[1] It is, rather, a question of which imaginable forms of audience participation in a performance can be described if the "specific materiality and mediality of theater" is to be found precisely "in the entangling of stage and audience. One can thus think, for instance, of rhythms and atmospheres of performances as interactions that the audience has a creative part in."[2] Against the backdrop of the theory of performance, it becomes plausible that the "investigation of a concrete performance must include the modes of experience of a concrete audience."

> As spectators, we are an integral component of performances. Only in our perception and through our experiences does the performance come into its own. In this, we are not just passive recipients who observe from the

DOI: 10.4324/9781003124863-6

orchestra what the stage has to say. We are rather called to a form of activity that does not only proceed intellectually but also affects each of us physically.[3]

Erika Fischer-Lichte and Jens Roselt have drawn attention to how Max Herrmann already designated the "creative activity of spectators" as a specific characteristic of theater performances; according to Herrmann, this activity develops "in a secret reliving, ... in a secret urge to perform the same movements, to produce the same vocal sounds in the throat."[4]

Roselt notes that a phenomenologically informed theory of art has had a decisive influence on such a conception of theater and perception. He writes, "What remains informative in the investigations from the twenties is the thought of conceiving aesthetics not just based on the artwork but on how the artwork is experienced."[5] This shift in perspective from the work to experience is accompanied by a reevaluation of perceptual processes: "The perception of art is thus not a secondary process of mere intake; the value or the being of art is instead contained in its experience."[6] In this, Roselt refers to, among others, Georg Bensch, who states the following on the history of phenomenological aesthetics and, more fundamentally, on phenomenologically oriented perspectives on art:

> Aesthetically perceiving an artwork means intently auscultating it for the feelings with which we bring it to life, but it also means being surprised by these feelings as if the artwork had produced them independently. The only thing that is fixed in the artwork is thus its ability to be brought to life. Meaning is only made when a perceiving subject makes use of this ability to be brought to life and actualizes it aesthetically.[7]

If one takes seriously the dissolution of the subject–object dichotomy as it is articulated in phenomenology,[8] then I, as an audience member perceiving a singing person in the opera, enter into a relation with this other.[9] The voice is then to be understood as the experience of a relation between producers and perceivers, in their copresence and covibration. Just as singing is a bodily process, a transfer of unique bodily characteristics into space, experiencing a voice is also a bodily process. The entangled process of singing, being heard, and listening can be understood as an intimate act of exchange.[10]

As already described by Herrmann, listening gives rise to the desire to imitate what one has just experienced, to participate actively. The cultural critic and scholar Wayne Koestenbaum describes this desire in the process of perception when one experiences an opera diva:

> A singer's voice sets up vibrations and resonances in the listener's body. First, there are the physiological sensations we call "hearing." Second, there are gestures of response with which the listener mimics the singer, expresses physical sympathy, appreciation, or exaltation: shudder, gasp, sigh; holding the body motionless, relaxing the shoulders, stiffening the

spine. Third, the singer has presence, an expressive relation to her body—and presence is contagious. I catch it. The dance of sound waves on the tympanum, and the sign I exhale in sympathy with the singer, persuade me that I have a body .... Forceful displays of singing insist that the diva has a body and so do you because your heartbeat shifts in uncanny affinity with her ascent.[11]

In the particular situation of perceiving opera, this "creative activity" (Herrmann) can become noticeable after intense experiences in, for example, bodily and vocal signs of exhaustion like breathlessness or hoarseness. It appears as if active perception effects a tension and exertion of precisely those body parts that are necessary for producing sounds: the breathing apparatus and the vocal cords. Or as one can read in an 1830 review of the tenor Giovanni Battista Rubini, who appeared in Vienna in a performance of Gioachino Rossini's *Tancredi*: "Instead of the singer, the listener loses his breath."[12]

A possible neurophysiological approach to explaining this can perhaps be seen in the resonance system of so-called mirror neurons, which have been described by the Parma brain researchers Vittorio Gallese and Giacomo Rizzolatti and which are possibly responsible for phenomena like echopraxia, the involuntary imitation of others when, for example, they yawn or laugh, and also for sympathy, the simulation of others.[13] But I do not want to push a neurophysiologically verifiable mechanism that determines, as an automatism, the perception of opera performances. I rather want to focus on the dimension of sensual experience with a phenomenological orientation and to acknowledge the subjectivity of the perceiver, which is foundational to every act of perception. This ineluctable subjectivity should not be viewed as an obstacle to academic engagement but rather, on the contrary, as a challenge and decisive factor for one to take on. Carolyn Abbate has rightly stated that renouncing the safe basis of formal and hermeneutic methods allocates a new, uncertain place for the perceiving and writing I:

This first person, this I who isn't going to forget, must be willing to walk onstage once what counts is the live performance that once took place, experienced only by those who were present .... There is no place to hide behind formalism's structural observations about works or texts .... A performance does not conceal a cryptic truth to be laid bare. But accepting its mortality, refusing to look away, may nevertheless be some form of wisdom.[14]

The present study discusses the experience and effects of performances based on the precondition, named above, that experience is also dependent on subjective dispositions, the goal of course not being to find out how a certain performance may have affected an entire audience. It is about addressing my own experience so as to point out aspects that are at work in a performance that are typically ignored or dismissed. If they are not the same effects that are triggered in others—and they can never be exactly the same—then one can, based on one's own experience, nevertheless transsubjectively infer that at least similar or even approximately the same mechanisms were at work in other audience members.[15] This is not about strengthening or reintroducing empirical methods for investigating how art is experienced.[16] Instead, by thematizing their own experience, scholars can—I can as a scholar—come to descriptions of this process that can then also lead, through reflection on them, to insights into more general processes of perception.

One of these insights could consist in going into greater detail about how the interplay of memory and expectation in our perception of time—in Edmund Husserl's terminology, the interplay of "retention" and "protention"[17]—is the basis for perceptual processes in opera: a primal impression such as a tone, a musical figure, or a voice is, in the process of perception, inscribed in memory and becomes part of retention. From this experience, a certain expectation develops for the continuation of the process, the expectation of a future impression, protention, is awoken.

This model describes the fundamentals of every act of perception; but it is particularly revealing with regard to the perception of bodies and voices witnessed live in music theater, in particular, when the material being performed is associated with heightened expectations because of its strong presence in the very small core repertoire of opera houses. I thus come to the theater as a preshaped listener with certain voices in my head when one of the works of the canonical repertoire is playing, works that allow me to anticipate and hear many phrases and tones in advance. The event of each moment then enters into a dynamic interaction with my experiences of the past and anticipations of the future. When my expectations are not met, it can trigger disappointment or boredom but also surprise or fascination, or because of surfeit fulfillment, both ecstasy and weariness.

In addition to this phenomenologically oriented theory of perception, the connection of two further theoretical directions is particularly interesting for this investigation. They are the theory of gestalt perception and the theory of intermodal integration. In his seminal work from 1956, *Emotion and Meaning in Music*, Leonard B. Meyer elaborated how the perception of music is subject to the gestalt principle and awakens expectations in the listener.[18] And in his investigations on the perception of time, Götz Pochat has pointed to the "intimate association of phenomenological temporal analysis and structural research based on gestalt psychology."[19] The corroboration of the processes of retention and protention in current brain research from a neuronal perspective (for example, in investigations of patients with an injury to the hippocampus)[20] underlines the current relevance of phenomenological aesthetics. Bringing together the named theories on perception makes it possible to illuminate in more detail the interplay and evaluation of auditory and visual impressions in the perceptual situation of an opera performance and to find out how music can be correlated with certain associations and how these associations can be further altered.

In engaging with the perceptual situation of opera performances, one question is of particular interest: How did widespread judgments like "that makes sense" or "that doesn't make any sense" arise, or, to be heard even more frequently, "that totally distracted me from the music," and also, though rarely, "I was never so concentrated on the music." What needs to be looked at here in more detail is the interplay of auditory and visual impressions in the perceptual situation of opera performances. In the first place, these are movements and visible scenic actions interacting with very familiar music that is also frequently auditorily comprehensible for audience members.

The familiarity of the music is based on knowledge of previous performances or on its presence in media like CDs, DVDs, television, and the Internet. When hearing it again, the familiar music initially evokes associations from when it was first encountered. Yet in connection with unfamiliar and unexpected visual impressions, it becomes tied to new associations and changes even as an auditory impression. What explanatory models do perceptual psychologists and physiologists offer for this so-called intermodal perception? Peter Mussbach, a psychiatrist and neurologist as well as an opera director and a former director of the Berlin Staatsoper Unter den Linden, wrote the following in the foreword to the program preview of his first season as the director of the Staatsoper in 2003: "The simultaneity of very different sensory impulses, the synchronicity of perceptual modes, animates us. Recent findings in perceptual psychology also indicate that we, for example, see more clearly when we hear, ([for example in] spatial orientation)." Klaus-Ernst Behne follows the same line of thought when he writes, "Experiments have shown that, for example, the visual threshold can be manipulated by strong or weak auditory stimuli, indeed that smells can intensify the acuity of vision."[21] For opera, this means that sound and movement or sights and sound intensify one another reciprocally.

Intermodal qualities appear to be more pronounced in children than in adults. Bernhard Waldenfels reports this with regard to spatial orientation in a mirror;[22] Helga de la Motte-Haber with regard to hearing colors.[23] The theory is also confirmed in the pedagogical practice of making the system of musical notes more accessible to children by using colors instead of letters. What is remarkable is that an above average number of children acquire absolute pitch through this method; that is, they are able to identify the precise pitch of an arbitrary tone when it sounds. The (at first arbitrary) ascription of a color to a tone may be able to better effect a sensibilization of the sense of hearing than writing or letters can; color strengthens the auditory mode of perception. This at least corroborates the thesis that a stimulus of one modality is capable of intensifying a stimulus of another modality.[24]

Yet intermodal perception is not only able to effect an intensification of the other modality but also a transformation. Just as tones are subject to a change of meaning depending on the harmonic and melodic context, the repeated perception of familiar music, for example, in different visual contexts, can change.[25] In this context, Behne refers to what physicists and sound technicians call the crosstalk effect, which results in events in one system modifying those in another.[26] He emphasizes, though, the quality of these modifications as negligible and refers to how the qualities of colors cannot be fundamentally influenced through auditory perceptions (that is, for example, red cannot become green). Only diffuse, labile, and relatively unclear perceptions can be modified.[27]

The music psychologist Helga de la Motte-Haber sees a basis for the possibility of such transformations in the laziness of human information processing. She means that we search for the fastest possible meaning, and she gives an account of the so-called McGurk effect: I see that someone says "ga" without hearing it. At the same time, I hear a "ba" over a speaker. What I then believe I perceive is neither one nor the other, that is, neither "ga" nor "ba," but rather a third sound, namely, "da," that is, something in between the two individual perceptions.[28] It is interesting in this case how individual perceptions are apparently changed in multimodal perception. Together, differing pieces of information lead to a new result. Visually perceivable scenic processes and bodily movements can change the perception of music, just as, vice versa, the specific sound of a musical phrase can change the perception of visual processes.

The neurologist and psychiatrist Hinderk Emrich goes a step further when he attempts to explain how one does not perceive singular data in multimodal phenomena but rather gestalts in the sense of gestalt theory. According to Emrich, intermodal integration is responsible for this. Different aspects of an object—like form, color, movement, surface structure, accompanying noise phenomena, and so on—can be related to each other in such a way that they are perceived as a "holistic unity" in the sense of gestalt theory. The question is then what mechanisms are at the basis of this intermodal integration ("binding"). There are indications, according to Emrich, that such intermodal unity can only be realized when different aspects of perception are related in the associative cortex based on evaluative structures in the limbic system.[29] He assumes that two modally different perceptions are unified through a binding executed by the limbic system. On the basis of this coupling by the brain's evaluative center of emotion, representations no longer appear as disconnected but rather as a meaningful unity.

In her essay "Musik und Bewegung: Wahrnehmungspsychologische Erkenntnisse" (Music and movement: Findings from perceptual psychology), Ursula Brandstätter summarizes Wolf Singer's thesis that "the temporal synchronization of neuronal patterns ... constitutes the neurobiological foundation for the integration of sense perceptions."[30] Brandstätter's reference to how "processes of synchronization are often associated with particular feelings of pleasure" is promising for better understanding the perceptual processes of heightened intensity that I treat in this study, both the positive and negative ones, enthusiasm and protest. She states "that the synchronization of phenomena or processes that are at first independent from one another is endowed with positive feelings of pleasure."[31] According to Brandstätter, this applies "in particular to the synchronization of music and bodily movement."[32]

In this study, I assume that the relations (correspondences or oppositions) between sounds and movements simultaneously experienced in opera performances are a manifestation of intermodal integration. With familiar operas, there is something like a habitualization or conditioning to such combinations or integrations. Intermodal integration thus refers to how visually perceived scenic actions are brought into a direct connection with acoustic events. The relative openness of music means that it is further determined by simultaneous visual experiences. One encounters a certain combination, perceives this combination as a gestalt, becomes accustomed to it, and then resists letting it go. This conditioning can be disturbed and irritated by new combinations. And then this irritation can lead to rejecting the new combination or to new conditioning, so, in the latter case, to an expansion of conditioning after a phase of becoming aware of the irritation. Emrich writes, "It is only because it is also possible to experience the improbable, the unforeseeable, that human subjects can adapt to completely new types of situations and develop adequate coping strategies in them."[33] From this, one could conclude that current performances of the familiar opera repertoire overload and interrupt the mechanisms of gestalt perception, resulting either in a satisfying feeling of pleasure in cases of successful integration or in irritation and rejection.

Notes

1 Roselt, *Phänomenologie des Theaters*, 321.
2 Roselt, 322.
3 Roselt, 322.
4 Max Herrmann, "Das theatralische Raumerlebnis," in *Vierter Kongress für Ästhetik und allgemeine Kunstwissenschaft, Hamburg, 7.–9. Oktober 1930: Bericht*, ed. Hermann Noack, supplemental volume to *Zeitschrift für Ästhetik und allgemeine Kunstwissenschaft* 25 (1931), 153; quoted from Fischer-Lichte and Roselt, "Attraktion des Augenblicks," 240.
5 Roselt, *Phänomenologie des Theaters*, 210.
6 Roselt, 210.
7 Georg Bensch, *Vom Kunstwerk zum ästhetischen Objekt: Zur Geschichte der phänomenologischen Ästhetik* (Munich: Wilhelm Fink, 1994), 172; quoted from Roselt, *Phänomenologie des Theaters*, 211.
8 On this, see also Maurice Merleau-Ponty, *Phenomenology of Perception*, trans. Donald A. Landes (Abingdon: Routledge, 2012); on its transfer to theater studies, see Jens Roselt, "Aufführungsparalyse," in Balme, Fischer-Lichte, and Grätzel, *Theater als Paradigma der Moderne*, 145–53; Jens Roselt, "Erfahrung im Verzug," in Fischer-Lichte, Risi, and Roselt, *Kunst der Aufführung*, 27–39; Roselt, *Phänomenologie des Theaters*.
9 On this approach, see for instance Bernhard Waldenfels, "Stimme am Leitfaden des Leibes," in Epping-Jäger and Linz, *Medien/Stimmen*, 19–35; Roland Barthes, "The Grain of the Voice," in *The Responsibility of Forms: Critical Essays on Music, Art, and Representation*, trans. Richard Howard (New York: Hill and Wang, 1985), 267–77; Risi, "Die bewegende Sängerin," 135–43; Sonja Galler and Clemens Risi, "Singstimme/Gesangstheorien," in Fischer-Lichte, Kolesch, and Warstat, *Metzler Lexikon Theatertheorie*, 325–28.
10 See Chapter 7.

11 Wayne Koestenbaum, *The Queen's Throat: Opera, Homosexuality, and the Mystery of Desire* (New York: Poseidon, 1993), 42.
12 Quoted from Konrad Huber, "Giovanni Battista Rubini als Donizetti-Interpret," in *Donizetti in Wien: Kongreßbericht (musikwissenschaftliches Symposion, 17–18. Oktober 1997)*, ed. Leopold M. Kantner (Vienna: Praesens, 1998), 117.
13 On this, see, for instance, Gerhard Roth, *Fühlen, Denken, Handeln: Wie das Gehirn unser Verhalten steuert* (Frankfurt am Main: Suhrkamp, 2001), 385.
14 Abbate, "Drastic or Gnostic?," 536.
15 On the claim that "descriptions of perceptions" make to "inter- and transsubjective validity," see Michael Weingarten, *Wahrnehmen* (Bielefeld: Aisthesis, 1999), 9.
16 Also see Roselt, *Phänomenologie des Theaters*, 324–25.
17 See, for instance, Edmund Husserl, *On the Phenomenology of the Consciousness of Internal Time (1893–1917)*, trans. John Barnett Brough, vol. 4 of *Collected Works*, ed. Rudolf Bernet (Dordrecht: Kluwer Academic, 1991), esp. 21–75; Edmund Husserl, *Die Bernauer Manuskripte über das Zeitbewusstsein (1917/18)*, ed. Rudolf Bernet and Dieter Lohmar, vol. 33 of *Husserliana: Gesammelte Werke* (Dordrecht: Kluwer Academic, 2001), esp. 3–49.
18 See Nicholas Cook and Nicola Dibben, "Emotion in Culture and History: Perspectives from Musicology," in *Handbook of Music and Emotion: Theory, Research, Applications*, ed. Patrick N. Juslin and John A. Sloboda (Oxford: Oxford University Press, 2010), 57.
19 Götz Pochat, "Erlebniszeit und bildende Kunst," in *Augenblick und Zeitpunkt: Studien zur Zeitstruktur und Zeitmetaphorik in Kunst und Wissenschaften*, ed. Hans Holländer and Christian W. Thomsen (Darmstadt: Wissenschaftliche Buchgesellschaft, 1984), 41.
20 See Karl K. Szpunar, Jason M. Watson, and Kathleen B. McDermott, "Neural Substrates of Envisioning the Future," *PNAS* 104, no. 2 (9 January 2007): 642–47; and Demis Hassabis et al., "Patients with Hippocampal Amnesia Cannot Imagine New Experiences," *PNAS* 104, no. 5 (30 January 2007): 1726–31.
21 Klaus-Ernst Behne, "Über die Untauglichkeit der Synästhesie als ästhetisches Paradigma," in *Der Sinn der Sinne*, ed. Kunst- und Ausstellungshalle der Bundesrepublik Deutschland (Göttingen: Steidl, 1998), 109.
22 "According to Merleau-Ponty, the senses can be translated into one another without an interpreter; they merge together on their own accord, without a mediating idea." Bernhard Waldenfels, *Das leibliche Selbst: Vorlesungen zur Phänomenologie des Leibes* (Frankfurt am Main: Suhrkamp, 2000), 92.
23 Helga la Motte-Haber, *Handbuch der Musikpsychologie*, 3rd ed. (Laaber: Laaber-Verlag, 2002), 327.
24 See Motte-Haber, 327.
25 Motte-Haber, 93.
26 Behne, "Untauglichkeit der Synästhesie," 110.
27 Behne, 110.
28 Helga de la Motte-Haber, "Wahrnehmung und ästhetische Erfahrung," *Positionen* 37 (1998): 6.
29 Hinderk M. Emrich, "Wirklichkeit der Wahrnehmung – Wahrnehmung der Wirklichkeit," in *Flamboyant: Schriften zum Theater* 9 (1999): 64.
30 Ursula Brandstätter, "Musik und Bewegung: Wahrnehmungspsychologische Erkenntnisse – exemplifiziert und falsifiziert an *Jagden und Formen* (Wolfgang Rihm/Sasha Waltz)," in *Neue Musik in Bewegung: Musik- und Tanztheater heute*, ed. Jörn Peter Hiekel (Mainz: Schott, 2011), 171. Brandstätter refers here to Wolf Singer, "Das Bild in uns – Vom Bild zur Wahrnehmung," in *Iconic Turn: Die neue Macht der Bilder*, ed. Christa Maar and Hubert Burda (Cologne: DuMont, 2005), 56–76.
31 Brandstätter, "Musik und Bewegung," 175.
32 Brandstätter, 175.
33 Emrich, "Wirklichkeit der Wahrnehmung," 65.

Part II
Analytical approaches

5 Symbioses and contestations
The interaction of auditory and visual elements

In discussions about opera productions, the question of how the music and scene interact—whether they complement, double, or even contradict one another—belongs to those most commonly posed. But the answers seldomly go beyond general observations. With intermodal integration and synchronization in the sense of gestalt perception, Chapter 4 discussed perception theory as a possible perspective for the integration of music and scene. And Chapter 1 concretely named one of the possible relationships between auditory and visual elements: the scenic substantiation or legitimation of formal or structural features in the musical sequence. Thus, as mentioned, both Peter Sellars in his staging of *Don Giovanni*[1] and Calixto Bieito in his stagings of *Don Giovanni*[2] and *Die Entführung aus dem Serail*[3] asked themselves how a change in affect and tempo from larghetto to allegretto moderato in Donna Anna's aria "Non mi dir" (Never say) in the second act[4] or Konstanze's endless chains of coloratura in her aria "Ach ich liebte, war so glücklich" (Oh, I was in love, so filled with joy)[5] can be legitimized and substantiated. The stagings found solutions in stimulating Donna Anna's and Konstanze's bodies through drugs or sex.

To further explain this technique of scenically legitimizing turning points in the musical dramaturgy, I would like to use a musicological text on opera that is already considered a classic: Carl Dahlhaus's essay "Zur Methode der Opern-Analyse" (On the method of analyzing opera),[6] which Dahlhaus understands as contributing to his attempts at developing "an aesthetics of opera that starts less with the linguistic and musical text and more with the theatrical event."[7] Using the example of Susanna and Figaro's duet from the finale of the fourth act of Mozart's *Le nozze di Figaro*, Dahlhaus names the technique of trying to legitimize musical features on the level of the plot—that is, the approach, also and especially practiced in so-called Regietheater, of scenically substantiating formal and structural features of the musical sequence—as decisive for staging operas. Dahlhaus writes:

> In its entirety, the duet has three parts, so it has the shape … of a cohesive form. Figaro's fake courtship of the "Countess" marks the beginning of the middle part …, the slap in the face with which Susanna believes she ends the game of hide and seek marks the beginning of the final part ….

DOI: 10.4324/9781003124863-8

72   *Analytical approaches*

> The musical caesuras are thus scenically justified such that the musical form manifests itself as a musical-dramatic form.[8]

A further productive example of scenically legitimizing musical and musical-textual peculiarities is Claus Guth's production of Mozart's *Le nozze di Figaro* at the 2006 Salzburg Festival, which was conducted by Nikolaus Harnoncourt. The finale of the opera exhibits a few points where the characters' affects and motivations are extremely different from one another, but the text in their joint ensemble is the same. Dahlhaus notes "complications" that

> result from the intrigues' foiling one another such that the characters are basically playing a game of chess not against one another but rather against an overpowering coincidence …. How Cherubino tries to seduce the Countess, who is disguised as Susanna, while Susanna, the Count, and Figaro comment on what is happening—each for him- or herself and unnoticed by the others—is scenically unmistakable as a situation without having to depend on the details of the text. When Susanna, the Count, and Figaro use the same words together in chorus ("Ah! nel sen mi batte il core"; My heart is racing!), each one means something different: Susanna sees the Countess's intrigue as endangered by Cherubino, the Count fears the thwarting of his rendezvous with "Susanna," and Figaro is plagued by jealousy.[9]

Yet according to Dahlhaus, even in the case of this imbroglio, the "principle of pantomimic intelligibility" is effective,[10] though only an actual staging could really demonstrate this.[11]

After Cherubino accidentally kisses the Count, then the Countess, the Count, Susanna, and Figaro all sing the text "Ah ci ho/ha fatto un bel guadagno" (Ha! So that is what you get; see Example 5.1),[12] though the conventional scenic realization isolates them spatially and affectively. So how can one realize in this case the "principle of pantomimic intelligibility"? Guth's staging provides a very impressive scenic answer: an angel (who is added to the well-known dramatis personae and appears as the alter ego of Cherubino) guides the characters as if they were on strings (see Figure 5.1) and momentarily unifies them all into a bundle.

One might even think that the staging follows another one of Dahlhaus's interpretive suggestions: the angel could be read as the embodiment of the—to speak with Dahlhaus—"overpowering coincidence" that reigns in this finale.[13] A similar situation comes about at the end of the performance with the expression "Ah tutti contenti" (Each and everyone happy again!), which promises reconciliation and is used very quickly, actually too quickly, after the Count's "Contessa perdono" (My Lady, forgive me)[14] when the angel organizes all the characters for the finale.

One can also make out examples of integrating music and scene in the sense of a legitimation and substantiation of musical particularities in Peter

Konwitschny's Hamburg production of Wagner's *Lohengrin*.[15] The composer himself already demanded that music and scene be intimately connected in staging practices in a way that had hardly ever been seen before him. Wagner's scenic instructions for performing *Lohengrin* in Weimar in 1850 read: "The

Example 5.1 Wolfgang Amadeus Mozart, *Le nozze di Figaro*, K. 492, ed. Ludwig Finscher, vols. 16.1–2 of *Neue Ausgabe sämtlicher Werke*, ser. 2, *Bühnenwerke*, group 5, *Opern und Singspiele* (Kassel: Bärenreiter, 1973), 526–27.

Reproduced by the permission of Bärenreiter-Verlag, Kassel.

74 *Analytical approaches*

Example 5.1 (Continued)

precise concurrence of moments of the plot with the music must be strictly maintained above all else."[16] That one can perceive such a great pleasure in the music in Konwitschny's staging—which produced moments where the music and scene were intimately integrated—can absolutely be understood as an answer to Wagner's demand. This will be demonstrated here in two situations: in the first act, in Elsa's appearance out of the closet and in the squeaky

Figure 5.1 *Le nozze di Figaro*, staging by Claus Guth, Salzburg Festival, 2006.
Photo courtesy of Monika Rittershaus.

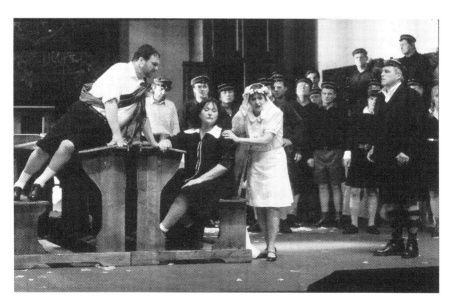

Figure 5.2 *Lohengrin*, staging by Peter Konwitschny, Thomas Moser as Lohengrin, Eva Marton as Ortrud, Inga Nielsen as Elsa, Hans-Joachim Ketelsen as Telramund, chorus, Staatsoper Hamburg, 1998.
Photo courtesy of Jörg Landsberg.

76 *Analytical approaches*

Figure 5.3 Lohengrin, staging by Peter Konwitschny, Emily Magee as Elsa, Gran Teatre del Liceu, Barcelona, 2006. Screenshot from the DVD recording.

© 2007 by Fundació del Gran Teatre del Liceu and EuroArts.

door of the classroom in which the entire plot was situated (see Figure 5.2),[17] and in Ortrud's actions as an organist at the end of the second act.

In many performances of *Lohengrin*, the audience is left asking why it actually takes so long, after the Herald's call and King Heinrich's many questions, for Elsa to finally sing her first notes and announce her first sentence: "Mein armer Bruder" (My hapless brother).[18] Why does everyone involved actually have to wait so long for her musically? The answer suggested by Peter Konwitschny's staging is very simple: she is so overwhelmed by the situation (the loss of her brother and the accusation that she killed him, an inordinate accusation that is hard to deal with) that she has hidden in the classroom closet. Elsa (played by Emily Magee in the DVD recording) does not want to face the situation; she cannot face it. She doesn't dare come out of her hiding place. That is, she does show signs of emerging from hiding several times when she slowly opens the closet door (see Figure 5.3), but her courage immediately leaves her, and she quickly closes the door again.

With this idea, these moments, which are musically extremely retarded by pauses—and are quite often filled with the singer playing Elsa making the most embarrassing mimic gestures—suddenly became clear. Shutting the closet door also produced a clearly audible additional sound, as did the classroom door, which, when the Herald called for Elsa's imagined champion to appear, one of the schoolgirls opened to look whether a champion was perhaps already standing outside. The classroom door squeaked, and it did so right in the middle of the general pause. As an audience member, my reaction to the squeaking was ambivalent. It first aroused resistance resulting from consternation with the fact that the silence of the music was being disturbed by something so profane as a squeak. But the disturbance also created a productive potential: the moment of silence was amplified by the disturbance. Indeed, the silence actually only became audible because it was perceived to be endangered. This experience points to a perceptual position that dominates opera performances, a position that is able to differentiate between welcome and unwelcome, relevant and irrelevant acoustic events and that also applies to the interaction of the auditory and the visual. In opera, the world also makes noises beyond those stipulated in the score, and operagoers have learned to disregard them. The shutting and squeaking of doors made one aware that in operatic performance practices there is an unwritten law that nothing should be heard except for the acoustic signs stipulated in the score. But Wagner himself absolutely had an affinity for the sounds of the world and accounted for them or even demanded them. Maybe not the squeaking or shutting of a door, but certainly, for instance, the noise of approaching horses. In the already cited scenic instructions for the 1850 Weimar performance, he proposed that for the arrival of the various troops in the third act, horses should come out just to the wings and then be led back. That horses would make their own sounds when they come out to the wings, that they would make sounds even if immediately led back, and that Wagner took this into account becomes unmistakably clear when one reads further that he even demanded substitute sounds if real horses were not available: "If horses are not at all an option, then one could experiment with how at least ... the sound of a galloping and halting rider can be imitated behind the scenes."[19] The door's squeaking was also such a sound of the world beyond musical notes, a sound that would have had to be imitated if it could be not produced naturally.

In the second situation from Konwitschny's staging of *Lohengrin* that I want to discuss here, the integration of musical-dramatic inflection and scenic action remained, on the auditory level, within the sonic texture of the music. On the front right edge of the classroom, which was also used as a minster and for the wedding ceremony in the second act, stood a positive organ. A student was sitting as the organist on a bench in front of it. At the end of the second act, during the wedding procession in the minster, Ortrud (played by Luana DeVol in the DVD recording) squeezed onto the organ bench, chased away the actual organ player, blowed in her hands like an artisan, and began to strike the keys with great ardor (see Figure 5.4). My first thought was: yes, of course Ortrud has to sit at the organ because the wedding music is going to be interrupted by the forbidden-question motif. The reason for the interruption is Ortrud, of course, so Ortrud is also going to play the forbidden-question motif herself and not—as usual—exchange portentous gazes with Elsa. But against my expectation, Ortrud did not interact with Elsa but savored playing the music with great relish without concerning herself at all with Elsa and the resounding forbidden-question motif.[20] The gnawing forbidden-question motif did not set in over Elsa through Ortrud's intervention but was rather already in Elsa herself—that was why Ortrud did not have to do anything more about it. The catastrophe would also take its course without Ortrud's interference, as Peter Konwitschny

78 *Analytical approaches*

Figure 5.4 *Lohengrin*, staging by Peter Konwitschny, Luana DeVol as Ortrud, Gran Teatre del Liceu, Barcelona, 2006. Screenshot from the DVD recording.

© 2007 by Fundació del Gran Teatre del Liceu and EuroArts.

and his dramaturg Werner Hintze once formulated it. The catastrophe lay in the system itself, the system of the forbidden question. Ortrud could devote herself entirely to the theatricality and pomp of a church scene and help shape it—musically. She, the queen of tragedy, who had earlier painted herself with war colors to invoke the "profaned gods," apparently had a penchant for impressive scenes.

Because of Ortrud's organ music, this performance made me think about two musical features of the finale—its arrangement as a musically grandiose church scene and the interruption by the forbidden-question motif. It may not have thereby changed my knowledge of the opera, but it did influence it in a new and lasting way.

The examples up to now have viewed the connection of music and scene, the integration of the auditory and the visual, from the perspective of the music, that is, from the starting material. How do scenic features explain musical features that were already present? From the perspective of perception, one can say that here the scenic realization reacts to musical events in the score and so that the music legitimizes the scene.

But the fascinating thing about the interaction of scene and music in opera performances is that it does not only function as intermodal integration and synchronization in this direction but rather can also function in the reverse direction. Then the musical effect can occur due to a visually perceivable event, or the acoustic effect of some music one believes to be familiar can

Figure 5.5 Tannhäuser, staging by Sebastian Baumgarten, Bayreuth Festival, 2011.
Photo courtesy of the Bayreuth Festival and Enrico Nawrath.

change in the moment of performance through a simultaneously perceived visual offering.

One of the central stage-design decisions of Sebastian Baumgarten's Bayreuth production of Wagner's *Tannhäuser*[21] was to have the whole staging play in a kind of installation (see Figure 5.5). It was an installation by the artist Joep van Lieshout, a sealed-off world like a factory in which the workers also lived and slept and in which both the Venusberg scenes and the Wartburg scenes took place. The Venusberg was situated under the platform for the Wartburg scene, a kind of cage for wild animals, animal-like people, and for Venus (see Figure 5.6). In this performance, I am particularly interested in the question of what happens with the well-known work and its dramatis personae when one views this setting, the installation, as a laboratory. What are the consequences or results of this experiment of having *Tannhäuser* play out in a closed system?

One of the first and most conspicuous consequences is that the performance casted an entirely new light on the music. My perception of the well-known music from *Tannhäuser* changed entirely. This was in large part thanks to the conducting of Thomas Hengelbrock and his interpretation of the score. He conceptualized his conducting from the perspective of Wagner's predecessors, from the perspective of German Romantic opera such as by Carl Maria von Weber. One heard a very light, transparent, and sometimes very fast Wagner with many unexpected tempo changes. But it was not only, perhaps not even primarily, Hengelbrock's conducting that made me perceive the music differently. Just seeing the installation on the stage—a space-filling

80 *Analytical approaches*

Figure 5.6 *Tannhäuser*, staging by Sebastian Baumgarten, Lars Cleveman as Tannhäuser, Bayreuth Festival, 2011.

Photo courtesy of the Bayreuth Festival and Enrico Nawrath.

factory with machines and workers—while I listened to the music fundamentally changed my perception of the music. It was the perception of what I saw, of the mechanized actions of the factory workers in this technicist ambience, that shaped my acoustic perception. I have seldomly heard the Venusberg sound less bombastic and so technical, so clear and virtuosic. One experienced how a performance, how a visual, scenic offering—here particularly the spatial installation and the actions performed by the extras and chorus in it and with it—can decisively shape one's perception of the music and lastingly change it in relation to the memories of the music (retention) one brings to the performance as an expectation.[22]

If the scenic reality primed auditory perception over the entire course of the performance in Baumgarten's *Tannhäuser*, then Kasper Holten's staging of *Lohengrin*[23] made possible a particular perceptual experience of the music from a single scene that one had believed to be familiar, namely, the prelude. To the prelude's ethereal music, the curtain opened on a battlefield in the state of devastation, that is, at the end of a battle, with innumerable dead and injured bodies. The performance began—when one relates it to the familiar libretto—sometime after the end of *Lohengrin* with the battle to which King Heinrich summons the men of Brabant, a battle that the staging apparently associated with great losses. We saw dead and wounded troops lying on the ground; women were going through the rows and searching for their men and would suddenly let out, like professional mourners, loud and anguished screams into the orchestral sounds of the prelude.

The ethereal, wondrous music in the prelude was transformed by what one simultaneously saw and heard into a funeral march, which I had never heard before in this music. The actually very short *fortissimo* middle part,[24] which is dominated by the brass section and precedes the prelude fading away again in *pp*, suddenly turned into an all-determining acoustic impression: instead of announcing a celestial wonder, it expressed lament, mourning, and rage.

It was not so much a reshaping of the emotional pitch as in the *Lohengrin* prelude or an atmospheric grounding as in *Tannhäuser* but rather a concrete transformation of temporal perception that shaped the interaction of the auditory and the visual in my experience of Jossi Wieler and Sergio Morabito's Stuttgart production of Verdi's *Don Carlo*.[25] The musical conclusion of the scene in which Carlo actually withdraws into the monastery of Yuste (San Giusto)—in the staging, the monastery turned out to be a circle of men reminiscent of Kendo fighters in their slow-motion movements and poses (see Figure 5.7)—seemed to me to be markedly slow, even protracted, with the renewed sounding of the friendship motif. But as the conclusion of a musical-scenic constellation where one primarily saw Kendo exercises, which also established the scene's temporal structure, the musical interpretation was very convincing, as if the rhythm of the movements had directly influenced it (even if one should presume that the conductor Lothar Zagrosek had his own

Figure 5.7 Don Carlo, staging and dramaturgy by Jossi Wieler and Sergio Morabito, Vladimir Kuzmenko as Don Carlo, Motti Kastón as Posa, Staatsoper Stuttgart, 2001.

Photo courtesy of A. T. Schaefer.

82 *Analytical approaches*

idea of tempo and had also asserted it). What is prescribed is "Tempo I,"[26] which refers to the beginning of the section "Allegro assai moderato."[27] The metronome specification reads: quarter = 84. I recall Zagrosek's Stuttgart quarter as being distinctly slower. But perhaps my subjective experience of time was overwriting my perception of musical tempo, and I just heard the end of the scene to be slower because of the visible actions. I assume that the visual rhythm had an effect on my perception of the musical rhythm. Even though my subjective memory is my only source for what I experienced, I could not resist measuring Zagrosek's tempo using a video recording of one of the performances. At the beginning of the friendship duet,[28] the tempo in the recording is in fact slower than what is prescribed (quarter = 76), and at the end of the scene even a little slower still (quarter = 72).

Yet another case of such a transformation of acoustic perception (here of an aria) through visually perceptible scenic actions—a case that particularly clarifies how expectations function—could be found in Balázs Kovalik's production of Verdi's *Il trovatore*[29] at the Staatstheater Nürnberg. At the beginning of the Conte di Luna's aria to the absent Leonora ("Il balen del suo sorriso"; The flashing of her smile[30]), an aria in which he sings of the heavenly beams of his desired but unobtainable Leonora (see Figure 5.8), the Conte found an undressed mannequin. He first directed his aria to the mannequin before using it to suggest sexual acts. Luna's aria is often one of the high points of *Trovatore* performances because, among other reasons, its high tessitura poses enormous challenges to any baritone. Due to its highly

Figure 5.8 *Il trovatore*, staging by Balász Kovalik, Mikolaj Zalasinski as Luna, Staatstheater Nürnberg, 2012.

Photo courtesy of Ludwig Olah and the Staatstheater Nürnberg.

demanding nature, singers often have to go to the limits of their capabilities and sometimes also beyond them, so the aria turns into a nerve-rattling experience for everyone involved—the singer and the audience. But from a dramatic perspective, this is absolutely conducive to the particular moment since it presents the scene as a liminal experience: extreme and unrequited love sometimes prevents one from controlling one's means of expression. This exceptionally emotional situation, which takes the moment of performance into consideration, was completely changed in Kovalik's staging, which sexualized and fetishized the scene on a visual level. The visible actions with the mannequin thus acutely irritated my anticipation (protention) of one of the outstanding love songs of operatic literature.[31] The scene painted over the expected effect of the aria, which never set in. At the same time, the scene produced such a discrepancy or friction between the auditory and visual levels that it actually really emphasized the features of each level and in the case of the musical level perhaps even first gave rise to them. I at least cannot recall whether I had ever so intensely expected to hear a "beautiful" love song ("beautiful" in the sense of not endangered, uncompromised) before experiencing this scene in the Nuremberg performance, or whether this expectation was first produced as such in the moment of disappointed or distraught expectation. The friction perhaps belatedly created an expectation that was not present before then.

This example can function as evidence for Jens Roselt's thesis that experiences of disappointed expectations in theater often have to do with the "diastatic displacement of cause and effect" formulated by phenomenology:

> If one is talking about expectations, one should not mechanically assume that spectators necessarily go to the theater with a finished list of expectations and check them off as if on a checklist so as to draw a balance at the end. Instead, expectations are first produced in the moment of their disappointment. This has to do with the diastatic displacement of cause and effect. Disappointment is, to a certain extent, the effect that precedes its cause, namely, expectation.[32]

A productive friction similar to the contradiction between music and scene in Luna's aria also took place in numerous scenes in Bieito's staging of Mozart's *Entführung aus dem Serail*, for example, in Konstanze's first aria "Ach ich liebte, war so glücklich."[33] Here the music offered a kind of consolation for the tortures the eyes had to endure. The possible perception of the musical events as an experience of beauty and as being outside of history entered in many passages into a productive contradiction to what could be seen on stage. A hopeful and redemptive dimension opened to the ear, a utopia that remained closed to the eyes.

How strongly the performance advanced such reconciliation, utopia, and a promise of healing was probably shown nowhere more clearly than at the beginning of the third act when Bassa Selim came very slowly from the back of the stage up to Konstanze and Belmonte at the front after their duet,[34] and, turning toward Konstanz, said: "Jetzt kommt der letzte Akt, Baby" (Here comes the last act, baby)—and then a long silence began. Bassa removed Konstanze's chains and released the safety catch on his pistol. The anticipation of what would come next after all the atrocities we had already seen paralyzed me and many other audience members with fear. The whole space of the theater (stage and auditorium) was filled with a long-lasting silence. Bassa handed the pistol over to Konstanze and thereby released her into freedom and also gave her the freedom to determine the end. She killed Selim and finally also herself. I am less interested in this changed finale than in the moment of silence. The silence on the stage was unbearable. The desire to release the tension through the freeing power of music became a corporeal desire, a desire that in turn finally manifested itself corporeally in one audience member's loud heckle: "Music!" The audience wanted music so as not to have to endure the silence. Here it was not the action or the emotion that substantiated the music as the only believable form of expression for a situation; rather, it was the situation that had become unbearable, and music was demanded so as to end it.[35]

The experience of Bieito's *Entführung* and the audience's reaction to it show how a scenic realization that is accompanied by an unexpected, long-lasting acoustic pause produces an anticipation of music to release pent-up tension. That such transformations of the musical level through the visual level not only take place in perception but rather that scenic moments of a performance unfold their own productive force with regard to performative processes—in other words, that they can have very concrete effects on the development of the music—was shown by a performance of Mozart's *Don Giovanni* I attended on 2 March 2002 in the production by Calixto Bieito at the Staatsoper Hannover.[36] On that evening, one heard the singers make multiple incorrect entrances and tempo transitions. In my experience, this was attributable to the high tempo and energy level of the performance. The singers seemed to me to be highly motivated and full of energy, taking their bodies and voices to the limits and, spurred on by a scenic drive, also to be musically outdoing the conductor's intended tempo. The conductor with his orchestra seemed unable to keep up with their energetic mood and forward push. In the drifting apart of voices and orchestra, tempo changes on the part of the singers were clearly noticeable. So a change had taken place not only in each different modality of perceiving the performance but apparently also in the production itself. The musical performance was influenced by the scenic performance.

If the singers and performers are influenced in their performances by the scenic realization and react differently on an individual basis, then it seems only logical and consistent that production teams take this awareness for performance into account and change the musical starting material.

This can occur through shortening or striking dialogues or recitatives, as is commonly practiced, through striking or adding arias or other numbers, and

Symbioses and contestations 85

Figure 5.9 Le nozze di Figaro, staging by Christoph Marthaler, Jürg Kienberger as recitativist, Salzburg Festival, 2001.
Photo courtesy of Ruth Walz.

also through new instrumental arrangements for certain passages. Particularly impressive in this respect was the invention of the role of the "recitativist" in Christoph Marthaler's Salzburg production of *Figaro*,[37] created for the musician, singer, and actor Jürg Kienberger and his highly virtuosic recitative accompaniments and insertions. In his review of the premiere, Claus Spahn writes:

> Jürg Kienberger not only uses his keyboard, he also plays arias with moistened fingers on tuned wine glasses [see Figure 5.9]. Once, suddenly gripped with passion, he begins to yodel between two scenes, and he can even blow a recitative accompaniment on two beer bottles. This is his most incredible trick: every swig from the bottle is measured so precisely that it produces an (almost) cleanly intonated cadence.[38]

86 *Analytical approaches*

The deployment of materials (and so also the musical material) seemed to follow a staging concept that could be described as the gathering of virtuosic eccentrics, of something never heard before. The performance was a plea for the peculiarities and absurdities of life, a moving and breathtaking presentation full of comedy and melancholy.

An even clearer alteration to the musical and dramaturgical continuities of an existing work, of a score, is found in cases in which instead of presenting new stagings of Mozart's *Figaro* and *Don Giovanni*, parts of the operas are put together from different contexts into a new whole, as was the case for the music-theater and dance-theater creation *Wolf, oder wie Mozart auf den Hund kam*, created by the choreographer Alain Platel and the conductor Sylvain Cambreling together with Les Ballets C de la B, three singers, the Klangforum Wien, and fifteen dogs.[39] Here there wasn't any work at all any more to which one could relate an interpretation. A different approach was needed from the start. One could describe *Wolf* as a piece about national and cultural conflicts in the suburbs, about isolation and neglect, inhumanity and hopelessness, about breakdowns in communication, and—above all—about the search for communication through music and movement. Everyone—dancers and singers—volunteered their bodies and voices as material for producing the performance.

The question of the performance's efficacy was spelled out explicitly when the deaf performer Kurt Vanmaeckelberghe, who presented himself in the performance because of his handicap as a social and artistic outsider, was supposed to experience, by seeing and feeling, what music is and what it is capable of doing through the "Domine Deus" from Mozart's Great Mass in C Minor, K. 427 (newly orchestrated with an accordion, two violas, two cellos, and a double bass). The singers Aleksandra Zamojska, Ingela Bohlin, and Marina Comparato let him feel the corporeality of the sound of singing on their bodies, and the dancer and trapeze artist Juliana Neves from Brazil let him see on the aerial silk how Mozart's music produces the breathtaking effect of a hovering body.

A different scene brought together Dorabella's aria "Smanie implacabili" (Remorseless longings) from the first act of *Così fan tutte*[40] and a break-dance number. Each of the two levels bore their own meaning, had their own context (for example, the knowledge of the dramaturgical function of the aria in *Così fan tutte* or Dorabella's anxiety and emotional confusion when she is confronted with the fact that her fiancé is going away). In the dialogue of song and movement, the means and contexts (Mozart's music, the singer's voice and activities, the dancer's movements) mixed into new questions and answers to the conditions of our present moment that the performative reality pushed before us: Who is scared of whom here? Who is trying to impress and to pressure whom? In addition, with regard to the employed materials, one was startled to discover how well the ductus of movement and rhythm fit Mozart's music and vice versa across the centuries.

In these two moments, the scene and music repeatedly drifted apart and united together again in an incredible way. Was the break-dancer following the singer's rhythm, or was it the singer who was following the break-dancer's rhythm? Were the dancers, who formed the counterweight in the background to the two aerial silks in which the acrobat was hovering, following the rhythm of the acrobat, who was in turn following the rhythm of the music, or was it the music that was following the acrobat's rhythm?

The undecidability, the impossibility of resolving the question of cause and effect determines the particular quality of such an intermodal perception of an opera performance. What particularly interests me in these examples is thus not the question of to what extent the scenic realizations encouraged something to become manifest that was already present and dormant in the scores before an interpretation brought it to light; rather, I am interested in what was added to the material of the score and interacted with (and chafed against) the supposedly familiar soundscape. Scene and music found themselves in a dialogue that let us hear the music differently, that let the music resound differently.

At the beginning of this chapter, I stated that as a scenic solution, the angel in Claus Guth's staging of *Figaro* could be interpreted as scenically substantiating certain musical features of the operatic composition. Yet neither the librettist Da Ponte nor the composer Mozart had such an angel in mind for their *Figaro*. Here something becomes clear that actually belongs to the fundamental characteristics of all operatic performances but is often overlooked when engaging with them: namely, the fact that every production adds something to the templates and so creates something new. That it enters into a dialogue, also indeed into a friction or even into a contradiction with the materials. This something "new"—which goes beyond a new (further) interpretation since it takes into account the reality, the here and now, produced in the performance—complements and expands the concept of opera as a dialogue and friction of two levels, as formulated, for instance, by Carl Dahlhaus in "Zur Methode der Opern-Analyse": "The 'real' text with which Figaro courts or pretends to court the 'Countess' is accompanied by an 'unreal' text with which Susanna vents her anger and whose language is music."[41] What Dahlhaus praises in opera—the possibility to speak on two levels at the same time and so to make a situation interesting through friction and contradiction—is precisely what so-called operatic Regietheater does with classics and what its opponents vehemently criticize it for: namely, adding yet another level to the layering of text and music, a level that enriches and complicates the network of relations, the *Beziehungszauber* or "relational magic" (as Dahlhaus so appropriately describes the event of opera).[42] New and unknown experiences that cannot be traced back to the templates become possible, experiences that, in dialogue with the well-known templates, make experiencing the performance interesting. The performance of an opera can thus not at all be thought of as the amplification of one side—of the text or the music—but rather always also creates something new in which nothing is predetermined and that can only become manifest in performance.

88 *Analytical approaches*

Notes

1 The premiere was at the Monadnock Music Festival in Manchester, New Hampshire, in 1980, with revivals at the PepsiCo Summerfare in Purchase, New York, in 1987 and at the Vienna Festival in 1989 with a video recording (London: Decca, 1991).
2 English National Opera, London, 2001; Staatsoper Hannover, 2002.
3 Komische Oper Berlin, 2004.
4 Mozart, *Don Giovanni*, 388; McClatchy, *Seven Mozart Librettos*, 649.
5 Mozart, *Entführung*, 129–30; McClatchy, *Seven Mozart Librettos*, 169.
6 Carl Dahlhaus, "Zur Methode der Opern-Analyse," in *Vom Musikdrama zur Literaturoper: Aufsätze zur neueren Operngeschichte* (Munich: Piper, 1989), 11–26.
7 Dahlhaus, 11.
8 Dahlhaus, 23.
9 Dahlhaus, 20. For the quoted passage, see Wolfgang Amadeus Mozart, *Le nozze di Figaro*, K. 492, ed. Ludwig Finscher, *Neue Ausgabe sämtlicher Werke*, ser. 2, Bühnenwerke, group 5, *Opern und Singspiele*, vols. 16.1–2 (Kassel: Bärenreiter, 1982), 521, m. 26; McClatchy, *Seven Mozart Librettos*, 471.
10 Dahlhaus, "Methode der Opern-Analyse," 20.
11 Here it becomes clear that there is a difference between Dahlhaus's conceptualization of the scenic and my own understanding of it. Since Dahlhaus never speaks in this text about concrete experiences of performances, he can actually only be concerned with imagined scenic and gestural moments acquired from the experience of reading and the dramaturgical analysis of the textual templates and the score. Strictly speaking, Dahlhaus's concept of the scenic would have to be replaced by the word *dramatic* since it has to do with a category referring to the textual versions of operas and their contexts before being realized in a concrete performance. See Dahlhaus, 20 and 23.
12 Mozart, *Le nozze di Figaro*, 527, m. 40; McClatchy, *Seven Mozart Librettos*, 475.
13 Dahlhaus, "Methode der Opern-Analyse," 20.
14 Mozart, *Le nozze di Figaro*, 579, m. 430; McClatchy, *Seven Mozart Librettos*, 493.
15 Staatsoper Hamburg, 1998; Gran Teatre del Liceu, Barcelona, 2000, with DVD recording (Stuttgart: EuroArts, 2006); Oper Leipzig, 2009. I attended the performances on 28 April 2001 in Hamburg and 18 December 2009 in Leipzig.
16 Richard Wagner, "Szenische Vorschriften für die Aufführung des *Lohengrin* in Weimar 1850," in *Sämtliche Schriften und Dichtungen*, vol. 16 (Leipzig: Breitkopf and Härtel, 1914), 73.
17 On the possible meanings of locating the plot in a classroom, see Chapter 6.
18 Richard Wagner, *Lohengrin*, WWV 75, ed. John Deathridge and Klaus Döge, vol. 7.1 of *Sämtliche Werke*, ed. Carl Dahlhaus, Egon Voss, et al. (Mainz: Schott, 1996), 45, mm. 308–9; English translation from Richard Wagner, *Lohengrin: Romantische Oper in drei Aufzügen*, trans. H. Corder and F. Corder (Leipzig: Breitkopf and Härtel, 1906), 61.
19 Wagner, "Szenische Vorschriften," 72.
20 Wagner, *Lohengrin*, 288, mm. 2099–100.
21 Bayreuth Festival, 2011. I attended the final dress rehearsal on 20 July 2011 and the performance on 19 August 2011.
22 On retention, see Chapter 4.
23 Deutsche Oper Berlin, 2012. I attended the performance on 25 April 2012.
24 Wagner, *Lohengrin*, 8, mm. 51–56.
25 Staatsoper Stuttgart, 2001. I attended the performance on 23 January 2001.
26 Giuseppe Verdi, *Don Carlos*, ed. Ursula Günther and Luciano Petazzoni, complete edition of the different versions in five and four acts, reduced vocal and piano score (Milan: Ricordi, 1980), 1:147.
27 Verdi, *Don Carlos*, 1:140.

28 Verdi, 1:140.
29 Staatstheater Nürnberg, 2012. I attended the performance on 3 November 2012.
30 See Giuseppe Verdi, *Il trovatore*, orchestral score, new rev. ed. (Milan: Ricordi, 1955), 179–205; English translation from William Weaver, trans., *Seven Verdi Librettos* (New York: W. W. Norton, 1975), 95.
31 On protention, see Chapter 4.
32 Roselt, "Erfahrung im Verzug," 36.
33 Mozart, *Entführung*, 119–31.
34 Mozart, 396.
35 This separation of music and scene can be, as described above, thoroughly fascinating and effective. The power of what one visually perceives enters into a contrast with the intensity of the experience of the music, and both levels strengthen each other reciprocally through contestation. But the separation can also weaken the perception of each different component. An unproductive discrepancy in this sense arose in the case of the *Entführung* when the music sounded too elegant or too light or too delicate or too beautiful or too slow for the graphic nature and tempo of the visible actions. Such a felt deficit can be formulated in both directions. Either from the perspective of the visible actions overwhelming the music or, vice versa, from the perspective of the music hampering the action. If one follows the first position, one possible consequence for a production is to change the visual side. If one follows the second position, one possible consequence for a production team is to change the acoustic side, that is, to alter the musical template.
36 Staatsoper Hannover, 2002.
37 Salzburg Festival, 2001. I attended the performance on 11 August 2001.
38 Claus Spahn, "Bräute in Weiß, nie abgeholt," *Die Zeit*, 2 August 2001.
39 World premiere at the 2003 Ruhrtriennale. I attended the performance on 8 June 2003 at the Volksbühne am Rosa-Luxemburg-Platz in Berlin and a performance on 17 May 2004 in the context of the Berlin Theatertreffen at the Haus der Berliner Festspiele.
40 See Wolfgang Amadeus Mozart, *Così fan tutte ossia La scuola degli amanti*, K. 588, ed. Faye Ferguson and Wolfgang Rehm, *Neue Ausgabe sämtlicher Werke*, ser. 2, *Bühnenwerke*, group 5, *Opern und Singspiele*, vols. 18.1–2 (Kassel: Bärenreiter, 1991), 120–29; McClatchy, *Seven Mozart Librettos*, 725.
41 Dahlhaus, "Methode der Opern-Analyse," 21.
42 Dahlhaus, 25–26.

6 The interplay of representation and presence in performance

Referring to performances by Maria Bengtsson in Bieto's *Entführung* and by David Moss in *Die Fledermaus*, I drew attention in Chapter 2 to one of the central features and appealing aspects of opera in performance: the interplay of representation and presence. In the following, I will discuss further exemplary moments in which this interplay has challenged audience members' perception. The details of its effects or possible effects can vary greatly. The sudden emphasis or focus on intense presence can strengthen the effect of the representational function—and so produce a possible meaning of the material—or it can interrupt, thwart, and alienate the representational function or also simply draw attention to one of the most important ingredients of a live performance: the inevitable risk of giving one's all to a performance, the lavish exertion of individual materialities such as bodies and voices. Finally, this interplay can bring to the fore completely new dimensions of a performance, such as the ideologically loaded performance history of a well-known opera, which I will discuss with the example of Wagner's *Die Meistersinger von Nürnberg* at the end of the chapter.

Hans Neuenfels's notorious 1981 Frankfurt production of Verdi's *Aida* can be described as a founding act of Regietheater in opera. Neuenfels had already made a name for himself a few years earlier in 1974 with a production of Verdi's *Troubadour* in Nuremberg and in 1976 with a production of Verdi's *Macbeth* in Frankfurt. Leo Karl Gerhartz wrote a lucid essay on the Frankfurt *Macbeth* in the 1980 volume *Werk und Wiedergabe* edited by Sigrid Wiesmann; the essay has the revealing title "Auch das 'hm-ta-ta' beim Wort genommen" (Taking even the "hm-ta-ta" literally).[1] There Gerhartz succinctly describes the proximity of Verdi's music theater to French melodrama, noting "that the juxtaposition in Verdi's music of entertainment and seriousness, pathos and 'hm-ta-ta,' which to many is troublesome or awkward, can only find its artistic truth from the perspective of a popular theater such as that of French melodrama."[2] For this "juxtaposition of balladic 'hm-ta-ta' and great melodic pathos, amusement and seriousness, in Verdi's music," Neuenfels had found, according to Gerhartz, "formulas that are as convincing as they are meaningful,"[3] such as when "with obscene movements, almost naked dancers literally and visibly celebrate Lady Macbeth's toast at the coronation ceremony in the second act as the beginning of a brutal and provocative power

DOI: 10.4324/9781003124863-9

The interplay of representation and presence 91

orgy" or when "the king's messengers, who announce the election of Macbeth as the Thane of Cawdor, dance happily on stage to Verdi's march and triple rhythms."[4]

Something similar could be seen in a very controversial scene from Neuenfels's staging of Verdi's *Nabucco*.[5] The premiere was almost cut short due to this scene, which often occurs with performances of Neuenfels's stagings. After the slow part of Abigaille's aria[6] (performed by Susan Neves in the premiere), the Babylonian priests (the men of the opera chorus) appeared in full-body bee costumes (see Figure 6.1) and moved their bee abdomens in rhythmic regularity to the fast second part of the aria, the cabaletta.[7] In the course of this cabaletta, the soprano has to manage several chains of trills and runs of coloratura.[8] During these virtuoso passages, Frank Frühkirch (Alexander Heidenreich)—the character Neuenfels added to the dramatis personae—tickled Susan Neves multiple times with a feather duster. In both cases (the rhythmic shaking and the tickling), the visible scenic occurrences and movements did not refer to any context beyond the sonic events. The pure joy of the contentless doubling and visualizing of the initially meaningless, stereotypical coloratura was thereby disavowed as mere ornament but was also especially exhibited, especially marked and emphasized, by the visual doubling as a musical element, and so it was perceived as something special. A trill that would have otherwise perhaps faded away unnoticed became imposing, though not meaningful. The mise-en-scène had no

Figure 6.1 Nabucco, staging by Hans Neuenfels, Susan Neves as Abigaille, chorus, Deutsche Oper Berlin, 2000.

Photo courtesy of Detlef Kurth.

meaning beyond manifesting the musical rhythm, but in the visible body movements, the specific materiality of the music (the rhythm, the ornaments like trills and coloraturas) came to the fore and became perceptible as such. This can be experienced as a doubling or redundancy,[9] or as a self-reference to music theater's means for visualizing and manifesting musical structures.[10] The movements enabled a quasi-tactile perception of the music. Through the corporeal realization, I was virtually able to touch the musical rhythm, to grasp it physically.

The Stuttgart production of Verdi's *Don Carlo* by Jossi Wieler and Sergio Morabito also made such an experience possible. In the Eboli–Carlo–Posa terzet, Eboli (Tichina Vaughn) took a revolver out of Posa's hand at the beginning of the Allegro agitato "Trema per te" (Tremble)[11] and aimed it at Posa and Carlo (see Figure 6.2). At the same time, she moved, indeed she danced, to the rhythm of the Allegro agitato for which there is no apparent reason in the expected logic of the plot. Finally, she shot rhythmically several times into the air in synchronicity with the syncopated stresses of the Più mosso.[12]

Both the dancing and the shots were parts of the mise-en-scène that only referred to the realization of the musical rhythm. Conspicuous and even seemingly curious repetitions of small bodily movements were directly related to repeated small movements in the music. The music could be experienced as translated into movement; the movement illustrated the rhythm and elicited laughter through the repeated doubling.[13] Like a burning mirror, this made

Figure 6.2 *Don Carlo*, staging and dramaturgy by Jossi Wieler and Sergio Morabito, Motti Kastón as Posa, Tichina Vaughn as Eboli, Staatsoper Stuttgart, 2001.

Photo courtesy of A. T. Schaefer.

visible what is particular in the composition. Without the visible scenic manifestations, I probably would not have perceived the excessively repeated musical phrases (the melody, motives, accompanying phrases). In addition, the shots played with a shocking moment in theater that is probably familiar to many—whenever a pistol appears on stage, I inwardly flinch in anticipation of a deafening bang—and this audibly thematized the noise that so often characterizes the final sequences of numbers by Verdi.

But in addition to this self-reference, which can be described as emphasizing the presence of the musical material, one can also draw semantic conclusions with regard to the level of representation precisely from this emphasis on musical characteristics. In the case of Abigaille's cabaletta, it is of course possible to relate the comical impression caused by the doubling of the musical rhythm and the rhythm of movement to the portrayal of a character, specifically, to the disavowal of a character. The steady movement back and forth of the abdomens of the bee costumes thus exposed the risibility of the cabaletta's martial aspects and so too the risibility of the Babylonians in their dramatic function as characters. This effect was already produced by the men of the chorus's rhythmic movements, which alone appeared comical and oafish, but it was further intensified by the bee costumes, which in turn opened up their own field of associations, such as with drones, which are not capable of taking care of themselves or of making their own decisions and only exist to mate with young queens and to be submissively devoted to them.

The intensive experience of the ostentatious body movements in interaction with the stereotypical nature of the musical sequence was intensified in my perception by how I believed to see a self-ironic devotion in the performers to their choreographic tasks. In my experience, this interplay in performances of Neuenfels's stagings is enjoyed in large by the audience and also usually by the performers on stage.

There used to be a recording of Abigaille's cabaletta from this Neuenfels staging on YouTube, though it was from a much later series of performances than the one I attended, namely, from February 2008, eight years after the premiere and conducted by Pietro Rizzo.[14] In this recording, the men of the chorus had noticeably lost both their rhythmic precision in dancing and their enjoyment in performing the scene. Abigaille was no longer played by Susan Neves but by Sylvie Valayre, and she apparently didn't want to be tickled so often or at all by Alexander Heidenreich with his feather duster; or these elements were simply practiced differently in the rehearsals for the revival than they were in the premiere series.

In actions like being tickled during demanding passages, singers always expose themselves and their audience to the danger that their vocal virtuosity could fail. As in any high-wire act, the anxiety over a possible failure amplifies the appeal of the moment through the protention; that is, it amplifies the intensity of the perception of these passages and increases the thrill of listening to the voice of the singer in the role of Abigaille. Anxiety and thrill arise from our knowledge of the necessary and now endangered balance of body and voice. It is no coincidence that Neuenfels once said: "It is ... very important, I think, that one sees a voice in opera and not only hears it."[15] This "seeing" the voice can amplify the present perception of such a moment extraordinarily.

Two of the most remarkable moments in a performance of Jossi Wieler and Sergio Morabito's staging of Verdi's *Un ballo in maschera* can be described in a very similar way.[16] In the finale of the first scene, Riccardo (Piotr Beczala) orders his entire court to disguise themselves for an excursion to the fortune teller Ulrica, who has been accused of witchcraft. Riccardo wants to test her abilities incognito to see if he should revoke the judgment. While the finale was still being performed, Piotr Beczala began to roll up the legs of his pants as the first step in donning his disguise in preparation for the next scene. To do this, he had to bend his torso far down, and since Riccardo is musically active more or less nonstop in the Allegro brillante e Presto[17]—that is, the stretta—he also had to sing simultaneously.

Jump ahead to the end of the performance: in the scene before the grand finale, the masked ball, Riccardo finds himself in a situation where he has to sign an order to dispatch his friend and rival Renato; this would mean that Renato's wife, who is Riccardo's secret lover, would leave as well. In addition, Riccardo has also received a letter from an unknown sender warning him of a disaster at the upcoming masked ball and urgently advising him to avoid the party. Riccardo decides to stick to his plans; he signs the deployment order and resolves to go to the masked ball despite the warning. As if Beczala wanted to underscore his determination and courage to follow these decisions, which are both difficult for Riccardo to make, Beczala lifted a really heavy-looking piece of furniture in the style of a bistro table up in the air while singing the Allegro ending "Sì, rivederti, Amelia" (Yes, to see you again, Amelia) of his romanza.[18]

In both cases, signs were produced on a bodily level, and then meanings were assigned that fit into the framework of representation. For the next scene with Ulrica, the character Riccardo had to dress up and fortify his courage and determination. With legible gestures, Riccardo indicated that he was ready for the upcoming events. But what I perceived at the same time, and what actually engraved itself in my memory, was my amazement and admiration for the fact that a singer could sing so flawlessly and rousingly in these postures, which seemed surprising and unusual to me even though Regietheater has been luring performers out of the only supposedly secure position of the upright, largely immobile vocal producer for decades. I perceived the dangerous vocal disposition of the singer, who, I assumed, should not be able to sing in certain extreme bodily positions (when bending his torso deep down or lifting a table with great force). I wondered how he could nevertheless succeed and how Piotr Beczala could possess the courage and willingness to take such risks. What would that do to his voice? How would his voice sound when he was simultaneously executing these rather extraordinary body movements? In both cases, the clearly legible signification of the bodily movements was counteracted and at the same time intensified by a much stronger effect in the dimension of presence, which only depended on how the self-referential actions touched me.

What comes to the fore in these examples is the physicality of singing actors, the physical challenges that actors face in performances of current stagings of operas. This new approach to physicality has shaped the history of Regietheater in opera since its beginnings.

It is thanks to directors such as Götz Friedrich, with his production of Wagner's *Tannhäuser* at the Bayreuth Festival in 1972, and Patrice Chéreau, with the Bayreuth centennial *Ring* from 1976 to 1980, that the body was liberated from the opulent garments of the previous Wagner stagings by Wieland and Wolfgang Wagner and became a central element of theatrical effect. In the case of Chéreau, this rediscovery of the body was blatantly accompanied by a certain casting politics, as is evident when one thinks of the former decathlete Peter Hofmann, who performed in the role of Siegmund with a bare upper body, or of Jeannine Altmeyer, who played Sieglinde with a flowing but widely cut white nightgown that constantly allowed her body to shine through, especially when she moved.

In Harry Kupfer's Bayreuth *Ring* cycle from 1988, the very physical joy of movement already practiced in Chéreau was increased to the point of athleticism. Hans Schavernoch's stage design mutated at times into a sports arena, for example, when the former athlete Peter Hofmann actually performed peak athletic feats as Siegmund in *Die Walküre* by daring to jump from a considerable height to take refuge in Hunding's hut. This downright excessive movement was also manifest in a *Siegfried* scene in which Graham Clark as Mime struggled with his whole body against Siegfried while also hanging on a ladder of his forge with one hand. Finally, the scene in the last act of *Walküre* in which Wotan (John Tomlinson) dragged his favorite daughter, Brünnhilde (Deborah Polaski; played by Anne Evans in the DVD recording), across the floor as punishment for disobeying his orders, was both impressive and dangerous.[19]

The singers in these performances did not only use their bodies to depict their characters' extreme movements; they themselves performed extreme actions and even ran the risk of real injuries. Gestures and actions did not stand for something else, such as the gesture of a character, but rather primarily referred to themselves, that is, to the gesture or action of the person on stage performing, who was exposed to real danger through his or her actions.[20] It was thus the phenomenal body in its materiality that demanded our attention and attracted us.

In my experience, an extreme example of emotional empathy and embarrassment for a performer who was facing an extraordinary situation in her phenomenal corporeality was the finale of the first act of Wagner's *Götterdämmerung* in Peter Konwitschny's Stuttgart production.[21] The production premiered as the last part of a *Ring* cycle in 2000; this Stuttgart cycle became famous because of, among other things, its division into four different directorial teams: Joachim Schlömer for *Rheingold*, Christof Nel for *Walküre*, Jossi Wieler and Sergio Morabito for *Siegfried*, and Peter

96 *Analytical approaches*

Konwitschny for *Götterdämmerung*. For me, one of the most impressive scenes of this entire *Ring* was the finale of the first act of *Götterdämmerung*, when Siegfried—disguised as Gunther—goes to Brünnhilde and forces her to submit to him. At this moment, Luana DeVol as Brünnhilde pulled down "her underpants and then [walked] slowly backward, her legs bound by them, into the chamber,"[22] as Stephan Mösch described it in *Opernwelt*. In an interview in the same magazine on the occasion of her selection as female singer of the year in 2000, Luana DeVol was asked by Mösch whether it had been difficult for her to implement this instruction. He himself believed that he had "never seen a stronger sign of rape on stage."[23] Luana DeVol answered:

> It was very hard for me. Very hard. And it still affects me deeply ... I can't just call up this gesture. I am an American and was very prudish growing up. But I do it because I know that it is very strong for Brünnhilde's character and in the scene.[24]

This reference to the singer's biography and to the psychological implications of these actions for Luana DeVol suggests the extent to which the effect of these gestures and actions went far beyond the expected representation of submission. The effect did not merely consist in signification; the performer's very personal consternation with how she was treating her body was also transferred to me as a spectator.

I also paid special attention to the physical disposition and effect of a performer in Neuenfels's staging of *Nabucco*. I was directly confronted with the phenomenal corporeality of the singer of Abigaille due to an unflattering costume. When I saw Susan Neves enter through a burning hoop in a puffed-out, knee-length, white, frilly dress, which reminded me of a circus princess, I ascribed meanings to it on the level of representation that made an explicit statement about the character of Abigaille. This act made Abigaille appear as a strong and undaunted woman; at the same time, the step through the burning circus hoop evoked an association with an animal that can be manipulated. But on the sensual level, that is, on the level of presence, I primarily perceived the singer's body in its very own materiality—as a thick body pressed into a circus princess costume that was too tight and unflattering. I could perhaps describe my feeling as embarrassment (I was embarrassed for this unflatteringly displayed body, because I imagined what it would be like if I had to present myself in such an unflattering condition).[25]

During the first part of her grand aria, the part *before* the cabaletta with the men of the chorus in bee costumes, Neves sang as Abigaille sitting in a rocking chair. Directly before the beginning of the aria, Frank Frühkirch (Alexander Heidenreich), the character Neuenfels added, set the rocking chair in motion (see Figure 6.3). An unexpected moment of tenderness then occurred, caused by how the rocking chair, which seemed to float, also let the heavy body float and made it seem light. This state of suspension coincided with the transition from the scena to the cantabile, with a moment that also musically occurred in suspension: a pause.[26] The state of suspension only set

The interplay of representation and presence 97

Figure 6.3 Nabucco, staging by Hans Neuenfels, Susan Neves as Abigaille, Alexander Heidenreich as Frank Frühkirch, Deutsche Oper Berlin, 2000.
Photo courtesy of Detlef Kurth.

in through how a specific corporeality with a specific motion interacted with the tension of the musical pause between the movements of her aria, and it was only thus that the body was transformed and that I experienced the singer's body with a special intensity—a moment of intensified presence, independent of any components of meaning, independent of all possible emotions.[27]

While the previous examples have focused in particular on singers' physical disposition, the interplay of representation and presence can also be experienced on the vocal level as an important consideration for the perception of opera in performance.

Moments in which a unique presence becomes manifest can naturally be found above all in cases where the perception of a performance seems to be noticeably influenced by the particular shape a performer is in on a particular day. This applies all the more when a singer is announced as indisposed before the beginning of a performance, as happened in a performance of Konwitschny's production of Mozart's *Don Giovanni*[28] at the Komische Oper Berlin on 6 November 2007 with Johannes Weisser in the role of the protagonist. The announcement of an indisposition usually puts me as a listener in an altered mode of attention. My listening is then always focused on how the voice sounds indisposed, on whether the indisposition becomes noticeable, and especially on whether singers who are so courageous (or even reckless) as to appear despite an indisposition are possibly overexerting themselves, possibly damaging their voices. This risk, which a singer actually always takes, is brought to the fore by an announced indisposition. Don Giovanni's famous canzonetta "Deh, vieni alla finestra" (Oh, come to the window),[29] which is directed toward Donna Elvira's lady-in-waiting, represents the protagonist's first conspicuously belcanto-like number, the first number in which the audience's attention is focused on virtuosic, exceptional singing. The recitative before the canzonetta ends with Giovanni's challenge to himself, "Ora cantiamo" (Time for a serenade[30]), a challenge that also intradiegetically characterizes the singing as singing. Bettina Bartz and Werner Hintze's translation of the libretto, which the Konwitschny staging was based on, reads: "Dann wollen wir mal singen" (Then let's sing)—in my memory, it was in a terse, dialectally colored intonation: "Dann woll'n wa ma singen." The announcement was audible and understandable to everyone and was spoken by the indisposed singer of Giovanni himself: now comes the famous canzonetta. An atmosphere set in as if the whole hall was inwardly praying, with sympathy and compassion for the ill singer, that the canzonetta would work out. One could hear a lot of people coughing and clearing their throats in the hall. To me, this seemed sympathetic, a touching moment, as if the audience was audibly asking itself the question: What if I had to sing the canzonetta now? The great tension and concentration were palpable; they were carried by the desire for him to succeed, for him to persevere, and they were tied to the question of why the canzonetta could not simply be left out or spontaneously taken over by someone else. This thought was all the more apparent since precisely this staging explicitly engaged with questioning the notion of a work's rigid structure in opera through multiple interruptions. At that moment, I experienced the singer (and all of us in the audience) as being forced into the score's and staging's corset of instructions and plans. The feeling that emerged was sympathy for the singer and outrage at the constraints imposed by decisions made beforehand. Johannes Weisser's voice sounded noticeably more limited, husky, and somewhat dull. The appeal it lacked can be experienced in the recording made under the direction of René Jacobs in the same year, 2007, and can also be listened to online.[31] In spite of a noticeable indisposition, Weisser sang the aria without interruptions or lapses, that is, in principle, flawlessly. After the canzonetta was over, there was more applause for the scene than for any other one that evening. The applause sounded like relief, like a thank you to the singer for daring to sing and for making it through it. But something else became clear as well: the presence of the unique performance, which was brought about by experiencing the voice's vulnerability, had effects on the level of representation. Suddenly, Don Giovanni no longer seemed like a womanizer but like a very vulnerable person. This raises the question of whether it was only the singer whom we the audience helped through encouragement and sympathy or rather it was not also—due to the special conditions of the performance that evening—the unique and unrepeatable version of the character Don Giovanni that arose in that performance.

As I have already suggested, one could experience several moments in Peter Konwitschny's staging as at least questioning widespread notions of a work's fixed structure and of a rigidly set dramaturgy; these included multiple interruptions, especially in Ottavio's second aria,[32] but also in the finale when the end of the opera materially evaporated in concrete terms through successive thinning of the instrumentation. The mise-en-scène, as it was planned by Konwitschny and his production team, also thematized the uniqueness of opera performances. But at least in the performance described here, these interruptions and thematizations of the uniqueness of opera performances, which were obviously planned by the staging, could not develop an effect nearly as impressive as that of the indisposed singer's nail-biting rendering of Giovanni's canzonetta, experienced in the here and now of performance with all its unpredictability.

The interplay of representation and presence is not only limited to the experience of individual, special moments; it can also define longer segments, entire scenes, acts, or even an entire performance.

In Peter Konwitschny's staging of Wagner's *Lohengrin*,[33] which I have already discussed above, the question of the possibilities of representation played a decisive role with regard to the phenomenal corporeality of the actors. In this performance, the actors, with the exception of the one playing Lohengrin, were occupied for the entire duration of the performance with the representational task of portraying juveniles with their own adult physiognomy. Konwitschny's *Lohengrin* was situated in a classroom reminiscent of the Wilhelmine period in its architectural design and furnishings; the costumes of the actors, who appeared as schoolchildren, also recalled this era. On the occasion of the Leipzig premiere, one could read on the website of the Oper Leipzig: "In the classroom, the world of grammar-school students, utopias are still believable, and young people are willing to change their idols quickly."[34] The director Peter Konwitschny has also commented on his concept:

> We are dealing here with immature people who have a great longing for something but do not know how they should live it. Young people experience their first love, fantasize about the future, and the only adult, Lohengrin, longs, after taking on responsibility, to return to childhood.[35]

The question that is always asked first in connection with this staging—why set *Lohengrin* in a classroom?—can be answered, also with recourse to Konwitschny's explanation, on the level of representation to the effect that this staging allowed one to experience a story dealing with the desires, fantasies, and projections of an immature and so all the more dangerous collective, be it a school class or a nation (an association suggested by the final image of the staging when the schoolchildren went with their knapsacks into what is intimated to be a battlefield of World War I). The staging revealed group-dynamic processes of inclusion and exclusion that could lead to violence against individuals and to revenge (collective processes of expulsion directed against Elsa, Telramund, and Ortrud). The associative framework of what one heard and saw can be outlined, in my view, as follows: violence and wars arise in the classroom. The dynamics and practices are habituated and tested in the classroom, in a supposedly protected space of bourgeois educational ideals. The move into a classroom—a space familiar to everyone in the audience, but one that seemed to be alienated again by the historical distance—made these processes close, comprehensible. As we could hear and see, processes of exclusion as well as conflicts of life and death are already fomented and habituated at school. The fact that this was a classroom in the actually distant Wilhelmine period allowed us to look into the abysses of our own history; it awakened a sudden horror in response to our own militaristic past, to our readiness to use violence, to nationalism that turns into racism, to our eagerness for war. The disastrous continuities in the history of German nationalism became painfully palpable to me, all the more intensely because the music of Wagner's *Lohengrin* is so well known and familiar and considering especially, of course, that works and composers can no longer be separated from their reception history and specifically how the works of Richard Wagner have been treated in the twentieth century.[36] Even if Wagner cannot be blamed for how later generations have appropriated him, the fusion of the work with its reception history is inseparably established in the collective consciousness. This knowledge of the reception clearly underpinned my perception of Konwitschny's *Lohengrin*.

But moving the setting into a classroom made it possible to experience another completely different dimension. It offered the opportunity for the most exuberant theater, for humorous, funny, even ridiculous scenes. It was this dimension of the emergence of the performers' presence that brought the events on stage much closer to us, the audience. Appearing in ridiculously short pants and skirts, hoisting themselves onto oversized school benches, but performing their (in a sense "adult") singing parts with the greatest seriousness and professionalism, the performers appeared in all their phenomenal physicality, which never receded in their actions behind the characters they were portraying. I often had to laugh. It was a joy to watch the performers' obvious glee in playing children, in allowing themselves to hog the limelight for once without feeling embarrassed. The squad of great singers who have taken incredible pleasure in the braided, precocious Ortrud encompasses the international who's who of Ortrud singers: Eva Marton at the Hamburg premiere in 1998, Gabriele Schnaut in a later Hamburg series and as a star stand-in at the Leipzig premiere in 2009, and Luana DeVol for the DVD recording in Barcelona in 2006 (see Figure 6.4).

The classroom setting seemed to produce a desire for theater in the performers, a desire that was also transferred to large parts of the audience. Their perceptible joy in performing drew attention to the fundamental duality of bodies and actions throughout the entire duration of the performance and allowed the act of music-theatrical portrayal to become a recurring theme. In this way, the astonishingly consistent layer of representation was joined by a strong experience of physicality and of the performers' presence, which could be simultaneously experienced as self-reflexive.

Yet another staging of *Lohengrin* should be discussed here. In Kasper Holten's production at the Deutsche Oper Berlin,[37] I saw a story (yet again different

Figure 6.4 Lohengrin, staging by Peter Konwitschny, Emily Magee as Elsa, Luana DeVol as Ortrud, chorus, Gran Teatre del Liceu Barcelona, 2006. Screenshot from the DVD recording.

© 2007 by Fundació del Gran Teatre del Liceu and EuroArts.

compared to the Konwitschny staging) that distinctly engaged me on the level of representation and encouraged me, as a spectator and listener, to assign specific meanings to what I saw and heard: Lohengrin was introduced as a talented director or magician who could manipulate crowds of people with the use of theatrical means. The means he employed—such as putting on swan wings at the back edge of the stage while the other characters were all looking forward or reading a cheat sheet during the Grail narrative—were visible to us spectators but not to the crowd gathered on the stage. As one could already see in the first scene when he put on the immense swan wings, the various means were adapted to their respective application, in this case, their application in rescuing a wrongly accused person in Brabant. Lohengrin thus also appeared like a skillful colonizer or missionary, employing the practices and signs of those to be colonized to convince or surprise them all the more effectively. During the King's (Albert Dohmen) prayer in front of the trial by ordeal, Telramund (Gordon Hawkins) knelt down and folded his hands. For a moment, this seemed to irritate Klaus Florian Vogt as Lohengrin, as if he didn't know this gesture, this ritual. But he did notice how everyone present thought he was sent by the power that they believed in and that Telramund was now kneeling to worship. So Lohengrin was able to adapt very quickly and even to outdo Telramund's gesture when Vogt first raised his arms like a priest or messiah while looking at the people and then sunk to his knees with an ostentatious, large gesture of folding his hands (see Figure 6.5). Lohengrin employed the rituals of the medieval Christians he encountered.

But Lohengrin, the magician—who also brought with him light and fog effects so as, for example, to blind Telramund in battle—possibly reached a

102 *Analytical approaches*

Figure 6.5 *Lohengrin*, staging by Kasper Holten, Klaus Florian Vogt as Lohengrin, Ricarda Merbeth as Elsa, Deutsche Oper Berlin, 2012.

Photo courtesy of Marcus Lieberenz.

little too deep into his bag of tricks with these swan wings, though they did not fail to achieve their effect when he first appeared. Ricarda Merbeth as Elsa first saw this Lohengrin with his swan wings later than the others, since she was wearing a blindfold at the beginning of the scene—as a symbol of her being accused—and Lohengrin only took the blindfold off after he had set his condition ("Nie sollst Du mich befragen"; These questions ask me never).[38] When Lohengrin removed her blindfold and Elsa beheld him very close in front of her, she was clearly startled. This costume was obviously inappropriately effusive in her eyes. Could Elsa see Lohengrin's cards? Everyone else present was still under the spell of his entrance, which was accompanied by instrumental music that also belonged, according to this interpretation, to the

The interplay of representation and presence 103

theatrical staging Lohengrin employed to bolster his effect. His brilliant entrance to the shimmering sounds of the strings dazzled everyone. Elsa saw him to the different, much more "earthly" music of when he prohibits her from asking about his identity, so the effect of his appearance was also different. She was irritated. But considering the predicament she found herself in, she apparently looked beyond the exaggerated staging of the newcomer.

Before the narrative of the Grail, Vogt (as Lohengrin) took white cards out of his skirt pocket: this Lohengrin had to cheat and take another look at the text for the climax of his self-staging. Apparently, he had also prepared something for this occasion—the Grail narrative could thus be understood as being staged to have an intended effect. Although Lohengrin did not know what came next by heart, it at the same time became clear that he had precisely foreseen and predetermined the course of the plot and for that reason had noted down the right words—those of the Grail narrative—on a piece of paper that apparently only the audience noticed. During the Grail narrative, the members of the chorus approached him as the people of Brabant and knelt around him as if he were a messiah, who—still dressed in his wings—now appeared to be an angel of death (see Figure 6.6).

In a way that could not have been foreseen in the very consistent representational space of this staging, the interplay of representation and presence occurred due to a unique constellation of planned staging intention and the unplanned daily condition of the participants. Klaus Florian Vogt had sung Lohengrin in the premiere but did not appear in the following two

Figure 6.6 Lohengrin, staging by Kasper Holten, Klaus Florian Vogt as Lohengrin, chorus, Deutsche Oper Berlin, 2012.

Photo courtesy of Marcus Lieberenz.

performances due to illness. In the performance I experienced, he was singing for the first time after his absence due to illness. In restless movements of his hands, which sometimes seemed like a tremor, I thought I could see Vogt's nervousness. In his otherwise so clear voice—which can also be perceived as boyish—one could hear traces of hoarseness. But maybe I only heard this because I knew that he was absent from the last two performances and that everyone in the audience, which apparently included many Vogt fans, was very nervous about whether he had completely recovered. Vogt's voice sounded a little throaty, throatier than otherwise, a little harder than usual, as if he were actually still a little ill. But all the exposed high notes came with the radiance and purity that one expects from him, albeit somewhat more short-winded than usual. As is often the case in such moments of an actual or assumed indisposition, we perceived the individual challenges of the parts—which produce concrete expectations due to their familiarity—even more intensely, which made successful passages all the more exhilarating.

What was so captivating about this constellation was, once again, watching how representation and presence were reciprocally dependent and reinforcing. The possibility that the singer Klaus Florian Vogt had not yet fully recovered from his cold and the ensuing impression that something of his former indisposition could still be heard strengthened in a peculiar (and unforeseeable) way what I have identified in the performance as Lohengrin's directorial function (that is, the level of representation): Lohengrin didn't seem to be a miracle sent by God but rather to be "only" a director or magician who was not immune to failure—just like a singer in his unique daily condition, who can be nervous or sound slightly hoarse. The perception of Vogt's imperfect voice in that performance strengthened—as an experience of heightened presence—the level of the performance that portrayed the character of Lohengrin as a humanly fallible con artist and manipulator instead of a superhuman, divine being.

While I have discussed physical and vocal experiences of presence in relation to the level of representation in the last two analyses of performances, my final analysis of a performance in this chapter will examine the interaction of representation and presence with regard to the integration of further elements of a performance into perception. In Katharina Wagner's 2007 Bayreuth production of Wagner's *Die Meistersinger von Nürnberg* (with Sebastian Weigle as the conductor and Robert Sollich as the dramaturg),[39] we did not experience the parade of the guilds in the third act at the beginning of the festival meadow, as envisaged in the original, but rather saw statues of Germany's intellectual and artistic geniuses—the so-called German masters (including Bach, Dürer, Goethe, Schiller, Beethoven, and Wagner)—brought to life with heads swollen to a disturbing size (see Figure 6.7). As if in a nightmare, the figures (extras wearing jumbo sculptures of heads) stormed Hans Sachs's workshop. They tied up Franz Hawlata as Hans Sachs and forced him to watch their grotesque dance, in which they mutilated one other and destroyed each other's body parts, always in harmony with the marches

Figure 6.7 Die Meistersinger von Nürnberg, staging by Katharina Wagner, Franz Hawlata as Hans Sachs, extras, Bayreuth Festival, 2007.

Photo courtesy of the Bayreuth Festival and Jochen Quast.

and melodies intended for presenting the respective guilds, such as the bakers, who extol their guild as fighting against famine. For me, these figures with swollen heads evoked an association with carnival and its customs as they are still practiced today in the metropolises of the Rhine and that become grotesque due to the simultaneity of comedy and threat. From that point forward, this atmosphere defined and colored the entire performance. Suddenly, the music of the festival meadow sounded changed, as if it had transformed itself according to the perception theory of intermodal integration and adopted the new atmosphere as its own, or as if the carnival had first tickled out this color.[40] After this thoroughly horrifying presentation, the figures with swollen heads bowed as if after a performance and brought on stage a "directorial team" with a "conductor" for applause. One master after the other disappeared (lastly Beethoven, Kleist, Schiller, and Wagner himself). Only the directorial team and conductor remained until they were finally put into a gray garbage bin by extras dressed as gray-clad cleaning personnel. At first I perceived this as a self-ironic punch line: what many traditionalists view as the destruction of art (Regietheater) belongs in the garbage can. And at the premiere, there was indeed spontaneous applause from parts of the audience. But when Sachs arrived a moment later, with his hands folded in front of his abdomen—a gesture that recordings of Hitler's speeches have inscribed into cultural visual memory—and lit the can, the scene and its effect abruptly changed (see Figure 6.8). Images of Nazi book burnings were immediately brought to mind, not only for me, but also for those in the auditorium who

106 *Analytical approaches*

Figure 6.8 Die Meistersinger von Nürnberg, staging by Katharina Wagner, Franz Hawlata as Hans Sachs, extras, Bayreuth Festival, 2007.

Photo courtesy of the Bayreuth Festival and Jörg Schulze.

had just been amused: they held their breath and halted their applause. The production was now obviously staging itself as an endangered cultural asset exposed to fascist persecution. The whole thing was ironically turned around yet again when Sachs finally took a golden prize statuette out of the fire. The statue could have been either a bellowing stag and so a sign of the petty German bourgeoisie or a Bambi and so a foreshadowing, as a quotation of a German media prize, of the transformation of Stolzing—who was then promptly awarded the same prize on the festival meadow—into a pop and entertainment star suitable for the masses and attributable to the culture industry.[41] I was confronted with representational means that very clearly referred to a visual language and aesthetic of National Socialism in the scene reminiscent of the book burnings but also even more clearly in Sachs's final speech. In this scene, Franz Hawlata appeared in the middle of an incredibly strong lighting effect that illuminated his face and upper body from below in a glaring chiaroscuro, as if he had emerged from a film by Leni Riefenstahl, and used gesticulation, articulation, and declamation that again evoked the poses and even the intonation of Hitler's addresses (see Figure 6.9).

Moreover, during the speech, two gigantic Goethe and Schiller statues were raised out of the stage floor; the more one could see of them, the more it was apparent that they were inspired by Arno Breker. What occurred here was not merely a reference to the visual language and aesthetics of National Socialism, not just a depiction of fascist means of staging on the level of representation. I rather perceived the staging to be using these means itself; that

The interplay of representation and presence 107

Figure 6.9 Die Meistersinger von Nürnberg, staging by Katharina Wagner, Franz Hawlata as Hans Sachs, Bayreuth Festival, 2007.

Photo courtesy of the Bayreuth Festival and Enrico Nawrath.

is, it made the means present and thus achieved a potentially overwhelming aesthetic and sensual effect. Even though the employed means—gestures, manners of articulation, light effects—unmistakably bore the index of National Socialist horror, I did not perceive their presentation as a distancing of the staging from these aesthetic procedures. Even though it was clear to my eyes and ears that what could be seen and heard was ideologically poisoned, it also became clear to me how receptive I was to the effect of these aesthetic means. This was a very painful experience, and many in the audience were unable to react to it other than with protest—a protest that was also directed against their own susceptibility.

108 *Analytical approaches*

The scandal of the staging, or rather what made it a scandal for many, lay in this duality of representation and presence in its means. Here the interplay of representation and presence became scandalous because it touched on a political and historical dimension that makes the performance history of Wagner's oeuvre, especially that of the *Meistersinger*, almost unbearable. Not only in these moments, but especially in them, I experienced the performance as productively provoking the audience, as challenging it to take a position. No one in the auditorium could sit back uninvolved. Everyone was called upon to take a stand. The performance was polarizing because it productively overtaxed the audience's senses by presenting scenic events ambivalently.

The meeting and merging of representation and the presence of performers, which is only manifest in a unique performance, constitutes one of the particular appeals of a performance of an opera staging from the well-known, canonical repertoire. This interplay is not only a perceptual event for the audience members but also—as I would like to argue—an occasion for the performers to heighten the intensity of the performance. It is thus able to spur the interminable process of the feedback loop between performers and audience members in an exceptional way.

Notes

1. Leo Karl Gerhartz, "Auch das 'hm-ta-ta' beim Wort genommen (Zur Frankfurter *Macbeth*-Inszenierung von Hans Neuenfels)," in Wiesmann, *Werk und Wiedergabe*, 311–19.
2. Gerhartz, 314.
3. Gerhartz, 317.
4. Gerhartz, 315.
5. Deutsche Oper Berlin, 2000; I attended the performances on 8 March 2000, 15 March 2000, 7 January 2001, and 30 October 2004.
6. Giuseppe Verdi, *Nabucodonosor*, ed. Roger Parker, vol. 3 of *The Works of Giuseppe Verdi*, ed. Philip Gossett et al., ser. 1, *Operas* (Chicago: University of Chicago Press; Milan: Ricordi, 1987), 226.
7. Verdi, 230–49.
8. Verdi, 238–39, 243–45.
9. See Horst Weber on the phenomenon of "Mickey Mousing" in "Vom 'treulos treuesten Freund': Eine Einführung in das produktive Dilemma des Regietheaters," in Weber, *Oper und Werktreue*, 10.
10. Katharina Wagner's production of Richard Wagner's *Die Meistersinger von Nürnberg* (Bayreuth Festival, 2007), which I will specifically engage with later in this chapter, also exhibited this pleasure in choreographically repeated sequences of movements in a kind of "Mickey Mousing," that is, a pleasure in visualizing musical rhythms and phrases, such as how the apprentices collectively wave their beer bottles at the beginning of the second act or how the participants in the fighting fugue similarly wave buckets of paint.
11. Giuseppe Verdi, *Don Carlos (Don Carlo)*, ed. Hans Swarowsky, piano score with German and Italian text, versions in four and five acts (Milan: Ricordi, 1967), 125–26.
12. Verdi, *Don Carlos*, 125, mm. 7–9.
13. See again Weber, "Vom 'treulos treuesten Freund.'"

14 https://www.youtube.com/watch?v=LCFNcEFZn38, accessed 30 April 2017, no longer accessible.
15 Hans Neuenfels, "Zwischen dramaturgischer Innovation und Werktreue: Zur Aktualität und Aktualisierbarkeit der *Aida*," in *Oper heute: Formen der Wirklichkeit im zeitgenössischen Musiktheater*, ed. Otto Kolleritsch (Vienna: Universal Edition, 1985), 38.
16 Staatsoper Berlin, 2008; I attended the performance on 22 May 2009.
17 See Giuseppe Verdi, *Un ballo in maschera: Melodramma in tre atti*, libretto by Antonio Somma, score, new rev. ed. (Milan: Ricordi, 1973), 69–92.
18 Verdi, *Un ballo in Maschera*, 453; Weaver, *Seven Verdi Librettos*, 257.
19 On this, see Bettina Brandl-Risi, "Die Körperlichkeit der Musik: Distanz und Überwältigung im Musiktheater Harry Kupfers," in Hintze, Risi, and Sollich, *Realistisches Musiktheater*, 77–96.
20 See Erika Fischer-Lichte, "Verwandlung als ästhetische Kategorie: Zur Entwicklung einer neuen Ästhetik des Performativen," in *Theater seit den 60er Jahren: Grenzgänge der Neo-Avantgarde*, ed. Fischer-Lichte, Friedemann Kreuder, and Isabel Pflug (Tübingen: A. Francke, 1998), 86.
21 Oper Stuttgart, 2000; I attended the performance on 7 October 2000.
22 Luana DeVol, "Auf der Jagd: Luana DeVol über Wachsen und Warten, Karrierekurven und Korrepetitoren, Lady Macbeth, Brünnhilde und die Praxis der permanenten Stimmpflege; Ein Interview," by Stephan Mösch, *Oper 2000: Das Jahrbuch*, yearbook of *Opernwelt*, October 2000, 8.
23 DeVol, 8.
24 DeVol, 8.
25 On this, see Jens Roselt, "Die Würde des Menschen ist antastbar: Der kreative Umgang mit der Scham," in *Erniedrigung genießen*, ed. Carl Hegemann (Berlin: Alexander, 2001), 47–59.
26 Verdi, *Nabucodonosor*, 222, m. 86.
27 See https://www.youtube.com/watch?v=i9AM7kskqZQ, accessed 30 April 2017, no longer accessible. Instead of Susan Neves, Sylvie Valayre was playing Abigaille in this video. The described moment of an experience of intensified presence through the lightness and floating of a heavy body did not take place with the recasting of a thin singer.
28 Komische Oper Berlin, 2003; I attended the performance on 6 November 2007.
29 McClatchy, *Seven Mozart Librettos*, 613.
30 McClatchy, 611.
31 https://www.youtube.com/watch?v=zo5aCqIUxM8, accessed 1 October 2020.
32 See Jürgen Schläder, "'… da der Tod der wahre Endzweck unsers lebens ist …': Theorie-Überlegungen zu Peter Konwitschnys Dekonstruktion der zweiten Ottavio-Arie," in *Mitten im Leben: Musiktheater von der Oper zur Everyday Performance*, ed. Anno Mungen (Würzburg: Königshausen and Neumann, 2011), 119–45.
33 Staatsoper Hamburg, 1998; Gran Teatre del Liceu Barcelona, 2000 (with a DVD recording in 2006); Oper Leipzig, 2009; I attended the performances on 28 April 2001 in Hamburg and on 18 December 2009 in Leipzig.
34 Website of the Oper Leipzig on the Leipzig premiere (18 December 2009), no longer available.
35 Quoted from the website of the Oper Leipzig on the Leipzig premiere (18 December 2009), no longer available.
36 See Sollich, "Staging Wagner," which refers to Walter Benjamin's idea of the "Nachreifen" (continued ripening) of works.
37 Deutsche Oper Berlin, 2012; I attended the performance on 25 April 2012.
38 Wagner, *Lohengrin*, trans. Corder, 141.
39 Bayreuth Festival, 2007; I attended the performances on 16 August 2007 and 27 July 2008.
40 On intermodal integration, see chapter 4.
41 Levin, "*Die Meistersinger von Nürnberg*," 263.

7 The voice and the body in opera performances

On the relationship between vocal production and gestures

This study has already thematized the relationship between the voice and the body in isolated instances, but this relationship can be called the central category of the performative aspect of opera—both with regard to individual singers and with regard to the interplay between singers and audience members. This chapter will specifically address this performative core of opera, beginning with a brief review of the history of performance practices in opera.

> Few singers … exhibit … a deep study of the scenic art; their movements are mostly dull and uniform, often ugly, such as the frequently occurring lifting of their arms in parallel and stretching them out alternately with a flat open hand.[1]

This observation, which found its way into the *Encyclopädie der gesammten musikalischen Wissenschaften* (Encyclopedia of all of music studies) in 1835, seems not to have lost its validity almost two hundred years later if one thinks of the gesture practices of some star singers in today's opera industry. What is deplored here can be roughly described as stereotypical singer gestures; these gestures have thoroughly recognizable historical roots. In their most basic form, they can be placed in a tradition that reaches from ancient rhetoric to baroque deictic gestures and the gestural code of the Enlightenment. But in addition to this tradition, there is, in my view, another powerful tradition at work here. One should not forget the influence of the usually long vocal studies and voice training that opera singers undergo. It is a very long process to acquire the projecting power that is necessary to be able to vocally hold one's own on the operatic stage. In order to learn how to operate the invisible and intangible instrument of the voice, budding singers are shown drawings of the larynx, tongue, and pharynx. If they are lucky enough to have teachers familiar with physiology, they are shown how to create the different positions of the larynx and the tongue that are responsible for phonation and resonance. But in the end, voice students have no choice but to imagine these processes as well as the steps and tactics necessary to perfect the vocal organ. They

DOI: 10.4324/9781003124863-10

imagine making a tone sound out in their forehead, the so-called mask, and not in their nose; they imagine making a tone float on a column of air so as to reach the back corner of an opera or concert hall, to prevent the pressure of the breath from pressing the tone, and to induce, caress, and embrace the tone. In order to gain control over the complex processes that take place in the throat, singers more or less involuntarily discover the potential of gestures that influence and guide the voice; they learn these gestures as autosuggestive tricks over many years of study. The discursive description of what one must imagine so as to master the voice may have made clear what these gestures are: the familiar operatic gestures that can be frequently seen independent of the text and the dramatic or theatrical situation. In this regard, it is interesting to note that these gestures of vocal production turn out to be much more excessive in situations (seemingly) without an audience, for example, in the context of a CD recording—that is, in situations distant from the grand operatic stage, situations where the singer is able to concentrate entirely on producing pure sound (and on the bodily control required for doing so)—than what we usually experience during a performance on stage.[2] It seems it is precisely the presence of the audience that prompts singers to hold back the intense and sometimes even intimate gestures that support the production of sound (or to use only the familiar operatic gestures).

In the case of gestures, we tend to postulate and diagnose a relationship between the inside and outside, a relationship between psychological or emotional states and bodily signs. Such a relationship also exists in the gestures of voice training, but here the relationship is between the inner bodily conditions for producing sounds and the external reflections of these bodily processes—that is, the relationship is unrelated to affective states and processes. Not only do singers grow up with these kinds of gestures, so does the opera audience. The audience connects this code with a certain expected type of operatic singing and is possibly never bothered by it.

Thus, in one of the earliest film recordings of an operatic scene—a 1911 performance of the sextet from Donizetti's *Lucia di Lammermoor*[3]—we not only recognize the ridiculous-looking rudimentary form of baroque or Enlightenment gestural practices and the singers' lack of imagination as they repeatedly perform a "lifting of their arms in parallel and stretching them out alternately with a flat open hand," exactly as described in the *Encyclopädie der gesammten musikalischen Wissenschaften*; these gestures also exhibit the influence of voice training. The actors in the film are not, however, singers but just actors and actresses imitating the typical gestural practices of singers—actors imitating the gestures of voice training! Since the film was recorded without sound—a soundtrack of an audio recording of singers was then added to it—the actors do not even need the gestures to produce sounds. Their act of mute imitation demonstrates, rather, how firmly the relationship between these gestures and the operatic voice was established in the audiences' consciousness and expectations at that time.

As already stated, this tradition can still be observed today, and not only as the standard and everyday practice on stage but also now ennobled in the

112 *Analytical approaches*

efforts of so-called historical or historically informed performance practices as an attempt to reconstruct how a director believes nineteenth-century singers gesticulated. This could be experienced, for example, in Pier'Alli's production of Verdi's *Oberto* at the 2007 Verdi Festival in Parma and Busseto.[4] The repertoire of gestures was not fundamentally different from the operatic gestures one usually sees, but they were performed in such a demonstrative manner that their rhetorical function clearly came to the fore and they became choreographically conspicuous (see Figure 7.1).

It was particularly noticeable how gestures were usually slowed down in the performance. There seems to be something like an established practice in operatic performance with regard to the question of timing—that is, with regard to the relationship between gesture and time—to slow down gestures according to the musical time. This practice optimally corresponds, of course, with the gestures of voice training, whose timing seems to have been taken directly from listening to musical time. The practice can already be found, with a theoretical and aesthetical explanation, in Pietro Lichtenthal's *Dizionario e bibliografia della musica* (Dictionary and bibliography of music) from 1826. In the entry "Attore" (Actor), by which is meant a "Cantante che fa una parte in un'Opera" (a singer who plays a part in an opera), Lichtenthal refers to the necessity that singers act; otherwise they are merely singers and not actors. But, he argues, they do not have to pay as much attention as actors to the "verità" (truth) of their performances, since the music already gives their performances an "anima" (soul).[5]

Figure 7.1 Oberto, staging by Pier'Alli, Francesca Sassu as Leonora, Giovanni Battista Parodi as Oberto, Teatro Verdi Busseto, 2007.

Photo courtesy of Roberto Ricci and the Teatro Regio di Parma.

Going back to early nineteenth-century acting theory is of decisive importance for discussing the relationship between the voice and the body with regard to the scenic actions of performers, since it was during this period—a few decades later in comparison to theater—that Enlightenment concepts of acting found their way into the practices of music theater, which made new demands on singers' ability to portray a role with their bodies (namely to make a performance appear convincing through gestural actions) and so assigned increasing importance to scenic actions in the process of performance. The offshoots of this new orientation in acting theory continue to shape the reality of performance and audiences' perceptual positions to this day, even though the aesthetic coordinate system of Regietheater is drastically different from that of late-Enlightenment music theater.

In 1785, Johann Jakob Engel indirectly granted singers the license not to subject themselves to the dictates of truth in acting, as long as they only paid attention to the beauty of their singing:

> Singing has so infinitely much sweetness; it captivates and enchants the soul so much through the most voluptuous of the subtle senses; it immerses the soul so deeply in the pleasure of the present moment that one either no longer notices or doesn't pay attention to the discord between expression and the state of the soul being expressed, the confusion of lyrical affect with dramatic affect. The truth of acting is of course weakened, and so too the effect; but what is lost in this respect is gained in another; what lacks truth is compensated with beauty.[6]

It was probably entirely in this spirit that the tenor Luigi Ferretti acted in a performance of the opera *Elena da Feltre* by Saverio Mercadante in Trieste in 1844, and a reviewer of the magazine *Il Figaro* did not reprimand him for doing so but rather came to his defense:

> [Ferretti's] voice is voluminous, wide-ranging, and has a very pleasant sound; his gestures are a bit sloppy; but if a tenor has a beautiful voice and knows how to use it, it doesn't matter if his acting is not the best.[7]

This was apparently common, and it is still used as a legitimate reason for many opera singers to leave the responsibility for affect and communication exclusively to the voice. But it is also a motivation for directors to work with singers on the theatrical plausibility of their gestures.

The 2007 *Oberto* in Busseto is an example of how the established practices regarding gestures and timing have been explicitly presented and staged as such in a current production. Outside of Italy, however, the trend of questioning entrenched practices is much more dominant in opera stagings. This results in performances that slow down the time of the gestures even further—to the point of slow motion—in order to focus attention on the force and energy of individual gestures and movements in their own materiality (such as in Robert Wilson's stagings of operas or in

114 *Analytical approaches*

Heiner Müller's production of *Tristan und Isolde* at the Bayreuth Festival in 1993). Or, conversely, the time of the gestures is accelerated, and the tempo for gestures is taken from the speed of musical figures, which has especially turned recent stagings of Handel's operas into athletic and dancing exhibitions of virtuosic movement, for example, in David McVicar's production of Handel's *Giulio Cesare* at the 2005 Glyndebourne Festival with William Christie as the conductor and Danielle de Niese as Cleopatra. Modeled on aerobics, Bollywood films, or MTV clips, musical movement was perceived in this production as translated into choreographic, rhythmic movements, with the focus less on gestures and their possible (affective) basis or meanings than on rhythmic formalization and thus on the artificiality of the music.[8]

But one can also discern in opera performances a trend to counteract the ingrained practice of stereotypical opera gestures with the means of psychological realism by seeming to take gestures from the language of everyday movement and the everyday perception of time. In Robert Carsen's 1999 Parisian production of Handel's *Alcina*, Morgana, the sister of the sorceress Alcina, appears as a maid. In her aria "Tornami a vagheggiar" (Come back to admire me), she explains her love to Bradamante, who has disguised herself as a man and has appeared under the name Ricciardo; Morgana does so with a wealth of gestures taken from everyday life (kneeling, rolling on the floor, straightening her clothes, arranging glasses and cutlery, unfolding napkins, filling a glass with wine, toasting). It was a pleasure not only to listen to the singer Natalie Dessay in her highly virtuosic flights and ornamentation but also to watch how she performs scenic actions while singing, actions that one would not expect based on the established practice of what one often experiences.[9]

Despite the trends outlined above to make gestures more noticeable in new ways in performances, the established practice of using gestures' function to support sound has remained influential as a habit and an expectation for opera performances. Only under the condition of this established practice and expectation did a moment in Jossi Wieler and Sergio Morabito's 2001 Stuttgart production of Verdi's *Don Carlo* unfold its effect. It was when the soprano Catherine Naglestad as Elisabetta *did not*, as expected, embrace sound in one of the most exposed passages at the end of an aria and *did not* raise or stretch out her arms in parallel to support the sound but rather put her hands brusquely into her coat pockets.[10] The contrast between expectation and experience, between the preimagined gestural code (protention) and the practice that violates it, intensified the moment, marking the scene in memory. The seemingly inappropriate gesture also intensified the sonic impression—*seemingly* inappropriate because it violated the familiar and expected gestural code but was also perfectly appropriate to the costume (a form-fitting coat) and Catherine Naglestad's posture during the aria.

These examples should demonstrate the potential of questioning operatic gestures that have been practiced in a similar form for almost two hundred years and can sometimes be explained in terms of voice physiology. Dissolving the bond between anticipated music and anticipated gestures also constantly changes the perception and effect of the music.

On the perception of voices in opera

While I have so far discussed the connection and interplay between physical gestures and vocal expression, it seems necessary to pay attention to voices in opera by themselves within the framework of an investigation on the performative dimension of opera. There are many ways to speak about voices. As I explained in Chapter 4, a phenomenological approach is the most profitable for the context of this study; phenomenological approaches are characterized by how they do not describe any event independently from one's own corporeal experience.[11] The particular ecstasy of the trained singing voice, with its energetic potential for effect, is able to create an intimate space of listening even over spatial distance and to affect listeners physically. Not what the singing voice is but how it is experienced individually is the question that comes to the fore. If the aesthetic effect of the singing voice cannot be grasped by categories such as register, timbre, and so on, then it must be examined as a dynamic medium between two bodies and as part of a subjective listening experience. According to Bernhard Waldenfels, the singing voice cannot be separated from its integration into the act of perception, since a voice is, in his view, always a "heard voice."[12]

In accordance with the corporeal understanding of experiencing the voice, the concrete reaction of listeners—applause, ovation (an extreme, sometimes almost animalistic sound)—can also be grasped as a reaction that seizes the body involuntarily. A review of a 1993 performance of Richard Strauss's *Ariadne auf Naxos* in Zurich with Edita Gruberová as Zerbinetta seems to be symptomatic of this:

> From the press ..., one knew that one should in any case expect something great. Edita Gruberová ... would ... undoubtedly shine. But in the end, it turned out completely different. For there was that moment. It was the moment that leaves connoisseurs and philistines speechless. A moment in which the entire audience leans forward in astonishment, where their breathing stops, where you can hear your neighbor's pulse—twelve minutes of paralyzed bewilderment .... And what followed was not a gesture, not a ritual of opera—but rather physical necessity. As if after a too generously measured transfusion, part of the sonic liquid had to find an outlet in wild cries of enthusiasm.[13]

The special fascination of a voice like Edita Gruberová's is based on a perceptual situation whose intensity is due to, among other things, a very particular relationship of the voice, the body, and sonic perception in space. With certain tones—primarily long-sustained tones in the extreme ranges of the third octave—I have felt as if Edita Gruberová's voice becomes detached from her body, as if her voice is floating bodilessly in space and is right next

116 *Analytical approaches*

to me, as if my entire body is enveloped and filled with the unique sound of this voice, whose sensual intensity cannot be remembered and so also cannot be anticipated.

The relationship between memory (retention) and expectation (protention) formulated by phenomenology for the perception of time plays a decisive role, if not *the* decisive role, with regard to the intensified perceptual situation of an operatic voice. For me, one characteristic of the complexity of perceiving an admired and celebrated opera singer is the perception of a history, a past that singers carry with them and that cannot be separated from the history the audience associates with a particular singer. What is decisive for recognizing something extraordinary in the case of an admired singer is not only the special presence of a voice but also just as much the perception of transience: Will it be like last time? How many times and for how long can it still be like this? With regard to the familiar and desired voices of famous singers, the existing concepts on the topic of temporal experience in opera must be expanded to include the times of musical (that is, vocal) realization: the times of a particular voice, the moment of a voice in correspondence to its own history. What I hear is the current sound, here and now, of, for example, Edita Gruberová, but it is also my expectation, the sound that I have in my ear even before it appears (before the performance), the oscillation between what she is currently producing and what I anticipate. There are always several Gruberovás on stage simultaneously.

This relationship between memory and expectation is not stable. It shifts through surprises, such as minor accidents after a scratched or failed tone that I did not expect. The tension grows, the worry that it could repeat itself, especially because one often knows what difficulties are still to come. The successful tones—which one had actually expected before the surprise, but which can no longer be taken for granted after the mishap—become all the more precious. The fragility and vulnerability of both the voice and the moment reinforce the appeal of the moment.

A particularly special and rare experience in the context of the performative relationship between the voice of a singer and an audience member is when you have the feeling that a certain singer is singing just for you, is looking right at you—an experience of exclusivity and intimacy.[14] A description of such an experience can be found in Gustave Flaubert's novel *Madame Bovary*. Emma Bovary is attending a performance of Donizetti's *Lucia di Lammermoor* at the opera in Rouen with a singer named Lagardy—who is described in more detail, also biographically, during the scene—in the role of Edgardo. During the sextet in the second act,

> a madness gripped her: he [Lagardy in the role of Edgardo] was gazing at her, for certain! She longed to run into his arms to take shelter in his strength, as in the embodiment of love itself, and to say to him, to cry out "Take me away, bear me away, let us begone! Yours, yours, all my fervour and all my dreams!"[15]

The voice and the body in opera performances 117

Based on my experience of a performance, I want to try to describe how such an impression of exclusivity gives rise to the special presence of a singer: the performance was that of soprano Iano Tamar in the title role of Luigi Cherubini's 2002 *Médée* at the Deutsche Oper Berlin in a production by Ursel and Karl-Ernst Herrmann.[16] But this attempt also shows that these impressions of exclusivity can never be securely or clearly fixed to exactly two participants. The relationship constantly develops, and it rarely comes to a concrete two-person relationship. It is more frequently the case that a singer also seeks an exclusive relationship, just not with the listener who feels that she or he has an exclusive two-person relationship with the singer.

Right from the beginning of the performance, Médée was all alone. Even before the overture started, the set, which tapered toward the back at an acute angle, opened up; far away at the back sat Médée, Iano Tamar, on a suitcase—a migrant, someone who had not yet arrived and never would. As the set opened, she appeared in its middle, in the center of the action; or conversely, the presence of the performer conveyed the impression that she had burst open the set to create space for her. Her power not only over the course of the drama but also over the course of the music became palpable in a moment when she turned to the audience and the orchestra, and then the overture began as she rose.

In the set, there was a kind of bridge from the stage to the orchestra pit: small steps led from the stage to a small platform that protruded into the orchestra pit at about the height of the prompter's box. On this platform, Médée appeared as someone cast off from the stage, but the platform could also be read as Médée's retreat from the world into the space of music, the orchestra pit (see Figure 7.2). The exclusive space also shook up the relationship between the stage and the auditorium. In her first aria, in which she tries to persuade Jason to let her have their children ("Vous voyez de vos fils la mère infortunée"; You see the unfortunate mother of your sons), it created the possibility of establishing a close relationship between Iano Tamar and her audience. She was actually imploring Jason, but her gaze went into the audience, past the stage apron, creating eye contact with the audience, with me in the sense of the exclusivity described above.

This exclusive relationship was established again in the performance with the aria in which Néris assures Médée that she will be faithful to her and follow her to her death ("Ah! Nos peines seront communes"; Oh! We will share our sorrows). Médée seemed to take little interest in the words of her confidante, and I paid just as little attention to the singer of Néris. The spell of Iano Tamar's radiance was too strong—a presence achieved through an enormous physical energy that was transferred directly to me as a listener and spectator; it bound my gaze to her and, above all, to her gaze.

A third moment from this performance should be mentioned. During the interlude between the second and third acts, it became clear how much the music was also contributing to strengthening the focus on Iano Tamar as Médée. In this interlude, the sorceress Médée prepares to poison her gift for her rival. The singer's body vibrated with each note of each new section; her

118 *Analytical approaches*

Figure 7.2 Médée, staging and set design by Ursel Herrmann and Karl-Ernst Herrmann, Iano Tamar as Médée, Deutsche Oper Berlin, 2002.

Photo courtesy of Bernd Uhlig.

breath visibly accelerated and intensified; her body and her gaze exclusively conveyed the music to the listener. The looks Tamar shot into the auditorium had a certain resemblance to the looks of silent-film divas—in the words of Gloria Swanson as Norma Desmond in Billy Wilder's *Sunset Boulevard* (1950): "We didn't need dialogue. We had faces!" By putting on her magical skirt, Tamar as Médée finally took over the entire stage space again; it was filled, overfilled, flooded with her presence. She thereby seemed to trigger both the thunderstorm and the thunderstorm music. Finally, she opened up the boundaries of the set (the walls moved apart) with her arms (or better, with her stage presence) and became the mistress of the entire space, the thunderstorm and the music.

In descriptions of the special relationship between the body and voice of a singer and an audience member, of this exclusive and even sometimes intimate two-person relationship, one finds in some authors who have dealt with the sensual dimension of opera singing an evocation of the erotic. This becomes very clear in formulations on the dissolution of the subject–object dichotomy, as described, for example, by Wayne Koestenbaum:

> The listener's inner body is illuminated, opened up: a singer doesn't expose her own throat, she exposes the listener's interior. Her voice enters me, makes me a "me," an interior, by virtue of the fact that I have been entered. The singer, through osmosis, passes through the self's porous membrane,

and discredits the fiction that bodies are separate, boundaried packages. The singer destroys the division between her body and our own, for her sound enters our system. I am sitting in the Met at Leontyne Price's recital in 1985 and Price's vibrations are *inside my body*.[17]

What Koestenbaum describes here is the unification of two actually separate bodies that takes place in the act of listening. Clearly audible is how he draws on Georges Bataille, who called the search for continuity a characteristic of eroticism:

> The whole business of eroticism is to destroy the self-contained character of the participators as they are in their normal lives. Stripping naked is the decisive action. Nakedness offers contrast to self-possession, to discontinuous existence, in other words. It is a state of communication revealing a quest for a possible continuance of being beyond the confines of the self.[18]

In eroticism, the dissolution of the subject–object dichotomy unfolds a very particular energy. In this sense, the entangled process of singing, being heard, and hearing can be understood as a very intimate act of exchange. To describe this process, Michel Poizat has brought into play the concept of jouissance, which has an explicitly sexual connotation.[19] In *S/Z*, Roland Barthes describes the experience of the singing voice in a very similar way:

> Singing (a characteristic generally ignored in aesthetics) has something coenesthetic about it, it is connected less to an "impression" than to an internal, muscular, humoral sensuality. The voice is a diffusion, an insinuation, it passes over the entire surface of the body, the skin .... Music, therefore, has an effect utterly different from sight; it can effect orgasm.[20]

The voice thus becomes a kind of drug that one can become addicted to. The prospect of hearing a certain voice creates very specific expectations of satisfying physical needs.

Eroticism has only received limited attention in the context of opera, such as with regard to certain patterns of action in seduction or possibilities of representing it, for example, in Mozart's *Don Giovanni*, Bizet's *Carmen*, Verdi's *La traviata*, Wagner's *Tannhäuser*, or Saint-Saëns's *Samson et Dalila*. Occasionally, theater historians have written about the amorous adventures of usually female performers (in opera and ballet) and their admirers in past epochs—often with amusement and usually as if they were reporting from an exotic world. When I refer to the eroticism in the special relationships between a singer and an audience member, I am not thinking of such representations of erotic mechanisms but rather of the phenomenal dimension of performance, that is, of the special relationship of vocality and corporeality between a singer and an audience member, a relationship in which desires play a decisive role.[21]

120 *Analytical approaches*

    Although eroticism is presumed to be one of the main driving forces for why operagoers want to experience the same perceptual situation repeatedly, it is usually not discussed. The potential force of eroticism is rarely considered as a category for analyzing the performative dimension.[22] But if one thinks of performances by Cecilia Bartoli, for example, then it seems to me to be almost unavoidable to venture such an attempt. In her live performances, one of the most exciting moments is when her voice gives the impression that the breakneck coloraturas in particular are visibly exploring all the parts of her body, that the sounds she is producing are making her body vibrate. Her performances suggest the existence of several resonating spaces in different bodily regions. This combination of voice and body movement triggers a very particular erotic fascination. The connection of her voice to her body is so strong, the use of her body creates such a lasting impression, that just listening to her recorded voice involuntarily brings it to mind, that my memory is able to evoke this body and its movements when listening to her recorded voice.

    The moment of expectation (protention) plays a decisive role in desire. Desire can be seen as a particular manifestation of the more fundamental perceptual stance of protention; conversely, protention can be understood as one of the mechanisms that lead to an erotic relationship. Two scenarios in particular are of interest here. On the one hand, there is the situation where I expect a very specific moment in an opera or in a phrase, and my anticipation dissipates because the moment does not live up to my expectation or does not even appear at all. But the opposite can also happen: a repetition of a familiar climax can surpass one's memory of it and so too one's expectation. There are events—such as a voice one has experienced several times singing certain phrases that one has heard multiple times—whose intensity simply cannot be remembered. One experiences a sound, one wants to hold on to it, to be sure of its appeal, but by then it is already gone, in the past.

    The appeal lies in the expectation or in the experience of the beginning, which triggers the expectation of an intensive experience. In Jean-Jacques Beineix's film *Diva* from 1981, such an experience can be seen in a filmic staging. After the entrance applause for the diva has ebbed, it takes a few seconds for the expected aria to begin. This moment of expectation in the film is intensified by cuts from shots of the singer from behind to a close-up of a fan who opens his lips a little (as in excited expectation of sensual pleasure) to the diva with closed eyes.[23] The extended pause between the entrance applause and the beginning is the moment that actually has no content and yet bears what is most important, namely, the moment of extremely intensified protention. With Barthes, one could also call these experiences erotic, though what he identifies as the "most erotic portion of a body" is here transferred into temporality, into the passing of moments of intense pleasure:

> Is not the most erotic portion of a body *where the garment gapes*? ... It is intermittence, as psychoanalysis has so rightly stated, which is erotic: the intermittence of skin flashing between two articles of clothing (trousers and sweater), between two edges (the open-necked shirt, the glove and the

The voice and the body in opera performances 121

sleeve); it is this flash itself which seduces, or rather: the staging of an appearance-as-disappearance.[24]

Ever since the primal scene of arousing song, the siren episode from the twelfth book of Homer's *Odyssey*, in which Odysseus has himself chained to the mast of his ship and exposes himself to the sirens' song, "hearing—like sexuality—has been suspected of being seductive and addictive."[25] The perception of the voice and its seductive power is linked here for the first time with the danger of losing oneself.[26] The singing voice is imbued with seduction and danger. In the view of Georges Bataille, the term *érotisme* represents "predominantly transgressive experiences of existential endangerment."[27] The aspect of transgression seems to me to be particularly profitable for this study, since it points to the ritual structure of erotic experience, and within this ritual structure, in particular to the moment of a liminal experience that challenges or even endangers existence. A symptom of the liminal experience provided by the erotic relationship may be a changed perception of the environment,[28] like what Koestenbaum experiences while listening to Anna Moffo's voice on record: "Her voice ..., like a breathing property, ... entered my system with a vector so naïve, unadulterated, and elemental ... that my drab bedroom shifted on its axis."[29] Defining the perception of opera performances in this respect as erotic and understanding eroticism in this context with Bataille as a threat to existence recalls the critiques and invectives that have been widespread since the beginning of theater and that have seen in it a danger to humanity.[30]

In the context of liminal experiences, one must assume that theater presents—in contrast to ritual—a special kind of transgression.[31] As a rule, liminal experiences in theater cannot be expected to result in any permanent change in life circumstances; they merely have to do with experiences of destabilization and disorientation for the duration of a performance: one falls in love temporarily with a voice or a singer, without drawing consequences from that for one's life beyond the performance—apart from the trace that the experience leaves in the body and that manifests itself in the fact that some listeners are so affected by a voice that they want to experience it again and again.[32]

Yet another central aspect of Bataille's concept of eroticism deserves attention here: incommunicability.

> My starting point is that eroticism is a solitary activity. At the least it is a matter difficult to discuss .... It cannot be public .... Somehow eroticism is outside ordinary life. In our experience taken as a whole it is cut off from the normal communication of emotions. There is a taboo in force .... The taboo is sufficiently active for me to be able to say by and large that eroticism, perhaps the most intense of emotions, is as if it did not exist as far as our existence is present to us in the form of speech and language.[33]

122 *Analytical approaches*

Roland Barthes also addresses the aspect of speechlessness with regard to pleasure:

> No "thesis" on the pleasure of the text is possible; ... [pleasure is] unable to speak itself ... (if I assert some pleasures of the text here, it is always in passing, in a very precarious, never regular fashion). In short, such a labor could not *be written*. I can only *circle* such a subject—and therefore better to do it briefly and in solitude than collectively and interminably.[34]

Writing about this motor that is so clearly at the heart of opera thus requires that one take into account this subjectivity of the object or the particular phenomenal dimension of the dissolution of the subject–object dichotomy. It is necessary to bring one's own subject into the description, to exhibit one's own subjectivity, to tell one's own story, to act autobiographically.[35]

Yet exhibiting one's own subjectivity, describing one's own experience, is associated with a risk, since it means admitting that one is susceptible to the seductions of opera and the voice. So as to conceal and hide this susceptibility—which is, I maintain, the reason for engaging with opera in the first place in most cases—most reviewers and authors of books about singers fall into an abstract, technical language. They concentrate on technical details of vocal production instead of writing about experiencing the voice. But when describing a voice in these abstract, technical details seems to work, then one can also assume that the voice has missed its actual goal, namely, to move. The fact that I have taken or have had to take a detour via singers' bodies or my own body to describe my intensive experiences with the voices of Cecilia Bartoli and Edita Gruberová is also indicative of the incommunicability diagnosed by Bataille.

Only in describing one's own experience can a trace of the performative or, more precisely, the erotic interrelation between the singer and audience member be articulated, if it is possible to do so at all. And this requires a certain courage—a bravery similar to the bravery that singers regularly demonstrate by exposing their vulnerability on stage. But the fear or shame of admitting that one is susceptible to the sensual stimuli of opera and of thereby making oneself assailable and vulnerable is—I would like to assert—the necessary first step toward describing a scenario of perception that shapes the aesthetics of the performative as it is uniquely manifested in opera: as an eroticism of the performative that defines opera as a special attraction.

Notes

1 Gustave Schilling, "Acteur," in *Encyclopädie der gesammten musikalischen Wissenschaften, oder Universal-Lexikon der Tonkunst*, ed. Gustav Schilling et al., vol. 1 (Stuttgart: Franz Heinrich Köhler, 1835), 47.
2 See, for example, Natalie Dessay and Ann Hallenberg during a CD recording of the Handel oratorium *Il trionfo del tempo e del disinganno* with Emmanuelle Haïm and Le Concert d'Astrée (in the quartet with Sonia Prina, and Pavol Breslik), https://www.youtube.com/watch?v=XtaXWqOvtCw, accessed 1 October 2020.

3 See "Unknown actors miming to 1908 Victor recording with Caruso etc., 1911," *The Art of Singing: Golden Voices of the Century* (Warner Music Vision, 1996), DVD, no. 2; https://www.youtube.com/watch?v=IeBpKNRpKZQ (starting at 2:10), accessed 1 October 2020.
4 Teatro Verdi Busseto, 2007; I attended the performance on 5 October 2007.
5 Pietro Lichtental, "Attore," in *Dizionario e bibliografia della musica*, 2nd ed., vol. 1 (Milan: Antonio Fontana, 1836), 74–75: "ATTORE s. m. Cantante che fa una parte in un'Opera. Non basta all'Attore d'essere eccellente cantante, se non è nello stesso tempo bravo pantomimo …. Oltre a ciò l'Attore non deve solo far sentire quello che dice, ma anche ciò che lascia dire alla musica…. I suoi passi, i suoi sguardi, i suoi gesti, tutto deve essere sempre d'accordo colla musica …. L'Attore lirico appoggiato al canto, il quale ha un linguaggio più attrattivo ancora della declamazione, e all'orchestra, che dà l'anima alla rappresentazione, è meno di tutti subordinato all'osservanza della rigorosa verità nella sua azione; mentre non di rado deve seguire il carattere della musica, e far concorrere il gesto colla musica stessa …. collocare e variar bene i gesti, senza sforzo e senza prodigalità; mettere un'armonia in tutti i moti del corpo, del volto, e della voce."
6 Johann Jakob Engel, *Ideen zu einer Mimik*, vol. 2 (Berlin: August Mylius, 1786), 72–73.
7 "La … voce [del Ferretti] è voluminosa, estesa e di suono assai simpatico: il gesto è un po' trasandato, ma quando un tenore ha bella voce e sa usarne a dovere poco monta se non agisce nel miglior modo." *Il Figaro*, 5 October 1844, 318.
8 See, for example, https://www.youtube.com/watch?v=X8wxblNNFx8, accessed 1 October 2020.
9 See https://www.youtube.com/watch?v=bnb3m90nl-E, accessed 1 October 2020.
10 Staatsoper Stuttgart, 2001; I attended the performance on 23 January 2001. For the passage from Elisabetta's aria, see Verdi, *Don Carlos*, vol. 2, 605, m. 2 ("il pianto mio").
11 On this approach, see, for example, Waldenfels, "Stimme"; Barthes, "Grain of the Voice"; Doris Kolesch, "Stimmlichkeit," in Fischer-Lichte, Kolesch, and Warstat, *Metzler Lexikon Theatertheorie*, 342–45; Jenny Schrödl, *Vokale Intensitäten: Zur Ästhetik der Stimme im postdramatischen Theater* (Bielefeld: Transcript, 2012).
12 Waldenfels, "Stimme"; also see Galler and Risi, "Singstimme/Gesangstheorien."
13 "Die Arie auf Naxos führte zum Orkan: Thomas Wördehoff über die Sensation Edita Gruberova," *Die Weltwoche*, 17 June 1993; quoted from Niel Rishoi, *Edita Gruberova: Ein Portrait* (Zurich: Atlantis, 1996), 92.
14 Also see Koestenbaum, *Queen's Throat*, 43: "The diva shatters the fourth wall dividing stage and audience when she stares straight into the crowd and finds a familiar fan's face."
15 Gustave Flaubert, *Madame Bovary: Provincial Morals*, trans. Adam Thorpe (London: Vintage Books, 2011), 214.
16 Deutsche Oper Berlin, 2002; I attended the dress rehearsal on 6 May 2002 and the performance on 28 May 2002.
17 Koestenbaum, *Queen's Throat*, 43.
18 Georges Bataille, *Erotism: Death and Sensuality*, trans. Mary Dalwood (San Francisco: City Lights Books, 1986), 22.
19 See Michel Poizat, *The Angel's Cry: Beyond the Pleasure Principle in Opera*, trans. Arthur Denner (Ithaca: Cornell University Press, 1992).
20 Roland Barthes, *S/Z*, trans. Richard Miller (New York: Hill and Wang, 1974), 110.
21 In this sense, the argument of eroticism has been profitably discussed with reference to the phenomenon of castrati in the seventeenth and eighteenth centuries. See, for example, Susan McClary, "Fetisch Stimme: Professionelle Sänger im Italien der frühen Neuzeit," in *Zwischen Rauschen und Offenbarung: Zur Kultur- und Mediengeschichte der Stimme*, ed. Friedrich Kittler, Thomas Macho, and Sigrid Weigel (Berlin: Akademie, 2002), 199–214.

124 *Analytical approaches*

22 The well-known exceptions include Roland Barthes, Wayne Koestenbaum, and Sam Abel with his *Opera in the Flesh: Sexuality in Operatic Performances* (Boulder: Westview, 1996). Susan Sontag also campaigned for an "erotics of art" in her famous essay "Against Intepretation."
23 https://www.dailymotion.com/video/xa50gr, accessed 1 October 2020.
24 Roland Barthes, *The Pleasure of the Text*, trans. Richard Miller (New York: Hill and Wang, 1975), 9–10.
25 Doris Kolesch, *Roland Barthes* (Frankfurt am Main: Campus, 1997), 125.
26 See Sigrid Weigel, "Die Stimme der Toten: Schnittpunkte zwischen Mythos, Literatur und Kulturwissenschaft," in Kittler, Macho, and Weigel, *Rauschen und Offenbarung*, 73–92.
27 Erik von Grawert-May, "Erotisch/Erotik/Erotismus," in *Ästhetische Grundbegriffe: Historisches Wörterbuch in sieben Bänden*, ed. Karlheinz Barck et al., vol. 2 (Stuttgart: J. B. Metzler, 2001), 311.
28 On the changed perception of the environment as an index and effect of a heightened aesthetic experience, see Martin Seel, *Aesthetics of Appearing*, trans. John Farrell (Stanford: Stanford University Press, 2005), 134.
29 Koestenbaum, *Queen's Throat*, 10.
30 See Erika Fischer-Lichte, "Zuschauen als Ansteckung," in *Ansteckung: Zur Körperlichkeit eines ästhetischen Prinzips*, ed. Fischer-Lichte, Mirjam Schaub, and Nicola Suthor (Munich: Wilhelm Fink, 2005), 35–50.
31 See Fischer-Lichte, *Ästhetische Erfahrung*, 355.
32 This affection becomes clear, for example, in the many fans who are fixated on certain singers, who provide information on social media and fan pages, and who talk with each other, in the targeted collecting of recordings of a certain singer, in the practice of illegally recording performances (without which we would not have any recordings of many singers today), and in travelling to attend as many performances by a certain singer as possible.
33 Bataille, *Erotism*, 252.
34 Barthes, *Pleasure of the Text*, 34.
35 It is thus only logical that two of the books that engage with corporeal reactions to singing begin with their authors' biographies: see Koestenbaum, *Queen's Throat*; and Abel, *Opera in the Flesh*. Roland Barthes demonstrates this exemplarily: "About music, no discourse can be sustained but that of difference—of evaluation." Barthes, "Music, Voice, Language," in *The Responsibility of Forms*, 279. See Kolesch, *Roland Barthes*, 128–29: "For Barthes, this level of evaluation is very concretely his own body, which is fascinated and is erotically aroused and which desires a voice. ... And since Barthes's discourse on music occurs in an erotic, sexual language of love, in which the subject displays itself in all its vulnerability, [this level of evaluation is] completely unprotected."

8 Rhythm and experiences of time in opera

The "other" time of opera performance

When the performative particularly has to do with events, processes, and actions, then time is actually its decisive dimension. But how can this dimension, which is decisive for the arts of music and theater as well as for the performative, be grasped conceptually and analytically? Whenever scholarship on opera discusses the problem of time, it is usually concerned with either differentiating between represented time and the time of representation (following the example of how narratology differentiates between the levels of narrated time and the time of narration) or with the three-times model of a production, according to which three layers of time are always simultaneously active in an opera performance, namely, the epoch of the plot, the epoch of the opera's creation (that is, the historicity of the text and the music), and the point in time of the performance. But if one is particularly interested in the performative dimension of opera, the focus necessarily shifts to experienced time—an aspect that is usually ignored in opera scholarship.

In his engagement with the experience of time in music and theater, the theater critic Alfred Kerr, known for his sharp tongue, already pointed out this phenomenon—that is, the difference between objective, so-called chronometric time and subjective or experienced time with a famous bon mot. About an unspecified performance, he is said to have reported: "The performance began at eight o'clock; when I looked at my watch two hours later, it was half past eight." While weather forecasting has only recently introduced the term *felt air temperature*, the concept of *perceived time* has been known for much longer.

In the context of this study, I am interested in two very specific experiences of time that have only played a role with regard to music in the scholarship since 1945, if at all.[1] On the one hand, there is the loss of one's sense of time, that is, a disorientation with regard to the passing of time caused by the acceleration and compression of time or by the dilation and intensification of time. Following Henri Bergson, one could call this a condition of "pure duration" or "durée";[2] it eludes measurability and consciousness. On the other hand, I am concerned with the conscious perception of time, the awareness of experiencing time. Finally, the second part of the chapter discusses a

DOI: 10.4324/9781003124863-11

specific parameter of experiencing time that is of decisive importance to the perception of time in both music and theater: rhythm.

The phenomenological approaches of Henri Bergson and Edmund Husserl had a great influence on twentieth-century thought regarding time. With clear recourse to ancient positions, they describe the experience of the present as central to the perception of temporality. The present is only conceivable through its constant reference to the past and future (retention and protention). Their positions were illustrated and differentiated by investigations in perceptual psychology and neurobiology, for example, with reference to the "psychic time of presence" (*psychische Präsenzzeit*)—the time span of about three to five seconds within which memory can process events as a gestalt—and in relation to human capacities to synthesize.[3]

Although the minimal differentiation between objective and subjective time seems to be generally accepted,[4] this distinction has also been criticized, for example, by Norbert Elias with his proposal for a sociological anchoring of the concept of time.[5] According to Elias, so-called objective time is also nothing more than an agreement made by people and between people to organize certain courses of action with varying degrees of standardization; watches, for example, have a very high degree of standardization. Our experience and perception of time are, so Elias, a matter of "relating together" situations and experiences.[6] This understanding makes one aware of how the experience of time can be understood as performative, as an activity.

But regardless of whether one speaks of differentiating between objective and subjective time or of differentiating between various subjective agreements—what is decisive is the potential for change, the variety of experiences of time, which are based on establishing a time that can always be newly observed in each experience. In this sense, one can speak, following Hans-Thies Lehmann, of creating "*another* time" of performance in relation to the performance of music or theater.[7] One must ask in this context what this "other time" contrasts with concretely. At least three criteria can be given for what it contrasts with: first, biological preconditions, such as the psychic time of presence and subjective predispositions; second, experiences with structures of time that an individual has collected from everyday life as well as from music and theater; and third, a current memory on whose basis the present is experienced and the future anticipated (retention and protention). The experience of the loss of temporal orientation through acceleration or dilation and the awareness of time through experiencing different layers of time can then be evaluated as "another time."

I am first of all interested in the two central experiences of time dilation and time compression. Through what means or parameters can these "other times" come about in performance? First, particular compositional structures can have an effect. Composers can operate against biological preconditions and have done so, consciously or unconsciously, by challenging and also overtaxing the perception of time shaped by our internal clocks. I am referring here to composers' attempts to break out of the divisible and thus predictable completion of harmonic progression in composition, such as Wagner does with his "endless melody" (*unendliche Melodie*)—here I am only thinking of the compositional perspective of the term, which is by no means uncontroversial[8]—or contemporary tendencies such as minimalism and presentism. Wagner's "art of transition" and his "endless melody" can be read as playing with the perception of temporal structures, as undermining the rules of gestalt based on the psychic time of presence, or as overtaxing the synthetic achievements of these forms.[9] Examples of what is generally identified with Wagner's "endless melody" in terms of compositional techniques include the grand scene with Isolde and Tristan from the second act of *Tristan und Isolde* or Isolde's *Liebestod* from the third act. Both scenes are characterized by, among other things, the fact that they cause a loss of the sense of time through dilation and intensification. After turning away from Wagner, Friedrich Nietzsche wrote polemically against "endless melody," but in doing so he underlines precisely the mode of effect referred to here:

> The artistic aim pursued by modern music in what now gets described in very strong, but vague terms as "infinite melody" can be made clear by going down into the sea, gradually losing our secure grip upon the bottom, and finally surrendering ourselves unconditionally to the billowing elements: we are supposed to be *swimming*. In the older music preceding this, one had to *dance* ...: where the measure ... demanded continual *self-possession* .... —Richard Wagner wanted a different sort of *movement of the soul*, one that is, as noted, related to swimming and floating .... His celebrated artistic technique ... —the "infinite melody"—strives to break ... all mathematical symmetry of tempo and energy .... He fears petrification, crystallization ... —and so he sets a three-beat rhythm against the two-beat one, frequently introduces the five- and seven-beat, repeats the same phrase immediately, but extending it so that it lasts two or three times as long.[10]

The result is a continuous stream of sound with a constantly delayed climax; it is the joyfully denied resolution or release of tension that contributes here to an experience of pure duration. The effect that sets in is that of time dilation. In order to underscore this view, I would like to refer to a model proposed by the philosopher and psychologist Wilhelm Keller in 1964. Based on the differentiation made by Husserl, his model relates the parameters of retention and protention—that is, a constant referring to both the past and an expectation of the future—to the present abundance of events:

> The *dilation of time* in the case of *great abundance* seems to be due to a simultaneously increased retention, that is, an intensified retaining of every particular.
> The dilation of time in the case of *limited abundance*, however, seems to be based on simultaneously intensified protention: then there is a stance of anticipation and expectation that is excessive because it remains empty (the longing for content in boredom).

128 *Analytical approaches*

> By contrast, the *compression of time* in the case of *great abundance* results when there is simultaneously a weakness of retention. Many things are indeed experienced, but they do not last, so time is compressed (classic example: stimulating, fast-paced entertainment!).
>
> Finally, the *compression* in the case of an *experienced emptiness* is due to a simultaneously reduced protention. There is then, even with so little content, no longer any excess expectation.[11]

In the examples I named above, there is, according to Keller's model, an increased protention with a limited abundance of events, that is, a dilation of time. The assessment of a limited abundance of events is based on the fact that no distinguishable parts of a melody or figures are in the foreground; instead, the impression of a single stream or flow of thought prevails.

"Other times" can also be experienced in performances of opera productions in the specific relationships of the music and the scene, of auditory and visual perception. When Siegmund and Sieglinde recognized each other textually and musically as twin siblings and, especially, as lovers in the forward-pushing, almost inflaming gesture of the music at the end of the first act in Patrice Chéreau's Bayreuth *Walküre* (1976–1980), one saw Jeannine Altmeyer as Sieglinde and Peter Hofmann as Siegmund fall to the ground in fervent physical movement and restless passionate hugs and then roll around on the floor. Their bodies positively attracted each other and seemed compelled to touch and virtually swallow each other (see Figure 8.1). By contrast, in Heiner Müller's 1993 production of *Tristan und Isolde* with the light-and-color cube by the stage designer Erich Wonder and with costumes by the Japanese fashion designer Yohji Yamamoto, the transgressive lovers and the audience were denied the confirmation of the love duet's orgiastic sounds in the second act, and an immense tension arose out of their distance: Siegfried Jerusalem as Tristan and Waltraud Meier as Isolde moved toward each other as if in slow motion and, at the moment of the musical climax,[12] stretched their palms toward each other. But before they could touch, their hands stopped as if frozen at a clearly recognizable distance from each other (see Figure 8.2). It was precisely this distance that was able to trigger, like a physical experiment, the greatest possible streams of energy between Waltraud Meier and Siegfried Jerusalem on the one hand and between the stage and the audience on the other. The gesture suggested pent-up energy in the physical tension between the two performers, a tension that could not be discharged and that, perhaps for this very reason, was transferred particularly strongly to the audience. Instead of the physical consummation of attraction, as the music might suggest, a physical attraction came into play with a tension through to their fingertips.[13]

Both moments are musically characterized in a similar manner by a forward-pushing, tension-building line, a sequential intensification of a group of four eighth notes (in *Tristan und Isolde*, however, slightly delayed by the dotted notes), that builds up to an unsurpassable extreme—in height and

Rhythm and experiences of time in opera 129

Figure 8.1 Die Walküre, staging by Patrice Chéreau, Peter Hofmann as Siegmund, Jeannine Altmeyer as Sieglinde, Bayreuth Festival, 1980.

Photo courtesy of Wilhelm Rauh and the Nationalarchiv der Richard-Wagner-Stiftung, Bayreuth, Zustiftung Wolfgang Wagner.

volume—and then explodes in a way that can be expected and heard in advance. The musical parallels are also obvious in the time signatures. In *Walküre*, one finds "Sehr belebt – Immer schneller" (Very animated—Ever faster) in 4/4 time; in *Tristan and Isolde*, "Immer belebter – Sehr lebhaft" (Ever more animated—Very lively) in 4/4 time.[14]

The great difference consists in the way in which the acoustic and visual levels are brought together, leading to two completely different experiences of time. To clarify this, I would like to turn to Keller's model. In the case of Chéreau's *Walküre*, one could perceive a parallelization of musical and scenic movement, a mutual intensification of the speed or acceleration. Keller's model explains the acceleration or compression of time in the following way: "The *compression of time* in the case of *great abundance* results when there is

130 *Analytical approaches*

Figure 8.2 Tristan und Isolde, staging by Heiner Müller, Siegfried Jerusalem as Tristan, Waltraud Meier as Isolde, Bayreuth Festival, 1999.

Photo courtesy of the Bayreuth Festival and Anne Kirchbach.

simultaneously a weakness of retention. Many things are indeed experienced, but they do not last, so time is compressed (classic example: stimulating, fast-paced entertainment!)."[15] The abundance of content consisted in the two performers' many, fast movements. This did not require any great effort of referring back to codes established in the performance; everything was comprehensible from basic, everyday experience; retention was reduced.

By contrast, the *Tristan* performance stirred up expectations of a parallelization of the music and movement, but they were not fulfilled. The movement faltered, and the music ran away from it. Through the collision of the two speeds, the slowness of the movement had an even more powerful effect. A dilation of time occurred: "The dilation of time in the case of *limited abundance*, however, seems to be based on simultaneously intensified protention: then there is a stance of anticipation and expectation that is excessive because it remains empty (the longing for content in boredom)."[16]

The large, unfulfilled expectation of the parallelization of the music and scene intensified the protention, while the slow motion was responsible for the limited abundance of content.

How new "other" times are created in the entangling of auditory and visual perception in an opera performance is also shown by the defining scenic moment in Peter Mussbach's 2003 production of Verdi's *La traviata*[17] at the Staatsoper Berlin. The black stage was shrouded by a gauze veil; behind it, light projections suggested a freeway on which Christine Schäfer, as Violetta, was staggering around like someone who has strayed from the path. Projections of raindrops were visible on the gauze veil, and at large intervals, an immense windshield wiper moved across the gauze veil from one side of the stage to the other. It gave the impression that we in the audience were sitting in a car driving on the freeway and had discovered a person at the side of the road who seemed to be lost.

The windshield wiper marked temporal breaks; the large intervals between the wiper movements referred to two different temporal levels. Between each movement of the windshield wiper, time stood virtually still and provided space for the plot of *La traviata*: for Violetta's monologues, which appeared as the inner monologues of a woman in the state of rapture, as well as for the rest of the musical plot, which also occurred only in the memory or fantasy of this person who had strayed from the path. The movement of the windshield wipers visibly brought to the fore what could be regarded as the passing of everyday, objective time and showed how the time of the opera performance was a completely different one, an extremely slowed down time that formed islands in time.

In Michael Thalheimer's 2005 production of Janáček's *Katja Kabanowa*[18] at the Staatsoper Berlin too, a concrete scenic means gave rise to an awareness for "another" passing of time. The central stage element was a mobile wall (see Figure 8.3) that extended diagonally across the stage from the front left to the back right. During the performance, this wall moved, as if on a hinge that could have been located at the front left, further and further forward up to the edge of the orchestra pit.

This advancing of the wall acted like a clock for the time that the evening would last—a measurement one could use to orient oneself. For as soon as the movable end of the wall extending diagonally across the stage would move all the way to the front, it would end at the orchestra pit and no more space would be left for performing. The stage and performance space would disappear. The inevitable end was thus announced from the very first moment, and everything would have to happen before it. The moving wall produced so much tension not only because it indicated the passing time of the performance, but also because it pointed so painfully to the finiteness of (dramatic) time. The wall posed the greatest danger to Katja (Melanie Diener). Its approach indicated that Katja's time was limited, that her end could not be deferred.

In the tradition still practiced today of maintaining the musical dramaturgy in its entirety and in its familiar sequence, the music that is heard in its familiar

132 Analytical approaches

Figure 8.3 Katja Kabanowa, staging by Michael Thalheimer, Stephen Rügamer as Boris, Melanie Diener as Katja, Staatsoper Berlin, 2005.

Photo courtesy of Monika Rittershaus.

order in a performance and that can, as familiar, be imagined in advance is also such a clock indicating the passing and end of time. Katja was given as much time as the music lasted. I could foresee how long the wall would take to sweep Katja's chair into the orchestra pit. When I got bored, I literally wanted to run onto the stage and accelerate the wall; when I saw that there was little time left, I wanted to stop it. By introducing the moving wall, the performance interacted with the perceptual mechanisms of retention and protection.

How space can create experiences of time became clear in a completely different way in Christof Loy's production of Janáček's *Jenůfa*[19] at the Deutsche Oper Berlin in 2012. The awareness of different, simultaneously occurring, and interacting layers of time—"other" times—again played an important role in my perception of the performance. The performance began with a silent scene. I saw a white box that looked like a prison cell. The Kostelnička (sacristan; played by Jennifer Larmore), who was obviously the cell's resident, was introduced (see Figure 8.4). It became clear that the staging was telling the story of Jenůfa from the perspective of the Kostelnička in retrospect. The Kostelnička was remembering the past, which would turn out to be the familiar story of Jenůfa.

The transition from the prison cell and the memory of the past to the remembered plot as the present occurred through a crack in the cell that opened up and through which one could see a cornfield and Jenůfa (Michaela Kaune). The box opened further, providing space for the beginning of the

Rhythm and experiences of time in opera 133

Figure 8.4 Jenůfa, staging by Christof Loy, Jennifer Larmore as the Kostelnička, Deutsche Oper Berlin, 2012.

Photo courtesy of Monika Rittershaus.

actual plot. In the final minutes of the first act, the entire village community looked at Laca (Will Hartmann) as the person guilty of injuring Jenůfa with a knife. Larmore as the Kostelnička entered the scene from behind with a serious face, at a significantly different speed than everyone who was frantically accusing Laca and also than Hartmann as Laca, who was clenching his fists to his forehead. Everyone present was duplicating the hectic tempo of the music, except for Larmore. This contrasting tempo made her conspicuous. What was

134 *Analytical approaches*

moving her? Was she now back in prison and so in the mode of memory? Or did she already recognize in this moment that Laca would initiate the coming catastrophe but also be its solution? This temporal contrast made the few seconds of the finale longer, denser, and thus more exciting. Regarding this impression, too, I would like to refer back to Wilhelm Keller's model. Keller considers the combination of great retention with great abundance to be responsible for the impression of time dilation. Great retention arose in my perception of the performance through the fact that I remembered what I thought I had recognized at the beginning with the prison cell and the establishment of the Kostelnička's mode of memory. The great abundance consisted in the presence of different rhythms of movement (hectic and static).

Again in the final seconds of the second act, an immense tension suddenly extinguished a prevailing lethargy. To the sentences of the Kostelnička— "Zavřte okno! ... Jako by sem smrt načuhovala!" (Close the window! ... As if death were peeping in here!)[20]—the music was accelerated through a combination of continuing the descending sixteenth-note figures in the woodwinds and strings and adding new sixteenth-note sextolets in the triangle and the brass (see the piano score in Example 8.1).[21] While the Kostelnička was hectically running back and forth to the table and looking around anxiously, Jenůfa remained next to the window and Laca on the left edge of the box as if rooted to it, as if frozen. The two established and embodied their own temporal level, while Larmore as the Kostelnička doubled the hectic pace of the musical time in the orchestra with her "real" time (see Figure 8.5).

The impression again came to my mind that the Kostelnička was in prison and looking back at this scene, experiencing it in a flashback. But if all three were moving in the same time, one could explain it by saying that the Kostelnička was looking into the future and saw the tragedy coming at her because of her crime, while Laca and Jenůfa did not (yet) suspect it at all. Jenůfa and Laca remained behind in a literal sense. They switched into a remote time, into an enraptured time; only the Kostelnička remained in the mode of advancing time, the time of the fate about to befall her, of which the others did not yet know anything—a time that could not be stopped.

While in Mussbach's *Traviata*, Thalheimer's *Katja Kabanowa*, and Loy's *Jenůfa*, it was the interaction of spatial concepts with specific experiences of movement that created "another" time of performance, in Sebastian Baumgarten's 2002 production of Jules Massenet's *Werther*[22] at the Deutsche Oper Berlin, it was a combination of a mediatized production of time (a film) and the live perception of the performance. At the beginning of the prelude to the fourth act, a screen made of wide white strips of paper shut off the stage like a curtain. To the sounds of the prelude, Werther and Charlotte's path to Werther's suicide was shown on this screen. In the plot, Albert forces Charlotte to hand over the pistols to Werther herself. Baumgarten showed this fatal situation as a psychological thriller in larger-than-life film images. As if with great calculation, Werther (Paul Charles Clarke) withdrew into a semiprivate, semipublic space—the changing room

Rhythm and experiences of time in opera 135

Example 8.1 Leoš Janáček, *Jenůfa: Její pastorkyňa (Ihre Ziehtochter)*, trans. Max Brod, piano score (Vienna: Universal-Edition, 1917), 176–77.
© by Universal Edition, Vienna, UE 13932 (previously UE 5821).

of a swimming pool—and prepared for his suicide. Charlotte (Charlotte Hellekant) was in the immediate vicinity, so she could have intervened, but she did not. The tension here arose from the voyeuristic arrangement. The voyeur (Charlotte) enjoys the horror of the forbidden, in this case, the horror of letting an act of violence happen that she could have prevented.

136 *Analytical approaches*

Figure 8.5 *Jenůfa*, staging by Christof Loy, Will Hartmann as Laca, Jennifer Larmore as the Kostelnička, Michaela Kaune as Jenůfa, Deutsche Oper Berlin, 2012.

Photo courtesy of Monika Rittershaus.

Every moment of delay was savored. Unlocking and releasing the revolver took place in slow motion, even the bullet's flight out of the barrel of the pistol was delayed. An intertitle like those from silent films was displayed: "Shot!"—for twenty-first-century filmic perception, a further delay. Deceleration also entailed that Werther's body sank into the swimming pool and did not suddenly fall over, which would have been conceivable after a shot. Finally, the water dragged out the actors' movements and the speed of the movements as if in a dream.

At the beginning of the second scene of the fourth act, Hellekant as Charlotte and Clarke as Werther then appeared in person in front of the screen. At the front of the stage, we saw a completely conventionally designed final scene, which was surprising in the context of this production: in historical costumes and with conventional operatic gestures, the dying Werther writhed about and Charlotte lamented his death for an agonizingly protracted length of time. The dream and the deceleration in the film sequence had opened up the otherwise extremely realistic setting of the staging to another temporal dimension, and then the conventionally designed final scene established yet another temporal dimension, which in my perception presented the genre of opera as historical, as moving at yet another different speed.

Here the particular quality of temporal perception resulted from working with different media contexts and expectations (opera dramaturgy, film dramaturgy, silent-film dramaturgy, and a citation of a conventional opera staging). With this abundance of temporal stratifications, it becomes evident that Keller's model can no longer simply be applied to classify the temporal structure. The accumulation led to an exhibition of the temporal structures themselves, an awareness of the perception of time. It was the experience of temporality as such that became perceptible to me in the performance.

Rhythms of opera performance

As mentioned at the beginning of this chapter, one musical category lends itself particularly well to differentiating further the experiences of temporality described so far: rhythm. Rhythm can be described as a paradigmatic instrument for analyzing performative processes, especially in the case of dealing with the performative dimension of opera performances, since rhythm always takes place in a field of tension between memory, expectation, and experience. In addition, the interplay between music and scene in each opera performance results in different and characteristic confrontations and collisions of different rhythms, which lead, as an interaction with the audience's own individual rhythms, to a completely new rhythm—the rhythm of the performance, first constituted in perception.

In 1875, Friedrich Nietzsche wrote the following about rhythm:

> The more excitable and original a person is, the more rhythm affects him—like a *compulsion* to reproduce a rhythm, producing that "blind attunement that precedes all judgment"; it is a compulsion usually tied to pleasure, but it can seize and overwhelm souls so suddenly that it is even more comparable to a painful cramp.[23]

What interests me about rhythm in this study is how it can be conceived as an underlying principle of every theatrical and operatic experience, namely, as the interaction and interplay of memory, experience, recognition, and anticipation, that is, of retention and protention, also as the interplay of representation and presence. As such, it is not limited to the perception of music, but rather is manifest precisely in the entangling of levels of perception in intermodal integration.

The term rhythm—from the Greek ῥυθμός—can be traced back to the verb ῥέω or ῥεῖν (to flow), and with the suffix θμός, it refers to a flowing in a regular ductus. Plato already characterized rhythm as an order of movement, in particular, of physical movement (*Laws* 664e).[24] Even though I must exclude the innumerable definitions of rhythm from the last centuries and even millennia, as well as musicological differentiations between rhythm, time signature, and meter,[25] the following thoughts are based on some basic foundations for speaking about rhythm.

Rhythm structures and organizes time, and so has something to do with order, more precisely, with a binary order such as the alternation between strong and weak in analogy to raising and lowering a foot, to arsis and thesis, to the heartbeat, or to breathing. This entails the regular repetition of contrasting or complementary elements.[26] And the fluidity of movement is of

138 *Analytical approaches*

particular relevance for understanding what forms the order. The phenomenologist Bernhard Waldenfels puts it in a nutshell: "Rhythm is only at home on the road."[27] It is this fundamental process-oriented quality of rhythm that distinguishes it as a performative element par excellence.

> Individual rhythmic movements are ... not functionally determined by reaching a goal, as is the case in the growth phases of a plant or the stages in the course of a disease; they are rather determined by the way in which the *movement is carried out*. What counts is not the where that the goal aims for and the what of the result, but the how of the movement.[28]

Since rhythm, as a category of "being in progress," simultaneously emphasizes and produces the processual, it becomes clear that when attempting to name criteria for an analysis oriented toward the performative dimension of opera, one cannot avoid rhythm—a perspective on performance that is not about a targeted or dramaturgical observation but rather about what is momentary, what is found in motion, about the sequence, about the processual.

When we talk about rhythm as order, we must necessarily also speak of perception, which often produces this order in the first place. Already for Plato, judgments about the order and disorder of movement are bound to human perception (aesthesis); the existence of rhythmic formations is thus dependent on a specific capacity of perception and the judgment of the human senses.[29] And according to Johann Georg Sulzer (1794), a "series of similar things" only becomes a rhythmic "sequence of equal beats according to equal divisions of time" when this sequence is structured by a person making or listening to music. Sulzer was convinced that every human being undertakes such structuring involuntarily.[30] This assumption was confirmed at the end of the nineteenth century by Wilhelm Wundt's and Thaddeus L. Bolton's studies in perceptual psychology, which proved the phenomenon of subjective rhythmization; according to this phenomenon, the structuring of events only takes place in the process of perception.[31]

Rhythm is not limited to a particular materiality or sensory modality: rhythms are phenomena that occur in time, whether they are acoustic, visual, or haptic. Already in the understanding of the Greek μουσική, rhythm simultaneously orders the movements of different materials: the movement of steps, gestures, syllables, and sounds.[32]

Rhythm has something to do with a past experience and an expectation directed toward the future. Since rhythm is always at work between a past experience and an expectation directed toward the future—between retention and protention—it proves to be a model for an understanding of performance in which staging and perception are always related to one another. An important aspect in the physiological perspective on the perception of rhythm is the ability, indeed the desire, to involuntarily continue rhythms one hears and experiences.[33] In order to perceive a rhythm as rhythm, one adapts to a certain temporal structure and anticipates the continuation of sequences or movements. It is a matter of becoming absorbed in something uniform, something familiar, so as then, against this background, to be receptive to deviations and surprises.[34] Igor Stravinsky also described this characteristic of rhythm in his *Poétique musicale* from 1939/40 with reference to the relationship between rhythm and meter in jazz:

> The isochronous beats are in this case merely a means of throwing the rhythmic invention of the soloist into relief. It is this that brings about surprise and produces the unexpected. On reflection we realize that without the real or implied presence of the beats we could not make out the meaning of this invention. Here we are enjoying a relationship. This example seems to me to clarify sufficiently the connections between meter and rhythm.[35]

On can also understand the following statement by the composer and director Heiner Goebbels in this sense: "In Neue Musik, rhythmic quality is no longer communicated, since rhythmic events are single events whose pulse is seen through only by conductors or musicians but not by the audience."[36]

Rhythm takes shape, just like atmosphere,[37] between a perceiving subject and a perceived object. "In every perception," writes Hanno Helbling, "there are two rhythms that must be brought into harmony: that of the object itself and that of the perceiving subject."[38] Every rhythmic process has to do with a relationship between fixed, produced rhythms and subjective rhythmizations. With this double perspective, one can now even more clearly formulate the claim that rhythm can serve as a model for an understanding of performance in which staging and perception are always related to one other. The staged rhythm is the rhythm presented, the rhythm that can be entered on a temporal axis; the rhythm brought into the performance is the individual bodily rhythm or the individual constitution at the time of perception. The rhythm of the performance takes shape in the meeting of these rhythms.

Various studies have shown that, first, our body is itself rhythmically organized and, second, that it allows its own rhythm to be influenced by heard, seen, and felt rhythms. What John Dewey claimed in his classic *Art as Experience* in 1934, namely that rhythm is a "universal scheme of existence,"[39] has been emphatically confirmed from a physiological point of view by Gerold Baier. All physiological processes in our bodies (like our heartbeat, breathing, muscle contractions in the gastrointestinal tract, hormone fluctuations in the blood, bodily movements in general) occur in rhythmic patterns, which means, for Baier, that they occur as a sequence of repeating events that obey an inner logic and are therefore comprehensible to other people.[40]

It is this rhythmic organization of our bodies that puts us in a productive relationship with perceived rhythms. Studies of patients with epilepsy and Parkinson's have shown the influence of musical, visual, and tactile rhythms (such as caressing) on rhythmic processes in the body.[41] And our own rhythmic disposition likewise has an influence on the perception of rhythms produced in performance. The effect of a performance thus depends to a considerable degree on the rhythmic processes of exchange between the participants.

140 *Analytical approaches*

What can the analysis of opera performances gain from this concept of rhythm? I will investigate this question using two performances at the Staatsoper Hannover; one of them is a performance of Calixto Bieito's production of Mozart's *Don Giovanni*[42] and the other a performance of Thomas Bischoff's production of Mozart's *Le nozze di Figaro*.[43]

Based on the assumption that rhythm is not limited to a specific materiality such as music or language but rather appears as a structuring moment in both acoustic and visual phenomena, I will deal in the following with possible relationships between acoustic and visual perception in opera performances. I will not provide a microscopic, detailed analysis of the musical rhythms of a particular number or phrase in relation to the movement of bodies within a time span, that is, the transformation of the score into movement in detail. I am rather interested in the fundamental possibilities of the relationship between prior experience, expectation, and experience with regard to what is sung, spoken, and played on an instrument and the movement of bodies in scenic configurations.

The fact that rhythm would play a central role in the effect of Bieito's scandalous sex-and-crime staging of Mozart's *Don Giovanni* quickly became clear to the audience. The psychologically realistic music theater, which was taken to the extremes, seemed as if it were precisely tuned to the rhythmic relations provided by the music. From the beginning of the scene with Donna Anna (Francesca Scaini) and Don Giovanni (Gary Magee), the constant alternation between hectic and static sequences of movement was striking. Clearly recognizable copulation on the back seat and hood of a car (see Figure 8.6) and hectic

Figure 8.6 *Don Giovanni*, staging by Calixto Bieito, Francesca Scaini as Donna Anna, Gary Magee as Don Giovanni, Staatsoper Hannover, 2002.

Photo courtesy of A. T. Schaefer.

running were followed by stiff, threatening gestures between Giovanni and the Commendatore (Hans-Peter Scheidegger); the animated scuffling was followed by the Commendatore's becoming rigid after falling victim to murder. With lots of fuss and anxiety, Donna Anna and Giovanni stuffed the Commendatore into the trunk of the car, jumped into it to leave the scene of the crime as quickly as possible, but then remained sitting there idle and motionless when the car failed to start. Donna Elvira (Christiane Iven), the woman who had been abandoned, manically emptied her shopping bags filled with junk food and then continued sobbing, lying between the bags. This list of sequences, fast–slow, hectic–static, could be effortlessly continued. They did not always coincide with the music, but in principle they followed the same binarity as the recitative and aria or as the tempo changes in the closed numbers. Binarity was the basic form of rhythm as a "universal scheme of existence" (John Dewey), as a succession of inhalation and exhalation, ebb and flow, slow and fast.[44] The visual rhythm affirmed the basic rhythm provided by the music.

A second perspective would probably emphasize, following Patrice Pavis, the contrast between the rhythm of the acting and the rhythm of the text,[45] a drifting apart of the usual combination of movement and sound. We were confronted with unusual movements accompanying the familiar sounds. For the presto stretta of the final scene,[46] Don Ottavio (José Montero) tied the womanizer to a kitchen chair with masking tape (!). Then all the participants of the final sextet stabbed, one after another, at Garry Magee as Don Giovanni with a kitchen knife. Several rhythms collided with one another. There is something like a habituation or expectation that a static tableau (the rhythm of what is to be seen) will accompany this sextet (the rhythm of the music)—habituation here means the rhythm of expectation that we bring with us. In Bieito's case, this anticipated rhythm was disturbed. With Pavis, one could say: "In such a moment, the rhythm no longer has the function of playing correctly, but … of alienating habitualized listening and spectating."[47] In the alienation, there was again, however, something affirmative, since the sound and movement of the figures' actions reciprocally intensified one another and sought, in this way, to overwhelm the audience. There was something downright violent about this rhythmic experience. The multiple killings kept one in suspense because the stage-acting of murdering someone was amplified by the musical rhythm in such a way that I thought I was physically suffering the stabs. As a spectator and listener, I let myself be drawn into the collision, let myself be gripped and carried away, and after the finale I was literally robbed of my breath.

Thomas Bischoff's production of *Figaro* showed that the usual combination of the rhythm of movement and the musical rhythm can also drift apart in a less sensational way that still remains, however, just as gripping. According to the libretto and score, Figaro tries to decide where to put his marriage bed in the first scene of the opera.[48] But during the overture of this staging, Susanna (Alla Kravchuk) and Figaro (Oliver Zwarg) were already sitting on a bed. In addition, considering that their wedding was imminent and that Susanna was,

142 *Analytical approaches*

according to her words, trying on her hat in front of the mirror while rejoicing musically, both of them seemed unexpectedly grumpy, wary, and annoyed. It quickly became apparent to me that this here and the entire performance was supposed to be a repetition, a reenactment of what had happened on the "crazy day," which had already occurred. Figaro and Susanna were dealing with their marriage problems by replaying their enraptured premarital whispers. The reciprocal injuries and proofs of mistrust had all already taken place and were now going to be relived again by everyone with masochistic zeal. This poisoned mood even succeeded in taking the forward thrust, the drive, out of the music. Suddenly, the music sounded annoying as well. It seemed as if the scenic actions were overwriting the musical rhythm. How could that be? I let myself be influenced by the faces of the characters and applied this influence to the music to realize an intermodal integration.

In my perception, repetition became the theme of the performance. The question was what happens to the material used (the text, the music) when it is also a repetition of a story familiar not only to the audience but also to the characters on stage. The story was familiar, the music was familiar, the text could even be read during the performance by means of the supertitles. What would this do to the characters and to the music? Would I hear the music differently?

As the central motif of the production, repetition was the decisive element for the rhythm; in this case, it was even a very demanding element, since *only* the repetition and not the exposition was presented. Furthermore, my identification of what happened on stage as a repetition produced a certain rhythm, since I was constantly observing two levels: the scenic present and the presumably hectic and turbulent withheld past. The rhythm of the past could be heard but not seen; the rhythm of the present could be seen but not heard. This resulted in an immense tension. Those who were not aware of this double perceptual possibility of the staging or who did not engage in it probably found the rhythm of the performance dull and sluggish.

Patrice Pavis argues that "the practices of breaks, of discontinuity, of the alienation effect, those recurrent techniques in contemporary art, further the perception of interruptions in performance: rhythmic syncopations thereby become all the more visible."[49] The performance held in store such surprising interruptions to rhythmic continuity in at least two places: in Marcellina's entrance with Bartolo in the first act and in the transition from Figaro's aria "Non più andrai" (No more now will you flutter by) to the Countess's cavatina "Porgi amor" (Grant me, Love), that is, actually the transition from the first to the second act, which took place in this staging without a change of scene or a curtain.[50] In both cases, one could hear the rhythm of the next number in advance because the dramatis personae for that number had already entered onto the stage (in the first case, Marcellina and Bartolo, and in the second, the Countess)—but this anticipated rhythm was interrupted by silence, sometimes for several minutes, which involuntarily led me to pay more attention to the visual rhythm. After his aria, Figaro (Oliver Zwarg) stopped and stood on the side of the stage and watched the Countess's (Christiane Iven) entrance. He

Rhythm and experiences of time in opera 143

wanted to exit, but she took a step toward him. Were they fellow sufferers? Did they share a common fate in the game of love and infidelity? A very short, touching moment occurred. The Countess sought consolation from Figaro or wanted to console him. Both knew so much; both had become so disappointed. But in all his bitterness, Figaro turned away; he did not want to act as a surrogate or to be pitied. Just as these scenes took place in the "in-between" of the actual numbers, something took place between the stage and the auditorium due to the break in continuity: an intense attention.

The rhythm of slow and fast, of stasis and movement, established in the performance of Bieito's production of *Don Giovanni* was a manifestation of the basic binary rhythm that was increased in its intensity to the extreme. This excessive fulfillment of the basic binary rhythm had a very convincing effect, sometimes even breathtaking. According to gestalt psychology, we are always looking for larger units in perception. Is a contrasting change such a unit? The desire for something fast following something slow is equal to the necessary completion of a unity; the fulfillment of this expectation produces pleasure, physical satisfaction. In the performance of Bischoff's production of *Figaro*, more complicated rhythmic relationships were dominant; the staging therefore seemed less catchy, less overwhelming, less superficially gripping. But if one is able to engage in differentiating the levels between past and present events and their different rhythms in perception, then such a rhythmic complication can certainly unfold very intense effects, since this combination challenges the body's capacity to absorb and resonate rhythms. The way in which visual and musical rhythms and anticipated rhythm interact with each other (correspondence or contrast on different levels) ultimately determines the rhythm of a performance and its effect: boredom, scandal, provocation, irritation.

If one posits the concept of an anticipated rhythm in music, then precisely such moments in which an expected development or a previously chosen temporal continuity—a rhythm that audience members have prepared themselves for—is interrupted are among the most striking and perceptually challenging moments of opera performances. This was made abundantly clear in the key scene of a staging that has become, though for completely different reasons, one of the most discussed opera stagings in recent decades: Hans Neuenfels's 2003 production of Mozart's *Idomeneo*[51] at the Deutsche Oper Berlin, which achieved international and mass-media fame three years later when the artistic director of the Deutsche Oper decided to stop performing the production because it represented "a security risk with an incalculable outcome."[52]

The last note of the premiere had faded away. Idomeneo (Charles Workman) entered once again into the echo, into the silence, with a white sack thrown over his shoulder; from this sack, he removed, one after another, the severed heads of Poseidon and the religious founders Jesus, Mohammed, and Buddha, and placed them on four chairs (see Figure 8.7).

In the few moments of this mute final scene, a palpable tension suddenly spread through the auditorium and was first discharged in isolated

144 *Analytical approaches*

Figure 8.7 Idomeneo, staging by Hans Neuenfels, Charles Workman as Idomeneo, Deutsche Oper Berlin, 2003.

Photo courtesy of Mara Eggert.

interjections like "Pfui" (boo) and then, after Idomeneo's concluding mad laughter, in a storm of protest that is customary at Neuenfels's premieres. What had happened? The statement of the final scene was really not that provocative. On the contrary, the scene provided a consistent end to the thoughts laid out in the staging about warlike conflicts between the powerful and the dependent, idols and servants. But what then provoked the booing? If it was not a consequence of the scene—that is, a conclusively interpretable result of the scene—then it was surely the sudden break from the foreseeable and anticipated continuity that finds its logical conclusion in the final note and falling curtain. This moment of irritation and disorientation—in which no one in the audience knew what was going to happen, in which no one knew how the otherwise seemingly restrained audience would react, whether the otherwise rather uniform flow of the staging would now be broken up by the audience's active intervention—turned out to be a moment of intense presence in which I became aware of my own perception, in which I could very distinctly feel the room, my neighbors, and the energy of the performance that was suddenly hanging in the room (an experience that was apparently shared in a similar way by numerous audience members).

It is always astonishing how much our knowledge of musical continuity and the adherence to that knowledge can be felt in opera performances of the classic repertoire. What I mean is the rhythm of a performance that is "faithful" to the score in its succession, a rhythm that audience members have "attuned" themselves to. When this succession is interrupted, it can feel like an injury, or at least like a great uncertainty. What makes us feel uneasy or fascinates us here lies in not knowing what exactly will happen, in the great expectation of an imagined but never really foreseeable or fore*hear*able future.

As a temporal art, music is ephemeral and so can only be perceived while it is in progress. What we want to hear and observe has actually always already passed by. The individual forms change continuously; the events cannot be grasped, since they flow and resound into each other. This applies to music theater and opera to an increased, potentiated degree, since the scenic elements such as the movements or facial expressions of performers (or also the lighting) are just as fleeting as the music, add their own fleeting temporality to the music's temporality, and contrast, conflict, or cooperate with it. Music and theater offer the unique chance to create "another time." The space of performance thus becomes a laboratory for testing the most diverse temporal stratifications and for reflecting on the act of perception itself.

Notes

1 On this, see, for example, Christa Brüstle, "Zeitbilder: Inszenierung von Klang und Aktion bei Lachenmann und Hespos," in Altenburg and Bayreuther, *Musik und kulturelle Identität*, vol. 3, 322–27.
2 On this, see Henri Bergson, "The Perception of Change," in *The Creative Mind: An Introduction to Metaphysics* (Mineola: Dover, 2007), 107–32.
3 On this, see, for example, Ernst Pöppel, "Die Rekonstruktion der Zeit," in *Das Phänomen Zeit in Kunst und Wissenschaft*, ed. Hannelore Paflik (Weinheim: VCH, 1987), 25–37.
4 This differentiation is also viewed as a foundation by experiments in music psychology: estimations of lengths of time are always based on comparing subjective estimates with the "actual" lengths of time. See Wolfgang Auhagen, Veronika Busch, and Simone Mahrenholz, "Zeit," in Finscher, *Musik in Geschichte und Gegenwart, Sachteil*, vol. 9 (Kassel: Bärenreiter, 1998), cols. 2221–22.
5 Norbert Elias, *An Essay on Time*, vol. 9 of *The Collected Works of Norbert Elias*, ed. Steven Loyal and Stephen Mennell (Dublin: University College Dublin Press, 2007).
6 Elias, 3, 10, 38–39, 97–98.
7 Hans-Thies Lehmann, *Postdramatisches Theater* (Frankfurt am Main: Verlag der Autoren, 1999), 317–19; Lehmann's book has also been partially translated into English, but the translation does not include this section. See Hans-Thies Lehmann, *Postdramatic Theatre*, trans. Karen Jürs-Munby (Abingdon: Routledge, 2006).
8 On the concept of endless melody and its manifestations, see Fritz Reckow, "Unendliche Melodie," in *Handwörterbuch der musikalischen Terminologie*, ed. Hans Heinrich Eggebrecht and Albrecht Riethmüller, binder 6 (Stuttgart: Franz Steiner, 1972–2005).
9 See Pöppel, "Rekonstruktion der Zeit."
10 Friedrich Nietzsche, *Human, All Too Human II*, trans. Gary Handwerk, vol. 4 of *The Complete Works of Friedrich Nietzsche*, ed. Alan D. Schrift and Duncan Large (Stanford: Stanford University Press, 2013), 58–59.
11 Wilhelm Keller, "Die Zeit des Bewußtseins," in *Das Zeitproblem im 20. Jahrhundert*, ed. Rudolf W. Meyer (Bern: A. Francke, 1964), 64–65.
12 Richard Wagner, *Tristan und Isolde*, WWV 90, ed. Isolde Vetter and Egon Voss, vol. 8.2 of *Sämtliche Werke* (Mainz: Schott, 1992), 62–63, mm. 551–56.

146 Analytical approaches

13 Heiner Müller's staging appears to be clearly influenced by the tendencies of so-called postdramatic theater and its concentration on materiality and duration—here following the example of Robert Wilson. See Lehmann, *Postdramatic Theater*, 156.
14 Richard Wagner, *Die Walküre*, WWV 86B, ed. Christa Jost, vol. 11.1 of *Sämtliche Werke* (Mainz: Schott, 2002), 183–90, mm. 1477–1523; Wagner, *Tristan und Isolde*, 60–65, mm. 529–67.
15 Keller, "Zeit des Bewußtseins," 64.
16 Keller, 64.
17 Staatsoper Berlin, 2003, Daniel Barenboim conducting; I attended the dress rehearsal on 10 April 2003.
18 Staatsoper Berlin, 2005, Julien Salemkour conducting, set design by Olaf Altmann; I attended the performance on 27 January 2005.
19 Deutsche Oper Berlin, 2012, Donald Runnicles conducting; I attended the performance on 20 April 2012.
20 Timothy Cheek, *Jenůfa*, vol. 3 of *The Janáček Opera Libretti: Translations and Pronunciations* (Lanham: Rowman and Littlefield, 2017), 20.
21 Leoš Janáček, *Jenufa: Její pastorkyňa (Ihre Ziehtochter)*, trans. Max Brod, piano score (Vienna: Universal-Edition, 1917), 176–77.
22 Deutsche Oper Berlin, 2002; I attended the performances on 21 September 2002, 20 December 2002, and 25 December 2002.
23 Friedrich Nietzsche, "Ueber den Rhythmus (1875)," in *Gesammelte Werke: Musarionausgabe*, vol. 5, *Vorlesungen: 1872–1876* (Munich: Musarion, 1922), 474–75.
24 See Wilhelm Seidel, "Rhythmus, Metrum, Takt," in Finscher, *Musik in Geschichte und Gegenwart, Sachteil*, vol. 8 (Kassel: Bärenreiter, 1998), cols. 257, 259, 264.
25 In contrast to the concept of time signature, which represents a virtual magnitude since it is a grouping of *the same kind* of note values that one does not necessarily hear—a temporal frame, so to say, that the rhythm stands out against—rhythm is a succession of *different note values*.
26 See Seidel, "Rhythmus, Metrum, Takt," col. 264. In 1854, Eduard Hanslick described the "changing, regular movement of individual parts in the tempo" as "rhythm at a small scale." Eduard Hanslick, *Vom Musikalisch-Schönen: Ein Beitrag zur Revision der Ästhetik der Tonkunst* (Leipzig: Rudolph Weigel, 1854; repr. Darmstadt: Wissenschaftliche Buchgesellschaft, 1965), 32; quoted from Carl Dahlhaus, "Rhythmus im Großen," *Melos: Neue Zeitschrift für Musik* 1 (1975): 439.
27 Bernhard Waldenfels, *Sinnesschwellen* (Frankfurt am Main: Suhrkamp, 1999), 64.
28 Waldenfels, 64.
29 Seidel, "Rhythmus, Metrum, Takt," col. 268.
30 See Johann Georg Sulzer, *Allgemeine Theorie der Schönen Künste*, 2nd ed., vol. 4 (Leipzig: Weidmannsche Buchhandlung), 92; quoted from Seidel "Rhythmus, Metrum, Takt," col. 293.
31 Motte-Haber, *Musikpsychologie*, 112. See also Manfred Spitzer, *Musik im Kopf: Hören, Musizieren, Verstehen, Erleben im neuronalen Netzwerk* (Stuttgart: Schattauer, 2002), 216: Rhythm is, "as it were, imposed by the perceiver on the perceived events."
32 Seidel, "Rhythmus, Metrum, Takt," col. 261.
33 Spitzer, *Musik im Kopf*, 221.
34 "The essence of rhythm is the preparation of a new event by the ending of a previous one." Susanne K. Langer, *Feeling and Form: A Theory of Art* (New York: Scribner, 1953), 126. "The essence of rhythm is not merely the perceived order (or pattern) of repetition (recurrence) of something; it is the demand, preparation and anticipation for something to come." Haili You, "Defining Rhythm: Aspects of an Anthropology of Rhythm," *Culture, Medicine and Psychiatry* 18 (1994):

363. With regard to language, Hans Ulrich Gumbrecht notes that rhythm in spoken language "only stands out ... between the echo of the preceding sound in retention and the anticipation of the following sound in protention." Gumbrecht, "Rhythm and Meaning," in Gumbrecht and Pfeiffer, *Materialities of Communication*, 173.
35 Igor Stravinsky, *Poetics of Music in the Form of Six Lessons*, trans. Arthur Knodel and Ingolf Dahl (Cambridge: Harvard University Press, 1970), 29.
36 Heiner Goebbels, "Rhythm in Neue Musik" (lecture, Mainz, 31 May 1999). See also, Heiner Goebbels, "Puls und Bruch: Zum Rhythmus in Sprache und Sprechtheater," in *Komposition als Inszenierung*, ed. Wolfgang Sandner (Berlin: Henschel, 2002), 106: "It testifies to a characteristic secrecy when contemporary composers grant themselves, the conductor, and the performing musicians the pleasure of the individual acoustic event's rhythmic deviation from the pulse with regard to the reference system of the time signatures visible in the score but withhold this experience from their audience because it remains inaudible."
37 On atmosphere as an intermediary process, see Gernot Böhme, *The Aesthetics of Atmospheres*, ed. Jean-Paul Thibaud (Abingdon: Routledge, 2017); as well as Sabine Schouten, *Sinnliches Spüren: Wahrnehmung und Erzeugung von Atmosphären im Theater* (Berlin: Theater der Zeit, 2007).
38 Hanno Helbling, *Rhythmus: Ein Versuch* (Frankfurt am Main: Suhrkamp, 1999), front flap of the dust jacket.
39 John Dewey, *Art as Experience*, ed. Jo Ann Boydston and Harriet Furst Simon, vol. 10 of *The Later Works, 1925–1953* (Carbondale: Southern Illinois University Press, 2008), 154; quoted from You, "Defining Rhythm," 362.
40 Gerold Baier, *Rhythmus: Tanz in Körper und Gehirn* (Reinbek bei Hamburg: Rowohlt, 2001), 23. What is actually novel about Baier's hypotheses is that he takes the known fact of the rhythmic organization of the entire body and then also draws consequences for analysis, diagnosis, and therapy. According to his position, sonic representations would be much more suited to representing complex processes in the body—its complex rhythms—than images. He advocates sonic techniques instead of imaging techniques to give an adequate expression to the rhythmic organization of our bodily functions. For example, the technique of Doppler ultrasonography of the cerebral arteries has been used for quite some time.
41 Baier, *Rhythmus*, 251, also see 170. See also Spitzer, *Musik im Kopf*, 213.
42 Staatsoper Hannover, 2002, David Parry conducting; I attended the performance on 2 March 2002.
43 Staatsoper Hannover, 2002, Shao-Chia Lü conducting; I attended the performance on 8 October 2002.
44 On this more generally, see also Pavis, *Semiotik der Theaterrezeption*, 95: "In performance, ... rhythm is perceptible in the perception of binary effects: silence–word, speed–slowness."
45 See Pavis, 91.
46 See Mozart, *Don Giovanni*, 473–86.
47 Pavis, *Semiotik der Theaterrezeption*, 94.
48 See Mozart, *Le nozze di Figaro*, 5–28, Sinfonia, 29–40, no. 1.
49 Pavis, *Semiotik der Theaterrezeption*, 96.
50 See Mozart, *Le nozze di Figaro*, 66, 160–61; McClatchy, *Seven Mozart Librettos*, 327, 329.
51 Lothar Zagrosek conducting; I attended the performances on 13 March 2003 and 3 May 2003.
52 For a representative report in the press, see Andreas Kilb et al., "Klammheimlicher Kniefall," *Frankfurter Allgemeine Zeitung*, 27 September 2006, http://www.faz.net/aktuell/feuilleton/debatten/deutsche-oper-klammheimlicher-kniefall-1354531.html, accessed 1 October 2020.

9 The future of opera?
On the mediated experience and distribution of opera performances

In view of the growing importance of mediatization in opera—be it through the use of videos on stage, the broadcasting of opera performances in cinemas, or the distribution of recordings online or on DVD—opera scholarship has vigorously taken up the debate in the fields of theater and performance studies on whether a performance is defined by how it only exists as a live event and cannot be recorded and repeated, or whether, on the contrary, mediatization can be both a component of a performance and even its model.[1] The question is whether Peggy Phelan's and Philip Auslander's arguments, which continue to serve as a basis for discussions in theater studies and performance theory, can also be productive in the debate on mediatization in opera.[2]

In my view, both positions are relevant to the performative dimension of opera, both Peggy Phelan's radical point of view that we can only speak of performance in the case of a live event and not in the case of a mediatized one and Auslander's criticism of this opposition between performance and mediatization, especially when it comes to questions of how fascination for the live event and for its effects is manifested or even provoked in mediatized forms. In this context, I am interested in the possibilities that media present for documenting and intensifying a characteristic of opera as a live event: the particular relationship between the singing performers and the perceiving audience, and the active perception of an operatic voice in performance. I want to discuss the distribution of single scenes, single arias, and also just of moments from live performances that fans either extract from DVDs or make directly in opera houses as bootleg recordings and that other opera fans then watch, especially on YouTube, and comment on.[3] What occurs here is a kind of mediatized form of a central aspect of opera as a live event, namely, active participation, which is manifested in speaking about the event, in commenting on it, in discourse.

The uniqueness of the live voice in the opera house—which, as discussed in Chapter 7, creates an intimacy between a singer and the audience even across a great distance and evokes a particular physical experience—would be a first argument for differentiating ontologically between opera as a live event and

DOI: 10.4324/9781003124863-12

its mediatized forms. Contrary to Auslander's view that every live performance is already influenced and shaped by the mediatized world surrounding us,[4] in opera there is a fundamental difference between a projecting voice produced live, which fills the room with its sound, and a microphoned voice. The difference is immediately audible even to an only limitedly trained ear. Much of what constitutes an operatic voice and makes it special is lost through a microphone.

Yet it is precisely this experience of the unique and particular nature of an operatic voice that can be disseminated and shared with others through media, especially on the Internet with its flexible and fast channels of communication. In mediatization, fans and Internet users are presented with a way to satisfy a longing to transfix the ephemeral, to make the unrepeatable repeatable, and to share one's own experience with others. Since its inception, the Internet video-portal YouTube has been an inexhaustible source for opera fans to view and listen to one-time operatic events that they could not participate in and to exchange information with a worldwide community of fans through the comments function.

As an example, we can take a clip from a longer film portrait of Edita Gruberová in which one can watch and listen to the end of the final aria from Gruberová's debut in the title role of Donizetti's *Lucrezia Borgia* in a concert performance in Barcelona from 2008. After the endlessly held high note (a high E♭), which goes beyond what is "humanly possible," and the last orchestral note, the celebrated opera diva makes three conspicuous bodily movements, gestures, or poses.[5] These three movements after the accomplished deed cannot be ascribed to the insane emotional state of the character she is portraying nor to an acknowledgment of her raging fans; they are rather, in my perception, solely due to Gruberová's physical and emotional state as a singer who has just accomplished something incredible—an unloading of tension that reveals more about how what we just heard and what she just achieved went beyond what is humanly possible than the moment of the performance did itself. Despite the fact that neither I nor most of the other users experienced this performance live, we are able to feel very close to Gruberová as she physically exerts herself and then relaxes thanks to YouTube and the documentary filmmaker's camera work. These last seconds seem as if the singer were divulging that this aria had cost her something and that she was letting herself go with relish. It is a very intimate moment and seems to be primarily intended for herself, but now everyone can share in it on YouTube. It was immediately noted and commented on, for example, by Mark alias "operadude 32" from Chicago: "I ABSOLUTELY love seeing her release her 'appoggio' after the final high note (you see her ribcage collapse). And then, when she throws her head back as if to say, 'I did it!'" (see Figure 9.1).[6]

One of the characteristics of the autopoietic feedback loop is that the process of influence does not only run in one direction—from the performers to the audience—but also has an effect back on the performers. The way in which a concrete performance actually takes place, with its intensity, effect,

150 *Analytical approaches*

Figure 9.1 Screenshot showing user comments on YouTube in response to a clip of Edita Gruberová performing the final aria in Donizetti's *Lucrezia Borgia* at the Gran Teatre del Liceu, Barcelona, 2008; clip from *Die Kunst des Belcanto*, directed by Claus Wischmann and Stefan Pannen (ZDF 2008); https://www.youtube.com/all_comments?v=fFOEISUIXeM, accessed 3 June 2011, no longer available.

and energetic force, depends on a unique, unrepeatable interaction between performers and audience members that only occurs in this unique constellation. This feedback loop of performance cannot, of course, be in any way active in the mediatized form of Gruberová's performance, yet as the comment shows, the mediatized performance in the clip produces its own feedback system—a new form of liveness that Nick Couldry has called "online liveness."[7] It is symptomatic that a nostalgic longing to remember a past live event as such is often expressed in the comments board to clips from live performances, as if those leaving a comment wanted to wrest the performance from ephemerality and also sometimes inscribe their own presence and participation in the performance into the event, as becomes clear in a comment by "asisecanta": "You can distinguish me between 1:56 and 1:58, at the left, with white shirt and glasses. I was there" (see Figure 9.2).[8]

This makes clear that mediatiziation does not dissolve or fray the boundaries between a live event and its mediatized forms but, to the contrary, makes those boundaries all the more prominent, as the longing for the lost live event becomes apparent on the comments board. This longing is not satisfied by the mediatized form but rather actually stimulated by it. The mediatization of opera thus clearly underscores the boundary between live and mediatized.

There are, however, aspects of opera that exist exclusively in mediatized forms, and they may herald its future. Using the career of the soprano Anna Netrebko as an example, I would like to show how media strategies were used to establish her as the "diva of the twenty-first century." The fact that opera

The future of opera? 151

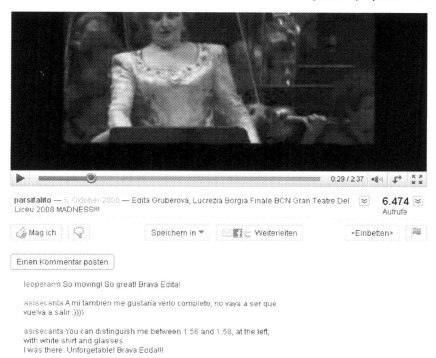

Figure 9.2 Screenshot showing user comments on YouTube in response to a clip of Edita Gruberová performing the final aria in Donizetti's *Lucrezia Borgia* at the Gran Teatre del Liceu, Barcelona, 2008; clip from *Die Kunst des Belcanto*; https://www.youtube.com/watch?v=DeJzZ0lUnIo, accessed 2 October 2013, user comment has since been removed.

divas employ media strategies of personal branding and marketing has been a well-known phenomenon ever since mass media such as newspapers, advertisements, cartes de visites, and steel engravings have been available, that is, at least since the second half of the nineteenth century.[9] What was new about the media strategies in Netrebko's case was how they unabashedly borrowed from the marketing of stars in the pop industry.[10] Netrebko was positioned and marketed entirely according to the mechanisms and rules of the pop market: with all-day appointments for interviews, artificially scarce tickets for her appearances, photo galleries in magazines such as *Gala* and *Stern*, appearances on Europe's most successful TV show at the time, *Wetten, dass …?*, advertising contracts for consumer products such as cell phones (with or instead of Franz Beckenbauer or Anke Engelke), a contract with the fashion label Escada, announcements intended for the society and gossip columns in newspapers, and the positioning of her CDs and her first DVD in the pop charts.

If one looks through the immense number of photographs of Anna Netrebko in circulation, especially from the beginning of her career, one principle becomes clear very quickly: she struck poses that aligned her with Maria Callas, both in the form of citing her and with reference to Callas as the "queen of the media event."[11] She often had herself photographed offstage, for example, in hotels or cafés. One can differentiate here between three groups of images or poses.

First, there are pictures in which the pose almost leaps out at one as a citation, as a restaging. In a photo from the booklet accompanying her second CD, *Sempre libera* (2004), she appears as a revenant of Callas (in Spontini's *La vestale*). With a flowing cape, her upper body is bent slightly forward as if frozen while floating—a movement that leads from the background into the foreground, that is, toward the viewer—her arms are stretched out from her body and caught in motion, and her gaze is absent and introverted.[12] Another photo recalls Audrey Hepburn—with a tiara in her pinned-up hair, bangs falling into her forehead in an orderly and disorderly fashion, eyebrows tapering clearly outward, eye shadow emphasizing the almond shape of her eyes, and long white gloves. This citation is, by the way, also conceivable as a double citation, since Callas was obsessed with wanting to look like Hepburn. In a black-and-white photo taken in the Hotel Sacher Salzburg for the *Süddeutsche Zeitung Magazin*, Netrebko appears like a cross between Maria Callas and Jackie Kennedy—with shoulder-length hair curled outward, a skirt ending just above the knees, high-heeled, pointed shoes, a cape that she holds in shape elegantly and seemingly effortlessly with her hands, and a look turned to the side, as if she feels both annoyed by the camera and challenged to pose at the same time, fully aware of the impression she is making.[13] Another portrait—in which she is laughing with her mouth wide open and has raised one leg as if to adjust the strap on her shoe while sitting on a bed in a red dress whose fabric is spread out over the bed—is obviously inspired by Marilyn Monroe.[14]

But many more pictures belong to a second category. In these photos, she appears with a bare navel or back, with a plunging neckline,[15] with pursed lips, a slightly opened mouth, and closed eyes,[16] with spread legs stretching upward, lounging on an armchair, her index finger lasciviously stuck in her mouth, or also in a supine pose, propped up on her naked arm or on her stomach on a white bearskin,[17] her gaze usually turned toward the viewer in a challenging manner. As if the director Willy Decker were restaging these poses of the media star in his 2005 Salzburg production of Verdi's *La traviata*, Anna Netrebko alias Violetta Valéry alias Anna Netrebko gets in trouble with the throng of male members of the chorus (Konzertvereinigung Wiener Staatsopernchor) while lying backward in a red dress on a sofa of the same color, her head and arms stretched back over the armrest, bare legs and feet extended out along the sofa, slightly spread out with a somewhat bent knee. The sofa is carried by some of the gentlemen of the chorus, while the majority stretch out their hands toward this unattainable erotic fantasy.[18] What can be seen here is the affirmation of a gender-specific role: the image of the erotically provocative woman who appeals to (male) sexual instincts and is staged as an object.[19]

The third group of images seems to want to correct this image. In these photos, Netrebko is staged as the nice girl next door, as a young woman in a private ambience, for example, in a flowered dress with an open, warm glow;[20] that she rides her bicycle to work fits this image.[21]

Particularly in the last two groups, the pictures seem to suggest a certain intimacy and availability, and the last group suggests a strategy that could be described as propagating naturalness and authenticity—a trend that has been continuously pursued in the pop sector as well as in various television formats for about twenty years.[22] It suggests that you can achieve everything if you just rely on your own potential and don't pretend to be someone else. The two biographies of Anna Netrebko that were published almost simultaneously in 2005 should also be mentioned in this context.[23] Their depiction of Netrebko's completely uninteresting, wholesome childhood has identificatory potential for a target group that strives for naturalness and authenticity. But what kind of intimacy is suggested? Ultimately, the impression of intimacy and availability is based (even exclusively) on a one-dimensional and clearly decipherable staging in images that have a high degree of brand recognition: the image of the Lolita who is as naive as she is precociously seductive.[24] The singer's own statements encourage this as well, such as her declaration (which she has since denied) in an interview with the magazine *Focus* that "In my dreams, I sing naked," a statement that can also be found on the back cover of her biography by Gregor Dolak. A scene on her DVD *The Woman, the Voice* from 2004 is also staged based on this model. The DVD was aggressively marketed and caused quite a stir, not least because the pop choreographer Vincent Paterson was engaged as the director. Before the Netrebko DVD, Paterson had choreographed Madonna's *Blond Ambition World Tour* and Michael Jackson's world tour *Bad*, among others. In the scene, Musetta's waltz from Puccini's *La bohème* is staged as a secret, passionate flirtation between an unfulfilled creature of luxury and her husband's chauffeur.[25]

But as a category for assigning the status of star or diva, intimacy needs a counterpart, a simultaneously palpable distance—we are talking about the dialectical tension between closeness and distance, between promise and rejection.[26] For fans of opera stars, the experience of standing in line at the box office for hours, sometimes even overnight, turns out to be such an experience of distance. Lines (and today also system failures when ordering tickets on the Internet) draw attention, which creates an even bigger line, which in turn attracts even further attention.[27] In steering Netrebko's early career, her management primarily pursued, in my view, two goals, both of a commercial nature. First, they attempted to transfer the mechanisms for constructing a media star into the world of opera; and second, they tried to attract a broader audience to opera by creating a pop superstar. With regard to the central criteria for becoming a star—box-office success, box-office lines, media presence, the dichotomy of intimacy and distance—one would be somewhat right to say that Netrebko was successfully established as a star. But this assessment should be qualified and made more precise.

154 *Analytical approaches*

As a characteristic for the reception of virtuosos and their position in the field of popular culture, Hans-Otto Hügel has proposed the concept of "popular listening":

> The mediation of music through the soloist's performance gestures eases the burden on the sense of hearing. The eye becomes a second organ for perceiving music, allowing for a deconcentrated listening, one that engages and disengages, that is, a popular listening.[28]

Through her poses—both those that are citations and the ones that exhibit naturalness—Anna Netrebko has pushed such "popular listening." Yet it was her self-branding and not her performances that first and foremost created her image as a singer. As this study has shown, the perception of a singer always oscillates between representation and presence, between meaning (the believed portrayal of a role) and sensuality (the physically experienced and admired qualities of the performers). The difference between the body and voice as signs and the phenomenal body constitutes a particular attraction of opera performances. In the case of Netrebko, the question shifted to an oscillation between the media image of Netrebko and what was assumed to be the real Netrebko, entirely following Madonna's motto: "I like that confusion of is it real or is it not real?"[29] Portrayed characters no longer played a role in these marketing strategies; the strategies and poses rather negotiated the tension between her media image and what was presumed to be the real Anna Netrebko.[30] She was completely assimilated by her image and brought what she presented as real with her into her appearances on stage.

While agencies have tried to secure the future of opera and its protagonists by transferring media branding strategies for stars from the pop industry, there have also been attempts to find the future of opera in the mediatization of production and distribution practices of opera performances. One such attempt was made in 2009 by Swiss Television (SF) with *La bohème im Hochhaus* (La bohème in a high-rise) in Bern's Gäbelbach quarter. This was a coproduction with the Stadttheater Bern and its production of Puccini's *La bohème*; it was staged as a live television event in high-rise apartments with participation from the residents.[31] The meeting of a performative-art form par excellence—opera performance—with the possibilities of mediatization produced a number of collisions that are of particular interest for defining the performative aspect of opera more precisely.[32] In the following, I particularly address the collision between two groups of spectators: the spectators who were moving within the performance space in the Gäbelbach quarter and the spectators in front of their televisions or computer screens.

At the beginning of the second act, which took place in the quarter's shopping mall—a mall based on the American model—the staging alludes to a currently very popular performance phenomenon in public space: so-called flash mobs. These are live performances that are recorded and posted on YouTube, where they sometimes achieve great popularity. Defined by the

The future of opera? 155

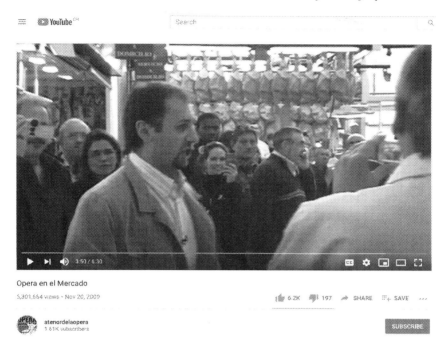

Figure 9.3 Screenshot showing the number of views on YouTube of "Opera en el Mercado," a video recording of an opera flash mob performing parts of Verdi's *La traviata* at the Mercado Central in Valencia on 13 November 2009, https://www.youtube.com/watch?v=Ds8ryWd5aFw, accessed 18 November 2020.

Oxford English Dictionary as a "large group of people organized by means of the internet, or mobile phones or other wireless devices, who assemble in public to perform a prearranged action together and then quickly disperse,"[33] flash mobs, and especially choreographed interventions in public places such as train stations and market halls, garner millions of clicks on YouTube. Quite a few flash mobs have explored the potential of classical music and opera. For example, a *La traviata* flash mob in the market hall in Valencia in 2009 now has over five million clicks (see Figure 9.3),[34] and a flash mob singing "Hallelujah" from Handel's *Messiah* in a food court in Niagara Falls in November 2010 has more than fifty-three million clicks (see Figure 9.4).[35]

The encounters between the ensemble and passers-by at the shopping mall in the Gäbelbach quarter at the beginning of the second act of the Bern *La bohème* have, at first glance, great similarities with encounters between flash mobbers and passers-by. The main characteristic of a flash mob, namely, the sudden beginning and ending of the performance, combined with catching people unaware who just happen to be there, is, of course, not present in the case of *La bohème im Hochhaus*. What constitutes the similarity—beyond the first impression—is another characteristic, namely, that a flash mob changes

156 *Analytical approaches*

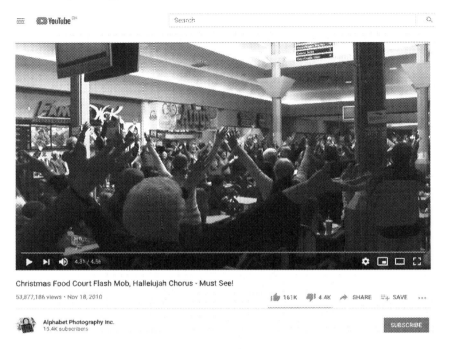

Figure 9.4 Screenshot showing the number of views on YouTube of "Christmas Food Court Flash Mob, Hallelujah Chorus – Must See!," a video recording of a flash mob performing the "Hallelujah" chorus from Handel's *Messiah* in the food court of a mall in Niagara Falls on 13 November 2010, https://www.youtube.com/watch?v=SXh7JR9oKVE, accessed 18 November 2020.

the perception of a public space through bodily movement and music as well as through different forms of participation. Flash mobs can transform a space that is identified as a space of isolation or separation—whether a shopping mall or a train station—into a space of participation, the form of participation differing depending on whether one is part of the choreographed or staged crowd of flash mobbers or an observer. Processes of inclusion and exclusion play a decisive role in the dynamics of the different forms of participation.

What connects a flash mob with a live performance in a theater is that a flash mob is a live event that only exists through and because of the simultaneous presence of performers and spectators. What has made flash mobs so popular, however, is their presence on social media, especially on YouTube, that is, the recorded versions of the live events, which are distributed in this form millions of times over. None of these mediatized documentations of flash mobs only show the flash mobbers; one also always sees the surprise and amazement of passers-by. A recurring motif in the recordings on YouTube are observers holding up their cell-phone cameras to capture the event that they are coincidentally, suddenly, and surprisingly participating in. This recurring motif is proof that the observers consider the experience important enough to record it. For those responsible for a flash mob, this is, of course, always a sign of the success of their performance: the performance has captivated people in such a way that they want to capture with their camera the event and the fact that they were there. So in the first seconds of the second act of *La bohème* in the shopping center of the Gäbelbach quarter, you can see numerous passers-by holding up their cameras as if to signal: "I was there, and I want to be able to prove it later!"

Yet the decisive difference remains: the intention and goal of this event was, from the very beginning, solely to record it and mediatize it. The spectators knew this or realized it immediately. As Christopher Morris has rightly remarked about a similar opera staging in a public space—*La traviata* in Zurich's main train station: "The production plays to and for the camera."[36] And so in the third act of this *La bohème*, one can also see a resident of the Gäbelbach quarter who pays no attention whatsoever to what was supposed to be the event—the plot of the opera—and instead only pays attention to what was actually the event, namely, the television broadcast. He behaves in a way that one often sees in the case of passers-by who happen to come within the recording radius of a reporter during a live news broadcast and wave into the TV camera. He too waves into the TV camera and seems to be calling someone with his cell phone, perhaps to let them know that he is on TV. In my view, this collision of different levels of participation and media awareness is what makes the staging so interesting: passers-by and residents switch between the roles of surprised flash-mob spectators and media-savvy participants, and the production team coproduces these oscillating roles between spectatorship and participation and brings them into the picture.

One motif common to all the variations on the mediatization of opera mentioned so far is that of repetition. From a certain point of view, the examples I have discussed all represent the desire to make the unrepeatable, the live event of opera in performance, repeatable in some way. As we have known at least since Kierkegaard, Deleuze, and Waldenfels, there can never be a repetition.[37] And yet there is an unsatiated and insatiable desire, especially in opera, to install repetition as an aesthetic practice and strategy. This longing does not come out of the blue, since repetition is one of the original ingredients of both operatic composition and the performative dimension of opera.

Opera lives from repetition, not only in voice training and rehearsals but also in the constant new productions of familiar and well-known operas. This is true even though every performance is—no matter how often it was repeated in rehearsal and no matter how often singers have repeated their phrases with their teachers since their studies—a liminal experience due to the risk associated with having to go to the limits in singing, and this liminal experience is directly transferred to the audience. Yet repetition determines both the programming politics—the practice of performing familiar pieces over and over again—and the audience's behavior when it demands repetitions of individual arias in the course of a performance.

Repetition also already has an effect on the level of compositional structures. In historically varied manifestations, repetition advanced to become a central structural element of composition within individual numbers. As a principle of musical construction, repetition can be seen as a strategy that allows listeners to experience the joy of recognition and deviation. At the same time, these structures of repetition inscribed in compositions—for example in the familiar form of the baroque da capo aria with an A part, a contrasting B part, and a third part that takes up the A part again—are an invitation to performers to bring out differences in repetition. On the level of composition, musical structures of repetition in arias already create structures that allow differences to become tangible in the smallest of spaces in ostensibly identical repetitions and that invite experimenting with the difference born out of repetition. Variations such as those created in a baroque da capo aria seem as if they emerged in the moment. In fact, the principle of variation can be practiced repeatedly in rehearsal, but it only becomes an event for the singer and listeners in the uncontrollable and uncontrolled live situation of the *hic et nunc*. Singers are thus put to the test in every performance: they know that fans want to go to the same operas again and again to experience their star in the same roles again and again. For the offer of repetition is eagerly accepted not only by the protagonists that produce opera but also by its protagonists in the audience, the fans, for whom always listening to the same singers and musical passages even becomes a need.

Opera houses possess a very special species of fans—a widespread species that is very important to the continuing success of the genre of opera: fans who do not want to experience the thrill of an opera performance only once but who want to preserve their experience and perception, share their experience, and transform its uniqueness into duration and an endlessly repeatable recording; fans who, against all the prohibitions, take recording devices into opera houses and secretly record their stars.

The film director Jean-Jacques Beineix erected a cinematic monument to this very special fan with his 1981 film *Diva*. The opera diva portrayed in the film refuses to make any records, so her fans are dependent on bootleg recordings, which set off the actual crime plot. As I have described in Chapter 7, in one scene we see a fan sitting in a concert, waiting for the aria "Ebben? Ne andrò lontana" (Well then? I'll go far away) from Alfredo Catalani's opera *La Wally*, surrounded by gangsters and bootleggers wearing black sunglasses. What is special about this short scene is, as already mentioned, the staging of a central perceptual event in the experience of a live opera performance: the anticipated repetition of a familiar aria. The physical perception of the fan is captured on screen by how he opens his lips in a close-up. This capturing of heightened perception—the attempt to make the impossible repetition of one's own experience possible—is precisely what the widespread practice of illegally recording opera performances is all about. This can be impressively demonstrated using a real bootleg recording that can be viewed on YouTube. In this video, Natalie Dessay can be seen performing the madness aria of Donizetti's *Lucia di Lammermoor* at the Opéra Bastille in Paris on

6 October 2006.[38] The fan who recorded the performance and who goes by the pseudonym "Akynou" on YouTube actually wants to let fellow fans share in Dessay's breathtaking performance of the madness aria. But what the clip also conveys is even more revealing. It is not the *image* of a physical response as in Beineix's film (the lips of the fan) but the *sound* of a physical response in anticipation of the repetition of a vocal tightrope act known in every detail. It is the audible breathing of the fan that grabs my attention. At the beginning of the aria, one can hear the fan breathing evenly every three seconds. Starting at 2:12, when Lucia's long solo cadenza begins with a fragile and highly demanding coloratura, the breathing becomes louder and louder, and the fan even starts to pant, until the moment when the voice begins the last phrase and the bootlegger awaits the final note, the high E♭, the touchstone of every Lucia singer. At this point (at 3:01)—that is, before the E♭—the fan holds his or her breath for a full twelve seconds, for three complete breaths. What becomes audible is a moment of intensely anticipating the repetition of the thrill of a high note already experienced in the past, an anticipation filled with concern for and pleasure in the possibility of difference.[39]

The fact that repeating the experience not only triggers a physical response but also active participation is impressively demonstrated in a series of video clips that show fans' very special identification with the stars they admire. I am referring to a performative technique of repetition that is more familiar from other contexts: lip syncing, also known in circles of opera fans as "lip-sync drag queening." At this point I would like to point out two examples, two versions of Cecilia Bartoli's interpretation of the aria "Agitata da due venti" (Agitated by two winds) from Antonio Vivaldi's opera *Griselda*, one performed by Roland Sandhovel and the other by Chris Jones alias "divoboy."[40] With regard to the longing to save a past and lost performance or to keep it alive in memory—a longing that appears in mediatized forms of live performances as discussed above—the practice of "lip-sync drag queening" could be described, following Simon Frith, as a "secondary performance."[41] Yet it is perhaps precisely the difference that appears in futile repetition (and the physical characteristics of the "lip syncers") that (to use Deleuze's language) is elicited from repetition as something new. And it is perhaps precisely this difference that repeatedly drives opera and its protagonists, both its performers and its audience, to repetition, which has its medial counterpart in the replay button.

Notes

1 See, for example, Morris, "Wagnervideo"; Morris, "Digital Diva."
2 Peggy Phelan, *Unmarked: The Politics of Performance* (Abingdon: Routledge, 1993); Philip Auslander, *Liveness: Performance in a Mediatized Culture*, 2nd ed. (Abingdon: Routledge, 2008).
3 The phenomenon of the opera fan is worthy of its own investigations. See, for example (though before the rise of the Internet), Koestenbaum, *Queen's Throat*; or also the sociological study by Claudio E. Benzecry, *The Opera Fanatic: Ethnography of an Obsession* (Chicago: University of Chicago Press, 2011).
4 Auslander, *Liveness*, 38.

160 *Analytical approaches*

5 https://www.youtube.com/watch?v=DeJzZ0lUnIo, accessed 1 November 2020.
6 This comment refers to the same clip as in footnote 5 but to a version of it uploaded by a different user whose YouTube account has since been deleted, so the comment is also no longer available online. https://www.youtube.com/all_comments?v=%20fFOEISUIXeM, accessed 3 June 2011.
7 Nick Couldry, "Liveness, 'Reality,' and the Mediated Habitus from Television to the Mobile Phone," *Communication Review* 7, no. 4 (2004): 353–61.
8 This comment was posted to the same video linked in footnote 5. The video can still be viewed, but the comment has since been removed. https://www.youtube.com/all_comments?v=DeJzZ0lUnIo, accessed 20 October 2013.
9 See Grotjahn, Schmidt, and Seedorf, eds., *Diva*.
10 See, for example, Hans-Otto Hügel, ed., *Handbuch Populäre Kultur: Begriffe, Theorien und Diskussionen* (Stuttgart: J. B. Metzler, 2003).
11 Elisabeth Bronfen and Barbara Straumann, *Die Diva: Eine Geschichte der Bewunderung* (Munich: Schirmer/Mosel, 2002), 51.
12 See, for example, https://portraits.klassik.com/musikzeitschriften/classix/anna_titel.jpg. On the image of Callas from 1954, see Michael Brix, ed., *Maria Callas: Aufführungen/Performances* (Munich: Schirmer/Mosel, 1994), 68.
13 Susanne Schneider, "Hallo Gott, hier singt Anna," *Süddeutsche Zeitung Magazin*, 16 January 2004; also see https://www.scribd.com/doc/264480792/Moment-26-2004.
14 http://annanetrebko.com/img/uploadedimages/portraits_015.jpg, accessed 31 August 2013, no longer accessible.
15 http://annanetrebko.com/img/uploadedimages/portraits_026.jpg, accessed 31 August 2013, no longer accessible.
16 For example, see http://www.sueddeutsche.de/kultur/370/405148/text/ or https://www.deutschegrammophon.com/en/showimg.htms?ID=a90184c4c935d0db2d93346c%2520be40e396, accessed 30 April 2017, no longer accessible.
17 http://annanetrebko.com/img/uploadedimages/portraits_024.jpg, accessed 31 August 2013, no longer accessible.
18 http://annanetrebko.com/img/uploadedimages/productions_046.jpg, accessed 31 August 2013, no longer accessible.
19 The only picture actually missing from this series is one of her scrubbing the floors of the Mariinsky Theatre as she was doing when, as legend has it, she was discovered by Valery Gergiev.
20 http://d1.stern.de/bilder/unterhaltung/2004/kw03/netrebko400_fitwidth_489.jpg or http://d1.stern.de/bilder/unterhaltung/2004/kw32/netrebkoneu_fitwidth_489.jpg, accessed 2 October 2013, no longer accessible.
21 http://annanetrebko.com/img/uploadedimages/personal_003.jpg, accessed 31 August 2013, no longer accessible.
22 Here one could name, for example, the formats *Popstars, Deutschland sucht den Superstar*, and *Big Brother* with the slogan "Leb so, wie du dich fühlst" (Live like you feel).
23 Gregor Dolak, *Anna Netrebko: Opernstar der neuen Generation* (Munich: Heyne, 2005); Marianne Reissinger, *Anna Netrebko: Ein Porträt* (Reinbek bei Hamburg: Rowohlt, 2005).
24 On this, see also Bronfen and Straumann, *Die Diva*, 58. They describe Marilyn Monroe as a "pale, artificially produced, sweet angel of female sexuality who needs protection" (61), and in their discussion of Madonna, who cites Monroe, they focus on Madonna's "voluptuously demonstrated game with the power of female sexuality, which characterized Marilyn Monroe just as much as her spectrally shimmering fragility did" (202).
25 See *Anna Netrebko: The Woman, the Voice*, directed by Vincent Paterson (Hamburg: Deutsche Grammophon, 2004), DVD, track 2. A clip of this track can be found here: https://www.youtube.com/watch?v=hCQrOiINhGc, accessed 1 November 2020.

26 See Carlo Michael Sommer, "Stars als Mittel der Identitätskonstruktion: Überlegungen zum Phänomen des Star-Kults aus sozialpsychologischer Sicht," in *Der Star: Geschichte, Rezeption, Bedeutung*, ed. Werner Faulstich and Helmut Korte (Munich: Wilhelm Fink, 1997), 118; Jens Thiele, "Künstlerisch-mediale Zeichen der Starinszenierung," in Faulstich and Korte, *Der Star*, 137.
27 A ticket line has seldom appeared so clearly as an index of the phenomenon of a star as during the guest performance of the Museum of Modern Art (MoMa) in Berlin in 2004. For weeks, the media only reported on the length of the line and announced new record waiting times. It was not the MoMa that was the star, as the posters promised, but the line.
28 Hans-Otto Hügel, "Virtuose," in Hügel, *Handbuch Populäre Kultur*, 491.
29 Madonna, interview by Vince Aletti, *Aperture*, no. 156 (Summer 1999): 46.
30 Netrebko's poses can also be read as a game with citations in the spirit of how Elisabeth Bronfen reads the stars Cindy Sherman and Madonna at the end of her book.
31 See, for example, https://www.bielertagblatt.ch/nachrichten/kultur/oper-la-boheme-im-%20hochhaus-weniger-populaer-als-la-traviata, accessed 30 April 2017, no longer accessible.
32 Alessandra Campana and Christopher Morris pointed out the aspect of collision in this staging in the exposé to the conference "Opera and the Space of Performance" at Tufts University in 2011: "Conventions [of costumes and gestures] collide with a video production style indebted to the aesthetics of reality TV."
33 *Oxford English Dictionary*, 3rd ed. (2013), s.v. "flash mob, *n.2*."
34 https://www.youtube.com/watch?v=Ds8ryWd5aFw, accessed 1 November 2020.
35 https://www.youtube.com/watch?v=SXh7JR9oKVE, accessed 1 November 2020.
36 Morris, "Digital Diva," 111: "It also relocates liveness, in that the production plays to and for the camera, while the audience in the train station are given only partial glimpses."
37 Søren Kierkegaard, *Repetition*, in *Repetition and Philosophical Crumbs*, trans. M. G. Piety (Oxford: Oxford University Press, 2009), 3; Gilles Deleuze, *Difference and Repetition*, trans. Paul Patton (London: Athlone, 1994), 70–85; Waldenfels, *Sinnesschwellen*, 79–83.
38 https://www.youtube.com/watch?v=tGRfVynf0GM, accessed 1 November 2020.
39 Following Michel Poizat, one could also ascribe this pleasure in repetition, in the repeated experience of the same passage or singer, to the insatiable desire to repeat the first cry that one made after being born or to experience this surprising, shocking, desirous moment again. Michel Poizat, "Das Wagnis der Musik oder 'Wozu Singen?,'" in Kittler, Macho, and Weigel, *Rauschen und Offenbarung*, 9–16.
40 https://www.youtube.com/watch?v=8ylrUbbY6zM, accessed 30 April 2017, no longer accessible; and https://www.youtube.com/watch?v=3LB1ZAesEAk, accessed 1 November 2020. The template is the recording of the aria "Agitata da due venti" from Antonio Vivaldi's opera *Griselda* sung by Cecilia Bartoli in a live concert in Paris (https://www.youtube.com/watch?v=rppj4LyucSw, accessed 1 November 2020).
41 Simon Frith, "Live Music Matters," *Scottish Music Review* 1, no. 1 (2007): 1–17, http://www.scottishmusicreview.org/Articles/1.1/Frith%3A%20Live%20Music%20Matters.pdf.

Conclusion

Repetition was one of the main themes I encountered in a performance of Thomas Bischoff's production of *Figaro* in Hannover in 2002. At the very beginning of the opera, all the characters gave the impression that the "crazy day" was already behind them and that they were now playing through it all over again. My perception of Sebastian Baumgarten's production of *Tannhäuser* in Bayreuth in 2011 was similarly shaped by the question of repetition. The staging was situated in an installation designed by Joep van Lieshout, and the inhabitants of this installation seemed to have been living in this very peculiar world, this closed system, for a very long time, as if they had been performing Wagner's *Tannhäuser* over and over again for themselves as their founding ritual. Everyone on stage seemed to know what would happen next. They were all just as familiar with the music, and they were often quite explicitly happy about individual musical moments, such as when the knights of the Wartburg began to sway to the music of the finale of the first act, or when the chorus swayed in the second act while Biterolf recited his compelling melody.

This laboratory setup in which a well-known set of ingredients is repeated over and over again illustrates a central aspect of our culture's practice of performing the same well-known operas over and over again: in performances of so-called repertoire classics, almost everyone in the auditorium knows how the story continues and ends, whereas we pretend that the characters on stage are experiencing the story for the first time. Yet in these two performances, the characters on stage had already experienced everything and were playing it through all over again. Characters who were not supposed to be on stage according to the libretto and score were present and watching what was happening. While everyone on stage could see everything and knew everything, in the auditorium, we were confronted with so many new and incomprehensible events with no relation to our previous knowledge of *Figaro* or *Tannhäuser* that we didn't have the slightest idea of how it would continue and come to an end. Doesn't this reversal provide a perfect metaphor for our experience of every performance of a classic opera? According to Hans Ulrich Gumbrecht, "in a meaning culture, ... the concept of the event is inseparably linked to the value of innovation and, as its consequence, to the

DOI: 10.4324/9781003124863-13

Conclusion 163

effect of surprise."[1] By contrast, "imagining a presence culture"—and this is how I would classify the performance practices of the operatic repertory system—implies

> the challenge of thinking a concept of eventness detached from innovation and surprise. Such a concept would remind us that even those regular changes and transformations that we can predict and expect imply a moment of discontinuity. We know, shortly after eight o'clock in the evening, the orchestra will begin to play an overture that we have heard many times. And yet the discontinuity that marks the moment in which the first sounds are produced will "hit" us—producing an effect of eventness that implies neither surprise nor innovation.[2]

The concept of eventness addresses exactly what I would call the tension between the familiar and the deviations from the familiar in a performance of an opera from the canonical repertoire. This tension evokes eventful moments of presence. In my opinion, the appeal of experiencing such an opera performance always consists in the experience of difference—in the tension that arises between the template one believes to be familiar and the experienced reality of the performance. How far can it go? How is this tension transferred to listeners and spectators? To what extent are expectations (of seeing and listening again to a beloved object—the work) fulfilled, excessively fulfilled, insufficiently fulfilled, or broken? How does the performance play with these expectations? For me, these questions are the central categories for understanding how and why a certain performance is effective, irritating, fascinating, or boring.

The method of dealing with a template as material in a playfully productive way, which is common in many other forms of art, often encounters bitter resistance in opera, both from those producing opera and from the audience. But if one eschews the productive energy of a contemporary artistic team (direction, musical direction, dramaturgy, performers), the potential of experiencing difference, particularly with the constantly repeated classics, will remain unexploited. After all, the addition of voices, bodies, scenes, and movements produces a plentitude of meanings that is just as unlimited as those of the text itself, resulting in a stimulating and challenging exponentiation of experience. A performance is capable of creating a new reality every evening. It is no longer the work or an interpretation of a work that is on stage, but a new aesthetic reality that is subject to its own laws—laws of the present moment—and at the same time questions them.

Heiner Goebbels has proposed a distinction that is provocatively generalizing but also very helpful between "theater as museum" and "theater as laboratory." He positions large opera companies and repertory stages on the side of "theater as museum," and independent, smaller, free, experimental, and innovative performance collectives on the side of "theater as laboratory."[3] By discussing performances of repertoire classics in opera houses that are committed to this repertoire, I have tried to show that it can be quite illuminating to bridge this divide between these two types of theater and to ask how performances of innovative opera stagings in the category of "theater as museum" can have an experimental, laboratory-like potential.

The performance of a text or a score—no matter how "faithful" the production tries or claims to be to an "original"—always influences and changes one's knowledge of the underlying work. Based on this fact, it is, in my view, only logical to conclude that a score or a text should be regarded as material for experimental setups that have to be constantly created anew. In each performance, a specific relationship arises between anticipation and momentary experience. It is this relationship that always newly determines the perception of an opera performance, be it a strong attraction or perhaps an even stronger repulsion. As the performances discussed in this study show, "theater as museum"—with its clear framings and narrow limits from constantly repeating repertoire classics—can present innovations that evoke strong emotional reactions and active participation, making it possible to continue to endow opera, time and again, with an intense presence.

Notes

1 Gumbrecht, *The Production of Presence*, 84.
2 Gumbrecht, 84.
3 Heiner Goebbels, "Theater als Museum oder Labor" (lecture, Neue Theaterrealitäten Symposium, Körber Studio Junge Regie, Hamburg, 2008), https://www.heinergoebbels.com/en/archive/texts/texts_by_heiner_goebbels/read/546.

List of performances discussed

Cherubini, Luigi. *Médée*. Staging and set design by Ursel Hermann und Karl-Ernst Herrmann. Fabio Luisi conducting. Deutsche Oper Berlin, 2002. Attended the dress rehearsal on 6 May 2002 and the performance on 28 May 2002.
Handel, Georg Friedrich. *Alcina*. Staging by Robert Carsen. William Christie conducting. Opéra Paris, 1999. Viewed a recording on YouTube.
Handel, Georg Friedrich. *Giulio Cesare*. Staging by David McVicar. William Christie conducting. Glyndebourne Festival, 2005. Viewed a recording.
Janáček, Leoš. *Jenůfa*. Staging by Christof Loy. Donald Runnicles conducting. Deutsche Oper Berlin, 2012. Attended the performance on 20 April 2012.
Janáček, Leoš. *Katja Kabanowa*. Staging by Michael Thalheimer. Julien Salemkour conducting. Staatsoper Berlin, 2005. Attended the performance on 27 January 2005.
Massenet, Jules. *Werther*. Staging by Sebastian Baumgarten. Antonello Allemandi conducting. Deutsche Oper Berlin, 2002. Attended the performances on 21 September 2002, 20 December 2002, and 25 December 2002.
Mozart, Wolfgang Amadeus. *Don Giovanni*. Staging by Calixto Bieito. David Parry conducting. Staatsoper Hannover, 2002. Attended the performance on 2 March 2002.
Mozart, Wolfgang Amadeus. *Don Giovanni*. Staging by Peter Konwitschny. Kirill Petrenko/Constantin Trinks conducting. Komische Oper Berlin, 2003. Attended the performance on 6 November 2007.
Mozart, Wolfgang Amadeus. *Don Giovanni*. Staging by Peter Sellars. Craig Smith conducting. Monadnock Music Festival, Manchester, New Hampshire, 1980; PepsiCo Summerfare, Purchase, New York, 1987; Vienna Festival, 1989. Viewed a recording of the production at the Vienna Festival from 1991.
Mozart, Wolfgang Amadeus. *Die Entführung aus dem Serail*. Staging by Calixto Bieito. Kirill Petrenko conducting. Komische Oper Berlin, 2004. Attended the dress rehearsal on 18 June 2004 and the performance on 10 December 2004.
Mozart, Wolfgang Amadeus. *Idomeneo*. Staging by Hans Neuenfels. Lothar Zagrosek conducting. Deutsche Oper Berlin, 2003. Attended the performances on 13 March 2003 and 3 May 2003.
Mozart, Wolfgang Amadeus. *Le nozze di Figaro*. Staging by Christoph Marthaler. Sylvain Cambreling conducting. Salzburg Festival, 2001. Attended the performance on 11 August 2001.

DOI: 10.4324/9781003124863-14

166 List of performances discussed

Mozart, Wolfgang Amadeus. *Le nozze di Figaro*. Staging by Claus Guth. Nikolaus Harnoncourt conducting. Salzburg Festival, 2006. Viewed a recording from 2006.

Mozart, Wolfgang Amadeus. *Le nozze di Figaro*. Staging by Thomas Bischoff. Shao-Chia Lü conducting. Staatsoper Hannover 2002. Attended the performance on 8 October 2002.

Puccini, Giacomo. *La bohème im Hochhaus*. Staging in the high-rise by Anja Horst. Television direction by Felix Breisach. Srboljub Dinic conducting. Production by the Stadttheater Bern. SF/ARTE Schweiz, 2009. Viewed the recording.

Strauss, Johann. *Die Fledermaus*. Staging by Hans Neuenfels. Marc Minkowski conducting. Salzburg Festival, 2001. Attended the performance on 22 August 2001.

Verdi, Giuseppe. *Un ballo in maschera*. Staging and dramaturgy by Jossi Wieler and Sergio Morabito. Philippe Jordan conducting. Staatsoper Berlin, 2008. Attended the performance on 22 May 2009.

Verdi, Giuseppe. *Don Carlo*. Staging and dramaturgy by Jossi Wieler and Sergio Morabito. Lothar Zagrosek conducting. Staatsoper Stuttgart, 2001. Attended the performance on 23 January 2001.

Verdi, Giuseppe. *Nabucco*. Staging by Hans Neuenfels. Marcello Viotti conducting. Deutsche Oper Berlin, 2000. Attended the performances on 8 March 2000, 15 March 2000, 7 January 2001, and 30 October 2004.

Verdi, Giuseppe. *Oberto*. Staging by Pier'Alli. Antonello Allemandi conducting. Teatro Verdi Busseto, 2007. Attended the performance on 5 October 2007.

Verdi, Giuseppe. *La traviata*. Staging by Peter Mussbach. Daniel Barenboim conducting. Staatsoper Berlin, 2003. Attended the dress rehearsal on 10 April 2003.

Verdi, Giuseppe. *Il trovatore*. Staging by Balázs Kovalik. Guido Johannes Rumstadt conducting. Staatstheater Nürnberg, 2012. Attended the performance on 3 November 2012.

Wagner, Richard. *Götterdämmerung*. Staging by Peter Konwitschny. Lothar Zagrosek conducting. Staatsoper Stuttgart, 2000. Attended the performance on 7 October 2000.

Wagner, Richard. *Lohengrin*. Staging by Kasper Holten. Donald Runnicles conducting. Deutsche Oper Berlin, 2012. Attended the performance on 25 April 2012.

Wagner, Richard. *Lohengrin*. Staging by Peter Konwitschny. Ingo Metzmacher/ Sebastian Weigle/Ulf Schirmer conducting. Staatsoper Hamburg, 1998; Gran Teatre del Liceu Barcelona, 2000 (with a DVD recording from 2006); Oper Leipzig, 2009. Attended the performances on 28 April 2001 in Hamburg and 18 December 2009 in Leipzig.

Wagner, Richard. *Die Meistersinger von Nürnberg*. Staging by Katharina Wagner. Sebastian Weigle conducting. Dramaturgy by Robert Sollich. Bayreuth Festival, 2007. Attended the performances on 16 August 2007 and 27 August 2008.

Wagner, Richard. *Der Ring des Nibelungen*. Staging by Harry Kupfer. Daniel Barenboim conducting. Bayreuth Festival, 1988. Viewed a recording from 1991.

Wagner, Richard. *Der Ring des Nibelungen*. Staging by Patrice Chéreau. Pierre Boulez conducting. Bayreuth Festival, 1976. Viewed a recording from 1980.

Wagner, Richard. *Tannhäuser*. Staging by Sebastian Baumgarten. Thomas Hengelbrock conducting. Bayreuth Festival 2011. Attended the dress rehearsal on 20 July 2011 and the performance on 19 August 2011.

Wagner, Richard. *Tristan und Isolde*. Staging by Heiner Müller, Daniel Barenboim conducting. Bayreuth Festival, 1993. Attended the performance on 6 August 1993.

List of performances discussed   167

Wolf, oder wie Mozart auf den Hund kam. Music by Wolfgang Amadeus Mozart. Staging and choreography by Alain Platel und Les Ballets C de la B. Sylvain Cambreling conducting. World premiere, 2003 Ruhrtriennale. Attended the performance on 8 June 2003 at the Volksbühne am Rosa-Luxemberg-Platz in Berlin and a performance on 17 May 2004 in the context of the Berlin Theatertreffen at the Haus der Berliner Festspiele.

Bibliography

Abbate, Carolyn. *In Search of Opera*. Princeton: Princeton University Press, 2001.

Abbate, Carolyn. "Music—Drastic or Gnostic?" *Critical Inquiry* 30, no. 3 (Spring 2004): 505–36.

Abbate, Carolyn. *Unsung Voices: Opera and Musical Narrative in the Nineteenth Century*. Princeton: Princeton University Press, 1991.

Abel, Sam. *Opera in the Flesh: Sexuality in Operatic Performances*. Boulder: Westview, 1996.

Altenburg, Detlef, and Rainer Bayreuther, eds. *Musik und kulturelle Identität: Bericht über den XIII. Internationalen Kongress der Gesellschaft für Musikforschung Weimar 2004*. Vol. 3. Kassel: Bärenreiter, 2012.

Auhagen, Wolfgang, Veronika Busch, and Simone Mahrenholz. "Zeit." In Finscher, *Musik in Geschichte und Gegenwart, Sachteil*, vol. 9, cols. 2220–51.

Auslander, Philip. *Liveness: Performance in a Mediatized Culture*. 2nd ed. Abingdon: Routledge, 2008.

Auslander, Philip. "Musical Personae." *Drama Review* 50, no. 1 (Spring 2006): 100–119.

Auslander, Philip. "Performance Analysis and Popular Music: A Manifesto." *Contemporary Theatre Review* 14, no. 1 (2004): 1–14.

Austin, J. L. *How to Do Things with Words*. Edited by J. O. Urmson and Marina Sbisà. 2nd ed. Cambridge: Harvard University Press, 1975.

Baier, Gerold. *Rhythmus: Tanz in Körper und Gehirn*. Reinbek bei Hamburg: Rowohlt, 2001.

Balme, Christopher. "Werktreue: Aufstieg und Niedergang eines fundamentalistischen Begriffs." In *Regietheater! Wie sich über Inszenierungen streiten lässt*, edited by Ortrud Gutjahr, 43–50. Würzburg: Königshausen and Neumann, 2008.

Balme, Christopher, Erika Fischer-Lichte, and Stephan Grätzel, eds. *Theater als Paradigma der Moderne? Positionen zwischen historischer Avantgarde und Medienzeitalter*. Tübingen: A. Francke, 2003.

Barthes, Roland. "The Grain of the Voice." In Barthes, *The Responsibility of Forms*, 268–77.

Barthes, Roland. "Music, Voice, Language." In Barthes, *The Responsibility of Forms*, 278–85.

Barthes, Roland. *The Pleasure of the Text*. Translated by Richard Miller. New York: Hill and Wang, 1975.

Barthes, Roland. *The Responsibility of Forms: Critical Essays on Music, Art, and Representation*. Translated by Richard Howard. New York: Hill and Wang, 1985.

Barthes, Roland. *S/Z*. Translated by Richard Miller. New York: Hill and Wang, 1974.

Bataille, Georges. *Erotism: Death and Sensuality*. Translated by Mary Dalwood. San Francisco: City Lights Books, 1986.
Baumgarten, Sebastian. "Aus dem Geist der Musik heraus das Heutige denken." In Beyer, *Warum Oper?*, 41–58.
Bayerdörfer, Hans-Peter, ed. *Musiktheater als Herausforderung: Interdisziplinäre Facetten von Theater- und Musikwissenschaft*. Tübingen: Max Niemeyer, 1999.
Becker, Heinz. "Zur Situation der Opernforschung." *Musikforschung* 27, no. 2 (April/June 1974): 153–64.
Behne, Klaus-Ernst. "Über die Untauglichkeit der Synästhesie als ästhetisches Paradigma." In *Der Sinn der Sinne*, edited by Kunst- und Ausstellungshalle der Bundesrepublik Deutschland, 104–25. Göttingen: Steidl, 1998.
Bensch, Georg. *Vom Kunstwerk zum ästhetischen Objekt: Zur Geschichte der phänomenologischen Ästhetik*. Munich: Wilhelm Fink, 1994.
Benzecry, Claudio E. *The Opera Fanatic: Ethnography of an Obsession*. Chicago: University of Chicago Press, 2011.
Bergson, Henri. "The Perception of Change." In *The Creative Mind: An Introduction to Metaphysics*, 107–32. Mineola: Dover, 2007.
Beyer, Barbara, ed. *Warum Oper? Gespräche mit Opernregisseuren*. Berlin: Alexander, 2005.
Blumenberg, Hans. *Arbeit am Mythos*. Frankfurt am Main: Suhrkamp, 1979.
Blumenberg, Hans. *Work on Myth*. Translated by Robert M. Wallace. Cambridge: MIT Press, 1985.
Böhme, Gernot. *The Aesthetics of Atmospheres*. Edited by Jean-Paul Thibaud. Abingdon: Routledge, 2017.
Böhme, Gernot. *Atmosphäre: Essays zur neuen Ästhetikchev*. Frankfurt am Main: Suhrkamp, 1995.
Brandl-Risi, Bettina. "Die Körperlichkeit der Musik: Distanz und Überwältigung im Musiktheater Harry Kupfers." In Hintze, Risi, and Sollich, *Realistisches Musiktheater*, 77–96.
Brandstätter, Ursula. "Musik und Bewegung: Wahrnehmungspsychologische Erkenntnisse – exemplifiziert und falsifiziert an *Jagden und Formen* (Wolfgang Rihm/Sasha Waltz)." In *Neue Musik in Bewegung: Musik- und Tanztheater heute*, edited by Jörn Peter Hiekel, 169–81. Mainz: Schott, 2011.
Braunmüller, Robert. "Auf dem Marsch durch die Institutionen: Götz Friedrichs Bayreuther *Tannhäuser* von 1972." In Hintze, Risi, and Sollich, *Realistisches Musiktheater*, 65–72.
Braunmüller, Robert. *Oper als Drama: Das realistische Musiktheater Walter Felsensteins*. Tübingen: Max Niemeyer, 2002.
Brix, Michael, ed. *Maria Callas: Aufführungen/Performances*. Munich: Schirmer/Mosel, 1994.
Bronfen, Elisabeth, and Barbara Straumann. *Die Diva: Eine Geschichte der Bewunderung*. Munich: Schirmer/Mosel, 2002.
Brüstle, Christa. "Klang als Performative Prägung von Räumlichkeiten." In *Kommunikation – Gedächtnis – Raum: Kulturwissenschaften nach dem "Spatial Turn,"* edited by Moritz Csáky and Christoph Leitgeb, 113–29. Bielefeld: Transcript, 2009.
Brüstle, Christa. "Performance/Performativität in der neuen Musik." In Fischer-Lichte and Wulf, *Theorien des Performativen*, 271–83.
Brüstle, Christa. "Selbstorganisation von Frauen in der Musik – Performativität des Kollektivs." In *Performativität und Performance: Geschlecht in Musik, Theater und*

MedienKunst, edited by Waltraud Ernst, Marion Gerards, and Martina Oster, 146–54. Münster: LIT, 2008.
Brüstle, Christa. "Zeitbilder: Inszenierung von Klang und Aktion bei Lachenmann und Hespos." In Altenburg and Bayreuther, *Musik und kulturelle Identität*, vol. 3, 322–27.
Brüstle, Christa, and Clemens Risi. "Aufführungsanalyse und -interpretation: Positionen und Fragen der 'Performance Studies' aus musik- und theaterwissenschaftlicher Sicht." In *Werk-Welten: Perspektiven der Interpretationsgeschichte*, edited by Andreas Ballstaedt and Hans-Joachim Hinrichsen, 108–32. Schliengen: Argus, 2008.
Butler, Judith. "Performative Acts and Gender Constitution: An Essay in Phenomenology and Feminist Theory." *Theatre Journal* 40, no. 4 (December 1988): 519–31.
Calico, Joy H. *Brecht at the Opera*. Berkeley: University of California Press, 2008.
Cheek, Timothy. *Jenůfa*. Vol. 3 of *The Janáček Opera Libretti: Translations and Pronunciations*. Lanham: Rowman and Littlefield, 2017.
Cook, Nicholas. "Analysing Performance and Performing Analysis." In *Rethinking Music*, edited by Nicholas Cook and Mark Everist, rev. ed., 239–61. Oxford: Oxford University Press, 2001.
Cook, Nicholas. "Between Process and Product: Music and/as Performance." *Music Theory Online* 7, no. 2 (April 2001). http://www.mtosmt.org/issues/mto.01.7.2/mto.01.7.2.cook.html.
Cook, Nicholas, and Nicola Dibben. "Emotion in Culture and History: Perspectives from Musicology." In *Handbook of Music and Emotion: Theory, Research, Applications*, edited by Patrick N. Juslin and John A. Sloboda, 45–72. Oxford: Oxford University Press, 2010.
Couldry, Nick. "Liveness, 'Reality,' and the Mediated Habitus from Television to the Mobile Phone." *Communication Review* 7, no. 4 (2004): 353–61.
Dahlhaus, Carl. "Rhythmus im Großen." *Melos: Neue Zeitschrift für Musik* 1 (1975): 439–41.
Dahlhaus, Carl. "Zur Methode der Opern-Analyse." In *Vom Musikdrama zur Literaturoper: Aufsätze zur neueren Operngeschichte*, 11–26. Munich: Piper, 1989.
Danuser, Hermann. "Interpretation." In Finscher, *Musik in Geschichte und Gegenwart*, *Sachteil*, vol. 4, cols. 1053–69.
Danuser, Hermann, ed. *Musikalische Interpretation*. Laaber: Laaber-Verlag, 1992.
Danuser, Hermann. "Zur Aktualität musikalischer Interpretationstheorie." *Musiktheorie* 11, no. 1 (1996): 39–51.
Deleuze, Gilles. *Difference and Repetition*. Translated by Paul Patton. London: Athlone, 1994.
DeVol, Luana. "Auf der Jagd: Luana DeVol über Wachsen und Warten, Karrierekurven und Korrepetitoren, Lady Macbeth, Brünnhilde und die Praxis der permanenten Stimmpflege; Ein Interview." By Stephan Mösch. *Oper 2000: Das Jahrbuch*, yearbook of *Opernwelt* (October 2000), 8.
Dewey, John. *Art as Experience*. Edited by Jo Ann Boydston and Harriet Furst Simon. Vol. 10 of *The Later Works, 1925–1953*. Carbondale: Southern Illinois University Press, 2008.
Döhring, Sieghart. "Beschreibung von theatraler Körperlichkeit am Beispiel von Maria Callas." In *Beschreibend wahrnehmen – wahrnehmend beschreiben*, edited by Christine Lubkoll and Peter Klotz, 247–58. Freiburg im Breisgau: Rombach, 2005.

Dolak, Gregor. *Anna Netrebko: Opernstar der neuen Generation*. Munich: Heyne, 2005.

Duncan, Michelle. "The Operatic Scandal of the Singing Body: Voice, Presence, Performativity." *Cambridge Opera Journal* 16, no. 3 (November 2004): 283–306.

Eggebrecht, Hans Heinrich. "Interpretation." In *Riemann Musik Lexikon*, updated 13th ed., edited by Wolfgang Ruf in collaboration with Annette van Dyck-Hemming, vol. 2, 449–50. Mainz: Schott, 2012.

Eggebrecht, Hans Heinrich. *Musik als Zeit*. Edited by Albrecht von Massow, Matteo Nanni, and Simon Obert. Wilhelmshaven: Noetzel, 2001.

Elias, Norbert. *An Essay on Time*. Edited by Steven Loyal and Stephen Mennell. Vol. 9 of *The Collected Works of Norbert Elias*. Dublin: University College Dublin Press, 2007.

Emrich, Hinderk M. "Wirklichkeit der Wahrnehmung – Wahrnehmung der Wirklichkeit." *Flamboyant: Schriften zum Theater* 9 (1999): 63–71.

Engel, Johann Jakob. *Ideen zu einer Mimik*. Vol. 2. Berlin: August Mylius, 1786.

Epping-Jäger, Cornelia, and Erika Linz, eds. *Medien/Stimmen*. Cologne: DuMont, 2003.

Faulstich, Werner, and Helmut Korte, eds. *Der Star: Geschichte, Rezeption, Bedeutung*. Munich: Wilhelm Fink, 1997.

Finscher, Ludwig, ed. *Die Musik in Geschichte und Gegenwart: Allgemeine Enzyklopädie der Musik begründet von Friedrich Blume*. 2nd rev. ed. 29 vols. Kassel: Bärenreiter, 1994–2008.

Fischer-Lichte, Erika. *Ästhetik des Performativen*. Frankfurt am Main: Suhrkamp, 2004.

Fischer-Lichte, Erika. *Ästhetische Erfahrung: Das Semiotische und das Performative*. Tübingen: A. Francke, 2001.

Fischer-Lichte, Erika. "Aufführung." In Fischer-Lichte, Kolesch, and Warstat, *Metzler Lexikon Theatertheorie*, 15–26.

Fischer-Lichte, Erika. "Einleitende Thesen zum Aufführungsbegriff." In Fischer-Lichte, Risi, and Roselt, *Kunst der Aufführung*, 11–26.

Fischer-Lichte, Erika. "Performativität/performativ." In Fischer-Lichte, Kolesch, and Warstat, *Metzler Lexikon Theatertheorie*, 251–58.

Fischer-Lichte, Erika. *The Semiotics of Theater*. Translated by Jeremy Gaines and Doris L. Jones. Bloomington: Indiana University Press, 1992.

Fischer-Lichte, Erika. *Semiotik des Theaters*. 3 vols. Tübingen: Gunter Narr, 1983.

Fischer-Lichte, Erika. *The Transformative Power of Performance: A New Aesthetics*. Translated by Saskya Iris Jain. Abingdon: Routledge, 2008.

Fischer-Lichte, Erika. "Verwandlung als ästhetische Kategorie: Zur Entwicklung einer neuen Ästhetik des Performativen." In *Theater seit den 60er Jahren: Grenzgänge der Neo-Avantgarde*, edited by Erika Fischer-Lichte, Friedemann Kreuder, and Isabel Pflug, 21–91. Tübingen: A. Francke, 1998.

Fischer-Lichte, Erika. "Was ist eine 'werkgetreue' Inszenierung? Überlegungen zum Prozess der Transformation eines Dramas in eine Aufführung." In *Das Drama und seine Inszenierung: Vorträge des internationalen literatur- und theatersemiotischen Kolloquiums, Frankfurt am Main, 1983*, edited by Erika Fischer-Lichte with assistance from Christel Weiler and Klaus Schwind, 37–50. Tübingen: Max Niemeyer, 1985.

Fischer-Lichte, Erika. "Zuschauen als Ansteckung." In *Ansteckung: Zur Körperlichkeit eines ästhetischen Prinzips*, edited by Erika Fischer-Lichte, Mirjam Schaub, and Nicola Suthor, 35–50. Munich: Wilhelm Fink, 2005.

172 Bibliography

Fischer-Lichte, Erika, and Christoph Wulf, eds. *Theorien des Performativen*. Special issue, *Paragrana: Internationale Zeitschrift für Historische Anthropologie* 10, no. 1 (2001).

Fischer-Lichte, Erika, and Jens Roselt. "Attraktion des Augenblicks – Aufführung, Performance, performativ und Performativität als theaterwissenschaftliche Begriffe." In Fischer-Lichte and Wulf, *Theorien des Performativen*, 237–54.

Fischer-Lichte, Erika, Clemens Risi, and Jens Roselt, eds. *Kunst der Aufführung – Aufführung der Kunst*. Berlin: Theater der Zeit, 2004.

Fischer-Lichte, Erika, Doris Kolesch, and Matthias Warstat, eds. *Metzler Lexikon Theatertheorie*. 2nd ed. Stuttgart: J. B. Metzler, 2014.

Flaubert, Gustave. *Madame Bovary: Provincial Morals*. Translated by Adam Thorpe. London: Vintage Books, 2011.

Frith, Simon. "Live Music Matters." *Scottish Music Review* 1, no. 1 (2007): 1–17. http://www.scottishmusicreview.org/Articles/1.1/Frith%3A%20Live%20Music%20Matters.pdf.

Früchtl, Josef, and Jörg Zimmermann, eds. *Ästhetik der Inszenierung: Dimensionen eines künstlerischen, kulturellen und gesellschaftlichen Phänomens*. Frankfurt am Main: Suhrkamp, 2001.

Galler, Sonja, and Clemens Risi. "Singstimme/Gesangstheorien." In Fischer-Lichte, Kolesch, and Warstat, *Metzler Lexikon Theatertheorie*, 325–28.

Gerhard, Anselm. "Was ist Werktreue? Ein Phantombegriff und die Sehnsucht nach 'Authentischem.'" In *Werktreue: Was ist Werk, was Treue?*, edited by Gerhard Brunner and Sarah Zalfen, 17–23. Vienna: Böhlau, 2011.

Gerhartz, Leo Karl. "Auch das 'hm-ta-ta' beim Wort genommen (Zur Frankfurter *Macbeth*-Inszenierung von Hans Neuenfels)." In Wiesmann, *Werk und Wiedergabe*, 311–19.

Goebbels, Heiner. "Puls und Bruch: Zum Rhythmus in Sprache und Sprechtheater." In *Komposition als Inszenierung*, edited by Wolfgang Sandner. Berlin: Henschel, 2002.

Goebbels, Heiner. "Rhythm in Neue Musik." Lecture, Mainz, 31 May 1999.

Goebbels, Heiner. "Theater als Museum oder Labor." Lecture, Neue Theaterrealitäten Symposium, Körber Studio Junge Regie, Hamburg, 2008. https://www.heinergoebbels.com/en/archive/texts/texts_by_heiner_goebbels/read/546.

Goehr, Lydia. *The Imaginary Museum of Musical Works: An Essay in the Philosophy of Music*. Oxford: Oxford University Press, 1992.

Gottschewski, Hermann. *Die Interpretation als Kunstwerk: Musikalische Zeitgestaltung und ihre Analyse am Beispiel von Welte-Mignon-Klavieraufnahmen aus dem Jahre 1905*. Laaber: Laaber-Verlag, 1993.

Gottschewski, Hermann. "Interpretation als Struktur." In *Musik als Text: Bericht über den internationalen Kongress der Gesellschaft für Musikforschung, Freiburg im Breisgau, 1993*, edited by Hermann Danuser and Tobias Plebuch, vol. 2, 155–59. Kassel: Bärenreiter, 1998.

Grawert-May, Erik von. "Erotisch/Erotik/Erotismus." In *Ästhetische Grundbegriffe: Historisches Wörterbuch in sieben Bänden*, edited by Karlheinz Barck, Martin Fontius, Dieter Schlenstedt, Burkhart Steinwachs, and Friedrich Wolfzettel, vol. 2, 310–37. Stuttgart: J. B. Metzler, 2001.

Grotjahn, Rebecca, Dörte Schmidt, and Thomas Seedorf, eds. *Diva – Die Inszenierung der übermenschlichen Frau: Interdisziplinäre Untersuchungen zu einem kulturellen Phänomen des 19. und 20. Jahrhunderts*. Schliengen: Argus, 2011.

Gumbrecht, Hans Ulrich. "Production of Presence, Interspersed with Absence: A Modernist View on Music, Libretti, and Staging." In *Music and the Aesthetics of*

Modernity: Essays, edited by Karol Berger and Anthony Newcomb, 343–56. Cambridge: Harvard University Press, 2005.
Gumbrecht, Hans Ulrich. *Production of Presence: What Meaning Cannot Convey.* Stanford: Stanford University Press, 2004.
Gumbrecht, Hans Ulrich. "Produktion von Präsenz, durchsetzt mit Absenz: Über Musik, Libretto und Inszenierung." In Früchtl and Zimmermann, *Ästhetik der Inszenierung*, 63–76.
Gumbrecht, Hans Ulrich. "Rhythm and Meaning." In Gumbrecht and Pfeiffer, *Materialities of Communication*, 170–82.
Gumbrecht, Hans Ulrich. "Rhythmus und Sinn." In Gumbrecht and Pfeiffer, *Materialität der Kommunikation*, 703–13.
Gumbrecht, Hans Ulrich, and K. Ludwig Pfeiffer, eds. *Materialität der Kommunikation*. Frankfurt am Main: Suhrkamp, 1988.
Gumbrecht, Hans Ulrich, and K. Ludwig Pfeiffer, eds. *Materialities of Communication*. Translated by William Whobrey. Stanford: Stanford University Press, 1994.
Hanslick, Eduard. *Vom Musikalisch-Schönen: Ein Beitrag zur Revision der Ästhetik der Tonkunst*. Leipzig: Rudolph Weigel, 1854. Reprinted Darmstadt: Wissenschaftliche Buchgesellschaft, 1965.
Hassabis, Demis, Dharshan Kumaran, Seralynne D. Vann, and Eleanor A. Maguire. "Patients with Hippocampal Amnesia Cannot Imagine New Experiences." *PNAS* 104, no. 5 (30 January 2007): 1726–31.
Haus, Andreas, Franck Hofmann, and Änne Söll, eds. *Material im Prozess: Strategien ästhetischer Produktivität*. Berlin: Reimer, 2000.
Hegel, Georg Wilhelm Friedrich. *Aesthetics: Lectures on Fine Art*. Translated by T. M. Knox. Vol. 1. Oxford: Oxford University Press, 1975.
Hegel, Georg Wilhelm Friedrich. *Vorlesungen über die Ästhetik*. Vols. 13–15 of *Werke in 20 Bänden*. Frankfurt am Main: Suhrkamp, 1986.
Helbling, Hanno. *Rhythmus: Ein Versuch*. Frankfurt am Main: Suhrkamp, 1999.
Herrmann, Max. "Das theatralische Raumerlebnis." In *Vierter Kongress für Ästhetik und allgemeine Kunstwissenschaft*, edited by Hermann Noack. Supplemental volume to *Zeitschrift für Ästhetik und allgemeine Kunstwissenschaft* 25 (1931): 152–63.
Hinrichsen, Hans-Joachim. "Musikwissenschaft: Musik – Interpretation – Wissenschaft." *Archiv für Musikwissenschaft* 57, no. 1 (2000): 78–90.
Hintze, Werner, Clemens Risi, and Robert Sollich, eds. *Realistisches Musiktheater: Walter Felsenstein; Geschichte, Erben, Gegenpositionen*. Berlin: Theater der Zeit, 2008.
Hiß, Guido. "Zur Aufführungsanalyse." In *Theaterwissenschaft heute: Eine Einführung*, edited by Renate Möhrmann, 56–80. Berlin: Dietrich Reimer, 1990.
Huber, Konrad. "Giovanni Battista Rubini als Donizetti-Interpret." In *Donizetti in Wien: Kongreßbericht (musikwissenschaftliches Symposion, 17.–18. Oktober 1997)*, edited by Leopold M. Kantner, 114–21. Vienna: Praesens, 1998.
Hügel, Hans-Otto, ed. *Handbuch Populäre Kultur: Begriffe, Theorien und Diskussionen*. Stuttgart: J. B. Metzler, 2003.
Husserl, Edmund. *Die Bernauer Manuskripte über das Zeitbewusstsein (1917/18)*, edited by Rudolf Bernet and Dieter Lohmar. Vol. 33 of *Husserliana: Gesammelte Werke*. Dordrecht: Kluwer Academic, 2001.
Husserl, Edmund. *On the Phenomenology of the Consciousness of Internal Time (1893–1917)*. Translated by John Barnett Brough. Vol. 4 of *Collected Works*, edited by Rudolf Bernet. Dordrecht: Kluwer Academic, 1991.

174 Bibliography

Husserl, Edmund. *Zur Phänomenologie des inneren Zeitbewusstseins (1893–1917)*. Edited by Rudolf Boehm. Vol. 10 of *Husserliana: Gesammelte Werke*. Haag: Martinus Nijhoff, 1966.

Hutcheon, Linda, and Michael Hutcheon. *Opera: Desire, Disease and Death*. Lincoln: University of Nebraska Press, 1996.

Hutcheon, Linda, and Michael Hutcheon. "Staging the Female Body." In Smart, *Siren Songs*, 204–21.

Jacobs, René. "Händel-Aufführung heute: Instrumente und Gesang in Oper und Oratorium." Lecture, "Alte Musik – live" series, Musikinstrumenten-Museum Berlin, 8 June 2008.

Janáček, Leoš. *Jenufa: Její pastorkyňa (Ihre Ziehtochter)*. Translated by Max Brod. Piano score. Vienna: Universal-Edition, 1917.

Kaden, Christian, Jan Brachmann, and Detlef Giese. "Zeichen." In Finscher, *Musik in Geschichte und Gegenwart, Sachteil*, vol. 9, cols. 2149–220.

Kapp, Reinhard. "Noch einmal: Tendenz des Materials." In Reinhard Kapp, *Musik*, 253–81. Notizbuch 5/6. Berlin: Medusa, 1982.

Keller, Wilhelm. "Die Zeit des Bewußtseins." In *Das Zeitproblem im 20. Jahrhundert*, edited by Rudolf W. Meyer, 44–69. Bern: A. Francke, 1964.

Kesting, Jürgen. *Maria Callas*. Düsseldorf: Claassen, 1991.

Kierkegaard, Søren. *Repetition*. In *Repetition and Philosophical Crumbs*, translated by M. G. Piety, 1–81. Oxford: Oxford University Press, 2009.

Kittler, Friedrich, Thomas Macho, and Sigrid Weigel, eds. *Zwischen Rauschen und Offenbarung: Zur Kultur- und Mediengeschichte der Stimme*. Berlin: Akademie, 2002.

Koestenbaum, Wayne. *The Queen's Throat: Opera, Homosexuality, and the Mystery of Desire*. New York: Poseidon, 1993.

Köhler, Sigrid G., Jan Christian Metzler, and Martina Wagner-Egelhaaf, eds. *Prima Materia: Beiträge zur transdisziplinären Materialitätsdebatte*. Königstein im Taunus: Ulrike Helmer, 2004.

Kolesch, Doris. *Roland Barthes*. Frankfurt am Main: Campus, 1997.

Kolesch, Doris. "Die Spur der Stimme." In Epping-Jäger and Linz, *Medien/Stimmen*, 267–81.

Kolesch, Doris. "Stimmlichkeit." In Fischer-Lichte, Kolesch, and Warstat, *Metzler Lexikon Theatertheorie*, 342–45.

König, Ekkehard, and Ulrike Bohle. "Zum Begriff des Performativen in der Sprachwissenschaft." In Fischer-Lichte and Wulf, *Theorien des Performativen*, 13–34.

Konold, Wulf, and Wolfgang Ruf. "Musiktheater." In Finscher, *Musik in Geschichte und Gegenwart, Sachteil*, vol. 6, cols. 1670–714.

Konwitschny, Peter. "Wir bauen die Katastrophen nach." In Beyer, *Warum Oper?*, 21–39.

Krämer, Sybille. "Negative Semiologie der Stimme." In Epping-Jäger and Linz, *Medien/Stimmen*, 65–84.

Krämer, Sybille, and Marco Stahlhut. "Das 'Performative' als Thema der Sprach- und Kulturphilosophie." In Fischer-Lichte and Wulf, *Theorien des Performativen*, 35–64.

Kreuzer, Gundula. "Authentizität, Visualisierung, Bewahrung: Das reisende 'Wagner-Theater' und die Konservierbarkeit von Inszenierungen." In Sollich, Risi, Reus, and Jöris, *Angst vor der Zerstörung*, 139–60.

Kreuzer, Gundula. "Voices from Beyond: Verdi's *Don Carlos* and the Modern Stage." *Cambridge Opera Journal* 18, no. 2 (July 2006): 151–79.

Kreuzer, Gundula. "*Wagner-Dampf*: Steam in *Der Ring des Nibelungen* and Operatic Production." *Opera Quarterly* 27, no. 2–3 (Spring/Summer 2011): 179–219.
Kreuzer, Gundula, and Clemens Risi. "Regietheater in Transition: An Introduction to Barbara Beyer's Interviews with Contemporary Opera Directors." *Opera Quarterly* 27, no. 2–3 (Spring/Summer 2011): 303–6.
Langer, Arne. *Der Regisseur und die Aufzeichnungspraxis der Opernregie im 19. Jahrhundert*. Frankfurt am Main: Peter Lang, 1997.
Langer, Susanne K. *Feeling and Form: A Theory of Art*. New York: Scribner, 1953.
Lehmann, Hans-Thies. "Die Gegenwart des Theaters." In *Transformationen: Theater der neunziger Jahre*, edited by Erika Fischer-Lichte, Doris Kolesch, and Christel Weiler, 13–26. Berlin: Theater der Zeit, 1999.
Lehmann, Hans-Thies. "Die Inszenierung: Probleme ihrer Analyse." *Zeitschrift für Semiotik* 11, no. 1 (1989): 29–49.
Lehmann, Hans-Thies. *Postdramatic Theatre*. Translated by Karen Jürs-Munby. Abingdon: Routledge, 2006.
Lehmann, Hans-Thies. *Postdramatisches Theater*. Frankfurt am Main: Verlag der Autoren, 1999.
Lehmann, Hans-Thies. "Über die Wünschbarkeit einer Kunst des Nichtverstehens." *Merkur*, May 1994, 426–31.
Levin, David J. "*Die Meistersinger von Nürnberg*: Drastisch oder gnostisch?" In Sollich, Risi, Reus, and Jöris, *Angst vor der Zerstörung*, 260–71.
Levin, David J. "The Mise-en-scène of Mediation: Wagner's *Götterdämmerung* (Stuttgart Opera, Peter Konwitchny, 2000–2005)." *Opera Quarterly* 27, no. 2–3 (Spring/Summer 2011): 219–34.
Levin, David J. "Reading a Staging/Staging a Reading." *Cambridge Opera Journal* 9, no. 1 (March 1997): 47–71.
Levin, David J. "Response to James Treadwell." *Cambridge Opera Journal* 10, no. 3 (November 1998): 307–11.
Levin, David J. *Unsettling Opera: Staging Mozart, Wagner, and Zemlinsky*. Chicago: University of Chicago Press, 2007.
Lévi-Strauss, Claude. "The Structural Study of Myth." *Journal of American Folklore* 68 (1955): 428–44.
Liebscher, Julia. "Funktion und Methodik der Bewegungsanalyse im Musiktheater: Achim Freyers *Freischütz*-Inszenierung (1980)." In *Bewegung im Blick: Beiträge zu einer theaterwissenschaftlichen Bewegungsforschung*, edited by Claudia Jeschke and Hans-Peter Bayerdörfer, 30–46. Berlin: Vorwerk, 2000.
Liebscher, Julia. "Schauspieler – Sängerdarsteller: Zur unterschiedlichen Aufführungssituation im Sprech- und Musiktheater, dargestellt am Beispiel der paralinguistischen Zeichen." In Bayerdörfer, *Musiktheater als Herausforderung*, 55–70.
Lichtental, Pietro. "Attore." In *Dizionario e bibliografia della musica*, 2nd ed., vol. 1, 74–75. Milan: Antonio Fontana, 1836.
Lütteken, Laurenz. "Wider den Zeitgeist der Beliebigkeit: Ein Plädoyer für die Freiheit des Textes und die Grenzen der Interpretation." *Wagnerspectrum* 2 (2005): 23–29.
Maehder, Jürgen. "Intellektualisierung des Musiktheaters – Selbstreflexion der Oper." *Neue Zeitschrift für Musik* 140 (1979): 342–49.
McClary, Susan. "Fetisch Stimme: Professionelle Sänger im Italien der frühen Neuzeit." In Kittler, Macho, and Weigel, *Rauschen und Offenbarung*, 199–214.
McClatchy, J. D., trans. *Seven Mozart Librettos*. New York: W. W. Norton, 2011.
Merleau-Ponty, Maurice. *Phenomenology of Perception*. Translated by Donald A. Landes. Abingdon: Routledge, 2012.

Mersch, Dieter. *Ereignis und Aura: Untersuchungen zu einer Ästhetik des Performativen*. Frankfurt am Main: Suhrkamp, 2002.
Morris, Christopher. "Digital Diva: Opera on Video." *Opera Quarterly* 26, no. 1 (Winter 2010): 96–119.
Morris, Christopher. "Wagnervideo." *Opera Quarterly* 27, no. 2–3 (Spring/Summer 2011): 235–55.
Mösch, Stephan. "Geistes Gegenwart? Überlegungen zur Ästhetik des Regietheaters in der Oper." In Mungen, *Mitten im Leben*, 85–103.
Mösch, Stephan. "Störung, Verstörung, Zerstörung: Regietheater als Rezeptionsproblem." In Sollich, Risi, Reus, and Jöris, *Angst vor der Zerstörung*, 216–32.
Motte-Haber, Helga de la. *Handbuch der Musikpsychologie*. 3rd ed. Laaber: Laaber-Verlag, 2002.
Motte-Haber, Helga de la. "Wahrnehmung und ästhetische Erfahrung." *Positionen* 37 (1998): 2–6.
Mozart, Wolfgang Amadeus. *Così fan tutte ossia La scuola degli amanti*, K. 588. Edited by Faye Ferguson and Wolfgang Rehm. Vols. 18.1–2 of *Neue Ausgabe sämtlicher Werke*, ser. 2, *Bühnenwerke*, group 5, *Opern und Singspiele*, Kassel: Bärenreiter, 1991.
Mozart, Wolfgang Amadeus. *Il dissoluto punito ossia il Don Giovanni*, K. 527. Edited by Wolfgang Plath and Wolfgang Rehm. Vol. 17 of *Neue Ausgabe sämtlicher Werke*, ser. 2, *Bühnenwerke*, group 5. *Opern und Singspiele*. Kassel: Bärenreiter, 1968.
Mozart, Wolfgang Amadeus. *Die Entführung aus dem Serail*, K. 384. Edited by Gerhard Croll. Vol. 12 of *Neue Ausgabe sämtlicher Werke*, ser. 2, *Bühnenwerke*, group 5, *Opern und Singspiele*. Kassel: Bärenreiter, 1982.
Mozart, Wolfgang Amadeus. *Le nozze di Figaro*, K. 492. Edited by Ludwig Finscher. Vols. 16.1–2 of *Neue Ausgabe sämtlicher Werke*, ser. 2, *Bühnenwerke*, group 5, *Opern und Singspiele*. Kassel: Bärenreiter, 1982.
Mungen, Anno, ed. *Mitten im Leben: Musiktheater von der Oper zur Everyday Performance*. Würzburg: Königshausen and Neumann, 2011.
Nancy, Jean-Luc. *The Birth to Presence*. Translated by Brian Holmes et al. Stanford: Stanford University Press, 1993.
Neuenfels, Hans. "Zwischen dramaturgischer Innovation und Werktreue: Zur Aktualität und Aktualisierbarkeit der *Aida*." In *Oper heute: Formen der Wirklichkeit im zeitgenössischen Musiktheater*, edited by Otto Kolleritsch, 34–47. Vienna: Universal Edition, 1985.
Nietzsche, Friedrich. *Human, All Too Human II*. Translated by Gary Handwerk. Vol. 4 of *The Complete Works of Friedrich Nietzsche*, edited by Alan D. Schrift and Duncan Large. Stanford: Stanford University Press, 2013.
Nietzsche, Friedrich. *Menschliches, Allzumenschliches 2*. Vol. 3 of *Werke: Kritische Gesamtausgabe*, edited by Giorgio Colli and Mazzino Montinari, part 4. Berlin: Walter de Gruyter, 1967.
Nietzsche, Friedrich. "Ueber den Rhythmus (1875)." In *Gesammelte Werke: Musarionausgabe*, vol. 5, *Vorlesungen: 1872–1876*, 473–76. Munich: Musarion, 1922.
Pavis, Patrice. "Die Inszenierung zwischen Text und Aufführung." *Zeitschrift für Semiotik* 11, no. 1 (1989): 13–27.
Pavis, Patrice. *Semiotik der Theaterrezeption*. Tübingen: Gunter Narr, 1988.
Pavis, Patrice. "Voice." In *Dictionary of the Theatre: Terms, Concepts, and Analysis*, translated by Christine Shantz, 435–36. Toronto: University of Toronto Press, 1998.
Phelan, Peggy. *Unmarked: The Politics of Performance*. Abingdon: Routledge, 1993.

Pochat, Götz. "Erlebniszeit und bildende Kunst." In *Augenblick und Zeitpunkt: Studien zur Zeitstruktur und Zeitmetaphorik in Kunst und Wissenschaften*, edited by Hans Holländer and Christian W. Thomsen, 22–46. Darmstadt: Wissenschaftliche Buchgesellschaft, 1984.

Poizat, Michel. *The Angel's Cry: Beyond the Pleasure Principle in Opera.* Translated by Arthur Denner. Ithaca: Cornell University Press, 1992.

Poizat, Michel. "Das Wagnis der Musik oder 'Wozu Singen?'" In Kittler, Macho, and Weigel, *Rauschen und Offenbarung*, 9–16.

Pöppel, Ernst. "Die Rekonstruktion der Zeit." In *Das Phänomen Zeit in Kunst und Wissenschaft*, edited by Hannelore Paflik, 25–37. Weinheim: VCH, 1987.

Rebstock, Matthias. "Analyse im neuen Musiktheater: Diskussion interdisziplinärer Ansätze." *Diskussion Musikpädagogik* 18 (2003): 26–32.

Reckow, Fritz. "Unendliche Melodie." In *Handwörterbuch der musikalischen Terminologie*, edited by Hans Heinrich Eggebrecht and Albrecht Riethmüller, binder 6. Stuttgart: Franz Steiner, 1972–2005.

Reininghaus, Frieder and Katja Schneider, eds. *Experimentelles Musik- und Tanztheater*. Laaber: Laaber-Verlag, 2004.

Reissinger, Marianne. *Anna Netrebko: Ein Porträt*. Reinbek bei Hamburg: Rowohlt, 2005.

Rienäcker, Gerd. "Begegnungen mit Felsensteins Musiktheater." In Hintze, Risi, and Sollich, *Realistisches Musiktheater*, 35–48.

Rienäcker, Gerd. *Musiktheater im Experiment: Fünfundzwanzig Aufsätze*. Berlin: Lukas, 2004.

Riethmüller, Albrecht. "Interpretation in der Musik." In *Interpretation*, edited by Gerhard Funke, Albrecht Riethmüller, and Otto Zwierlein, 17–30. Stuttgart: Franz Steiner, 1998.

Rishoi, Niel. *Edita Gruberova: Ein Portrait*. Zurich: Atlantis, 1996.

Risi, Clemens. "Am Puls der Sinne: Der Rhythmus einer Opernaufführung zwischen Repräsentation und Präsenz – zu Mozart-Inszenierungen von Calixto Bieito und Thomas Bischoff." In *TheorieTheaterPraxis*, edited by Hajo Kurzenberger and Annemarie Matzke, 117–27. Berlin: Theater der Zeit, 2004.

Risi, Clemens. "Arbeit an der Oper als Arbeit am Mythos: Medea und die Präsenz des Mythos bei Iano Tamar und Maria Callas." In *Medeamorphosen: Die Künste und der Mythos*, edited by Nike Bätzner, Matthias Dreyer, Erika Fischer-Lichte, and Astrid Silvia Schönhagen, 34–43. Munich: Wilhelm Fink, 2010.

Risi, Clemens. "Barockoper heute: Ein Versuch über den Begriff der historisch informierten Aufführungspraxis." In *Musiktheater im Fokus*, edited by Sieghart Döhring and Stefanie Rauch, 387–94. Sinzig: Studiopunkt, 2014.

Risi, Clemens. "Bühne als Labor: Die Bayreuther Festspiele im 21. Jahrhundert." In *Richard Wagner: Persönlichkeit, Werk und Wirkung*, edited by Helmut Loos, 327–34. Markkleeberg: Sax, 2013.

Risi, Clemens. "'Die andere Zeit': Zur Zeiterfahrung und Performativität von Opernaufführungen." In Altenburg and Bayreuther, *Musik und kulturelle Identität*, vol. 3, 463–69.

Risi, Clemens. "Die bewegende Sängerin: Zu stimmlichen und körperlichen Austausch-Prozessen in Opernaufführungen." In *Klang und Bewegung: Beiträge zu einer Grundkonstellation*, edited by Christa Brüstle and Albrecht Riethmüller, 135–43. Aachen: Shaker, 2004.

Risi, Clemens. "David Moss in Salzburg, oder: Die Aufführung als Provokation einer Musiktheaterwissenschaft." In *Strahlkräfte: Festschrift für Erika Fischer-Lichte*, edited by Christel Weiler, Jens Roselt, and Clemens Risi, 54–65. Berlin: Theater der Zeit, 2008.

Risi, Clemens. "Diva Poses by Anna Netrebko: On the Perception of the Extraordinary in the Twenty-First Century." In *Technology and the Diva: Sopranos, Opera and the Media from Romanticism to the Digital Age*, edited by Karen Henson, 150–58. Cambridge: Cambridge University Press, 2016.

Risi, Clemens. "The Diva's Fans: Opera and Bodily Participation." In *On Participation and Synchronisation*, edited by Kai van Eikels, Bettina Brandl-Risi, and Ric Allsopp, 49–54. Special issue, *Performance Research* 16, no. 3 (2011).

Risi, Clemens. "'Gefühlte Zeit': Zur Performativität von Opernaufführungen." In *Möglichkeitsräume: Zur Performativität von sensorischer Wahrnehmung*, edited by Christina Lechtermann, Kirsten Wagner, and Horst Wenzel, 153–62. Berlin: Erich Schmidt, 2007.

Risi, Clemens. "Hören und Gehört werden als körperlicher Akt: Zur feedback-Schleife in der Oper und der Erotik der Sängerstimme." In *Wege der Wahrnehmung: Authentizität, Reflexivität und Aufmerksamkeit im zeitgenössischen Theater*, edited by Erika Fischer-Lichte, Barbara Gronau, Sabine Schouten, and Christel Weiler, 98–113. Berlin: Theater der Zeit, 2006.

Risi, Clemens. "'Keinen Wagner-Kult mehr. Sondern Theater, Theater, Theater': Der Ring des Nibelungen und das Regietheater." In *Von der Zukunft einer unmöglichen Kunst: 21 Perspektiven zum Musiktheater*, edited by Bettina Knauer and Peter Krause, 139–47. Bielefeld: Aisthesis, 2006.

Risi, Clemens. "Koloratur des Wahnsinns – Wahnsinn der Koloratur." In *Genie – Virtuose – Dilettant: Konfigurationen romantischer Schöpfungsästhetik*, edited by Gabriele Brandstetter and Gerhard Neumann, 171–77. Würzburg: Königshausen and Neumann, 2011.

Risi, Clemens. "*Lohengrin* im Klassenzimmer und die Lust der Inszenierung an der Musik." *Rampenlicht: Oper Leipzig* 3/4 (2010): 14–15.

Risi, Clemens. "'Martern aller Arten': Calixto Bieitos Suche nach der Wahrheit des Musiktheaters." In Hintze, Risi, and Sollich, *Realistisches Musiktheater*, 132–47.

Risi, Clemens. "Mozart-Musiktheater: Wege des Performativen." In *Wege zur Klassik*, edited by Dagmar Hoffmann-Axthelm. Special issue, *Basler Jahrbuch für historische Musikpraxis* 30 (2006): 137–48.

Risi, Clemens. "Die neuen *Meistersinger* und die Angst vor der Zerstörung." In Sollich, Risi, Reus, and Jöris, *Angst vor der Zerstörung*, 272–79.

Risi, Clemens. "Opera in Performance: In Search of New Analytical Approaches." *Opera Quarterly* 27, no. 2–3 (Spring/Summer 2011): 283–95.

Risi, Clemens. "Opern-Gesten: Zur Aufführungspraxis der Oper des 19. Jahrhunderts in historischer und aktueller Perspektive." In *Gesten: Inszenierung, Aufführung, Praxis*, edited by Christoph Wulf and Erika Fischer-Lichte, 154–62. Munich: Wilhelm Fink, 2010.

Risi, Clemens. "The Performativity of Operatic Performances as Academic Provocation: Response to David J. Levin." In *Verdi 2001: Atti del Convegno internazionale; Proceedings of the International Conference; Parma – New York – New Haven; 24 January – 1 February 2001*, edited by Fabrizio Della Seta, Roberta Montemorra Marvin, and Marco Marica, vol. 2, 489–96. Florence: Leo S. Olschki, 2003.

Risi, Clemens. "Performing Wagner for the Twenty-First Century." *New Theatre Quarterly* 29, no. 4 (November 2013): 349–59.

Risi, Clemens. "Die Posen der Diva: Inszenierung und Wahrnehmung der Außergewöhnlichen heute: Anna Netrebko 'gegen' Edita Gruberova." In Grotjahn, Schmidt, and Seedorf, *Diva*, 195–206.

Risi, Clemens. "Rhythmen der Aufführung: Rhythmus-Kollisionen bei Steve Reich und Heiner Goebbels." In Fischer-Lichte, Risi, and Roselt, *Kunst der Aufführung*, 165–77.
Risi, Clemens. "Shedding Light on the Audience: Hans Neuenfels and Peter Konwitschny Stage Verdi (and Verdians)." *Cambridge Opera Journal* 14, no. 1–2 (March 2002): 201–10.
Risi, Clemens. "Sinn und Sinnlichkeit in der Oper: Zu Hans Neuenfels' *Idomeneo* an der Deutschen Oper Berlin." *Theater der Zeit* 58, no. 6 (2003): 38–39.
Risi, Clemens. "Die Stimme in der Oper zwischen Mittel des Ausdrucks und leiblicher Affizierung." In *Die Zukunft der Oper: Zwischen Hermeneutik und Performativität*, edited by Barbara Beyer, Susanne Kogler, and Roman Lemberg, 267–75. Berlin: Theater der Zeit, 2014.
Risi, Clemens. "Das Surplus der Performance oder der 'Beziehungszauber' der Aufführung: Dahlhaus' *Figaro*-Analysen im Lichte aktueller Inszenierungen." In *Carl Dahlhaus und die Musikwissenschaft: Werk, Wirkung, Aktualität*, edited by Hermann Danuser, Peter Gülke, and Norbert Miller, 142–47. Schliengen: Argus, 2011.
Risi, Clemens. "Verdi, das Hmtata und der Opernchor bei Hans Neuenfels." In *Chöre und Chorisches Singen: Festschrift für Christoph-Hellmut Mahling zum 75. Geburtstag*, edited by Ursula Kramer, 219–25. Mainz: Are, 2009.
Risi, Clemens. "Verdi und Wagner auf dem Theater." In *Verdi und Wagner: Kulturen der Oper*, edited by Arnold Jacobshagen, 321–34. Cologne: Böhlau, 2014.
Risi, Clemens. "Von (den) Sinnen in der Oper: Überlegungen zur Aufführungsanalyse im Musiktheater." In Balme, Fischer-Lichte, and Grätzel, *Theater als Paradigma der Moderne*, 353–63.
Risi, Clemens. "Wagner and German Regietheater: In Search of New Analytical Approaches." *Wagner Journal* 3, no. 1 (March 2009): 14–19.
Roselt, Jens. "Aufführungsparalyse." In Balme, Fischer-Lichte, and Grätzel, *Theater als Paradigma der Moderne*, 145–53.
Roselt, Jens. "Erfahrung im Verzug." In Fischer-Lichte, Risi, and Roselt, *Kunst der Aufführung*, 27–39.
Roselt, Jens. *Phänomenologie des Theaters*. Munich: Wilhelm Fink, 2008.
Roselt, Jens. "Die Würde des Menschen ist antastbar: Der kreative Umgang mit der Scham." In *Erniedrigung genießen*, edited by Carl Hegemann, 47–59. Berlin: Alexander, 2001.
Roth, Gerhard. *Fühlen, Denken, Handeln: Wie das Gehirn unser Verhalten steuert*. Frankfurt am Main: Suhrkamp, 2001.
Schachtsiek, Mark. "'Missachtung von Form ist Verlust an Sinn': Von Ruth Berghaus' besonderem Umgang mit der Kunstform Oper." In Hintze, Risi, and Sollich, *Realistisches Musiktheater*, 188–202.
Schechner, Richard. "Drama, Script, Theatre, and Performance." *Drama Review* 17, no. 3 (September 1973): 5–36.
Schilling, Gustav. "Acteur." In *Encyclopädie der gesammten musikalischen Wissenschaften, oder Universal-Lexikon der Tonkunst*, edited by Gustav Schilling et al., vol. 1, 47. Stuttgart: Franz Heinrich Köhler, 1835.
Schläder, Jürgen. "'… da der Tod der wahre Endzweck unsers lebens ist …': Theorie-Überlegungen zu Peter Konwitschnys Dekonstruktion der zweiten Ottavio-Arie." In Mungen, *Mitten im Leben*, 119–45.
Schläder, Jürgen. "Kontinuität fragmentarischer Bildwelten: Postmoderne Verfahren im Stuttgarter Ring von 1999/2000." In *OperMachtTheaterBilder: Neue Wirklichkeiten des Regietheaters*, edited by Jürgen Schläder, 191–218. Leipzig: Henschel, 2006.

Schläder, Jürgen. "Musikalisches Theater." In *Theaterwissenschaft heute: Eine Einführung*, edited by Renate Möhrmann, 129–48. Berlin: Dietrich Reimer, 1990.
Schläder, Jürgen. "Strategien der Opern-Bilder: Überlegungen zur Typologie der Klassikerinszenierungen im musikalischen Theater." In Früchtl and Zimmermann, *Ästhetik der Inszenierung*, 183–97.
Schläder, Jürgen. "Über die Veränderung in den Köpfen: Gedanken zur Werktreue in der Oper." *Neue Zeitschrift für Musik* 153, no. 5 (1992): 12–19.
Schouten, Sabine. *Sinnliches Spüren: Wahrnehmung und Erzeugung von Atmosphären im Theater*. Berlin: Theater der Zeit, 2007.
Schrödl, Jenny. *Vokale Intensitäten: Zur Ästhetik der Stimme im postdramatischen Theater*. Bielefeld: Transcript, 2012.
Seel, Martin. *Aesthetics of Appearing*. Translated by John Farrell. Stanford: Stanford University Press, 2005.
Seel, Martin. *Ästhetik des Erscheinens*. Munich: Carl Hanser, 2000.
Seel, Martin. "Ereignis: Eine kleine Phänomenologie." In *Ereignis: Eine fundamentale Kategorie der Zeiterfahrung; Anspruch und Aporien*, edited by Nikolaus Müller-Schöll, 37–47. Bielefeld: Transcript, 2003.
Seidel, Wilhelm. "Rhythmus, Metrum, Takt." In Finscher, *Musik in Geschichte und Gegenwart, Sachteil*, vol. 8, cols. 257–317.
Singer, Wolf. "Das Bild in uns – Vom Bild zur Wahrnehmung." In *Iconic Turn: Die neue Macht der Bilder*, edited by Christa Maar and Hubert Burda, 56–76. Cologne: DuMont, 2005.
Smart, Mary Ann. *Mimomania: Music and Gesture in Nineteenth-Century Opera*. Berkeley: University of California Press, 2004.
Smart, Mary Ann. "Resisting Rossini or Marlon Brando Plays Figaro." *Opera Quarterly* 27, no. 2–3 (Spring/Summer 2011): 153–78.
Smart, Mary Ann, ed. *Siren Songs: Representation of Gender and Sexuality in Opera*. Princeton: Princeton University Press, 2000.
Sollich, Robert. "Staging Wagner – and Its History: Die Meistersinger von Nürnberg on a Contemporary Stage." *Wagner Journal* 3, no. 1 (March 2009): 5–13.
Sollich, Robert. "Die verkehrte Welt ist die bessere Welt: Peter Konwitschnys Musiktheater zwischen den Traditionen." In Hintze, Risi, and Sollich, *Realistisches Musiktheater*, 203–21.
Sollich, Robert, Clemens Risi, Sebastian Reus, and Stephan Jöris, eds. *Angst vor der Zerstörung: Der Meister Künste zwischen Archiv und Erneuerung*. Berlin: Theater der Zeit, 2008.
Sommer, Carlo Michael. "Stars als Mittel der Identitätskonstruktion: Überlegungen zum Phänomen des Star-Kults aus sozialpsychologischer Sicht." In Faulstich and Korte, *Der Star*, 114–24.
Sontag, Susan. "Against Interpretation." In *Essays of the 1960s and 70s*, edited by David Rieff, 10–20. New York: Library of America, 2013.
Spitzer, Manfred. *Musik im Kopf: Hören, Musizieren, Verstehen, Erleben im neuronalen Netzwerk*. Stuttgart: Schattauer, 2002.
Steinbeck, Dietrich. "Die Oper als theatralische Form: Notizen und Anmerkungen zu einer Theorie." *Musikforschung* 20 (1967): 252–62.
Strauss, Johann. *Die Fledermaus: Operette in 3 Akten*, RV 503. Libretto by Richard Genée. Edited by Michael Rot. Vol. 3 of *Neue Johann Strauss Gesamtausgabe*, ser. 1, group 2. Vienna: Strauss Edition, 1999.
Stravinsky, Igor. *Poetics of Music in the Form of Six Lessons*. Translated by Arthur Knodel and Ingolf Dahl. Cambridge: Harvard University Press, 1970.

Sulzer, Johann Georg. *Allgemeine Theorie der Schönen Künste*. 2nd ed., vol. 4. Leipzig: Weidmannsche Buchhandlung, 1794.
Szpunar, Karl K., Jason M. Watson, and Kathleen B. McDermott. "Neural Substrates of Envisioning the Future." *PNAS* 104, no. 2 (9 January 2007): 642–47.
Thiele, Jens. "Künstlerisch-mediale Zeichen der Starinszenierung." In Faulstich and Korte, *Der Star*, 136–45.
Treadwell, James. "Reading and Staging Again." *Cambridge Opera Journal* 10, no. 2 (July 1998): 205–20.
Ullrich, Wolfgang. "'Die Kunst ist Ausdruck ihrer Zeit': Genese und Problematik eines Topos der Kunsttheorie." In Sollich, Risi, Reus, and Jöris, *Angst vor der Zerstörung*, 233–46.
Verdi, Giuseppe. *Un ballo in maschera: Melodramma in tre atti*. Libretto by Antonio Somma. Score. New rev. ed. Milan: Ricordi, 1973.
Verdi, Giuseppe. *Don Carlos (Don Carlo)*. Edited by Hans Swarowsky. Piano score with German and Italian text, versions in four and five acts. Milan: Ricordi, 1967.
Verdi, Giuseppe. *Don Carlos*. Edited by Ursula Günther and Luciano Petazzoni. Complete edition of the different versions in five and four acts, reduced vocal and piano score. Milan: Ricordi, 1980.
Verdi, Giuseppe. *Nabucodonosor*. Edited by Roger Parker. Vol. 3 of *The Works of Giuseppe Verdi*, edited by Philip Gossett, Julian Budden, Martin Chusid, Francesco Degrada, Ursula Günther, Giorgio Pestelli, Pierluigi Petrobelli, and Gabriele Dotto, ser. 1, *Operas*. Chicago: University of Chicago Press; Milan: Ricordi, 1987.
Verdi, Giuseppe. *Il trovatore*. Orchestral score. New rev. ed. Milan: Ricordi, 1955.
Wagner, Richard. *Lohengrin*, WWV 75. Edited by John Deathridge and Klaus Döge. Vol. 7.1 of *Sämtliche Werke*. Mainz: Schott, 1996.
Wagner, Richard. *Lohengrin: Romantische Oper in drei Aufzügen*. Translated by H. Corder and F. Corder. Leipzig: Breitkopf and Härtel, 1906.
Wagner, Richard. *Sämtliche Werke*. Edited by Carl Dahlhaus, Egon Voss, Christa Jost, Peter Jost, and Reinhard Kapp. Mainz: Schott, 1970–.
Wagner, Richard. "Szenische Vorschriften für die Aufführung des *Lohengrin* in Weimar 1850." In *Sämtliche Schriften und Dichtungen*, vol. 16, 63–73. Leipzig: Breitkopf and Härtel, 1914.
Wagner, Richard. *Tristan und Isolde*, WWV 90. Edited by Isolde Vetter and Egon Voss. Vol. 8.2 of *Sämtliche Werke*. Mainz: Schott, 1992.
Wagner, Richard. *Die Walküre*, WWV 86B. Edited by Christa Jost. Vol. 11.1 of *Sämtliche Werke*. Mainz: Schott, 2002.
Waldenfels, Bernhard. "Das Lautwerden der Stimme." In *Stimme: Annäherung an ein Phänomen*, edited by Doris Kolesch and Sybille Krämer, 191–210. Frankfurt am Main: Suhrkamp, 2006.
Waldenfels, Bernhard. *Das leibliche Selbst: Vorlesungen zur Phänomenologie des Leibes*. Frankfurt am Main: Suhrkamp, 2000.
Waldenfels, Bernhard. "Responsivität des Leibes: Spuren des Anderen in Merleau-Pontys Leib-Denken." In *Merleau-Ponty und die Kulturwissenschaft*, edited by Regula Giuliani, 305–20. Munich: Wilhelm Fink, 2000.
Waldenfels, Bernhard. "Responsivity of the Body: Traces of the Other in Merleau-Ponty's Theory of Body and Flesh." In *Interrogating Ethics: Embodying the Good in Merleau-Ponty*, edited by James Hatley, Janice McLane, and Christian Diehm, 91–106. Pittsburgh: Duquesne University Press, 2006.
Waldenfels, Bernhard. *Sinnesschwellen*. Frankfurt am Main: Suhrkamp, 1999.

Waldenfels, Bernhard. "Stimme am Leitfaden des Leibes." In Epping-Jäger and Linz, *Medien/Stimmen*, 19–35.

Weaver, William, trans. *Seven Verdi Librettos*. New York: W. W. Norton, 1975.

Weber, Horst, ed. *Oper und Werktreue*. Stuttgart: J. B. Metzler, 1994.

Weber, Horst. "Vom 'treulos treuesten Freund': Eine Einführung in das produktive Dilemma des Regietheaters." In Weber, *Oper und Werktreue*, 1–16.

Weber-Lucks, Theda. "Vokale Performancekunst: Zur Verknüpfung von Stimme, Körper, Emotion – Meredith Monk und Diamanda Galas." *Positionen: Beiträge zur Neuen Musik* 40 (1999): 28–32.

Weigel, Sigrid. "Die Stimme der Toten: Schnittpunkte zwischen Mythos, Literatur und Kulturwissenschaft." In Kittler, Macho, and Weigel, *Rauschen und Offenbarung*, 73–92.

Weingarten, Michael. *Wahrnehmen*. Bielefeld: Aisthesis, 1999.

Wellmer, Albrecht. "Werke und ihre Wirkungen: Kein Beitrag zur Rezeptionstheorie des Musiktheaters." In *Zukunftsbilder: Richard Wagners Revolution und ihre Folgen in Kunst und Politik*, edited by Hermann Danuser and Herfried Münkler, 257–73. Schliengen: Argus, 2002.

Wieler, Jossi, and Sergio Morabito. "Es gibt keine richtige Interpretation." In Beyer, *Warum Oper?*, 59–80.

Wiesmann, Sigrid, ed. *Werk und Wiedergabe: Musiktheater exemplarisch interpretiert*. Bayreuth: Mühl'scher Universitätsverlag Bayreuth Werner Fehr, 1980.

You, Haili. "Defining Rhythm: Aspects of an Anthropology of Rhythm." *Culture, Medicine and Psychiatry* 18 (1994): 361–84.

Zumthor, Paul. "Body and Performance." In Gumbrecht and Pfeiffer, *Materialities of Communication*, 217–26.

Zumthor, Paul. "Körper und Performanz." In Gumbrecht and Pfeiffer, *Materialität der Kommunikation*, 703–13.

Index

Page numbers in *italic* indicate figures; Page numbers followed by n indicate chapter notes.

Abbate, Carolyn 8, 32, 47, 62
Adorno, Theodor W. 38
Aida (Giuseppe Verdi) 90
Alcina (Georg Friedrich Händel) 114
Alden, David 16n36
Altmeyer, Jeannine 95, 128, *129*
Ariadne auf Naxos (Richard Strauss) 115
Arthaus 3
Ästhetik des Performativen (The Transformative Power of Performance) (Erika Fischer-Lichte) 50–51, 53–54
audience: behavior 157; bodily responsivity 38; consciousness 111; expectations 34, 111; interaction with performers 4, 9, 30–31, 51, 150; interaction with singers 110, 122, 148; sensory perception 39
auditory and visual elements, interaction of 63–64, 71–87
Auslander, Philip 148–149
Austin, J. L., 54–55, 58n19
autodeixis 8
autopoietic feedback loop 40, 51, 149

Bad (Michael Jackson) 153
Baier, Gerold 139, 147n40
Barthes, Roland 46, 119–122, 124n35
Bartoli, Cecilia 13, 120, 122, 159
Bartz, Bettina 98
Bataille, Georges 119, 121
Baumgarten, Sebastian 5, 12, 79–80, *80*, 134, 162
Bayreuther Festspiele 5, 13, *80*, 95, *105–107*, 109n39, 114, 128, *129*, *130*
Beckenbauer, Franz 151
Beczala, Piotr 94

Behne, Klaus-Ernst 64–65
Beineix, Jean-Jacques 120, 158–159
Bengtsson, Maria 1, *2*, 13, 21, *28*, 37, 39, 46, 90
Bensch, Georg 61
Berghaus, Ruth 5
Bergson, Henri 125–126
Beyer, Barbara 5, 33–34
Bieito, Calixto 1, *2*, 10–12, 21, 25, *25*, 28, *28*, 71, 83–84, 90, 140, *140*, 141, 143
Bischoff, Thomas 12, 140–141, 162
Blond Ambition World Tour (Madonna) 153
Blumenberg, Hans 35
body in opera performance 110–122
Bohle, Ulrike 55–56
Bohlin, Ingela 86
Bolton, Thaddeus L., 138
Brandl-Risi, Bettina 16n37, 109n19
Brandstätter, Ursula 65
Braunmüller, Robert 8
Breker, Arno 106
Bronfen, Elisabeth 161n30
Brüstle, Christa 42n54
Bülow, Hans von 31–32
Butler, Judith 38, 54–55

Calico, Joy 8
Callas, Maria 152
Cambreling, Sylvain 86
Campana, Alessandra 161n32
canonization 14n12
Carsen, Robert 114
Catalani, Alfredo 158
Centre de musique baroque de Versailles 6

characterization 3, 8, 44–45, 56–57, 93, 98, 115, 127–128, 137, 160n24
Chéreau, Patrice 5, 12, 95, 128–129, *129*
Cherubini, Luigi 12, 117
Christie, William 114
chronometric time 125
Clark, Graham 95
Clarke, Paul Charles 134, 136
Cleveman, Lars *80*
Comparato, Marina 86
contestations 71–87
Cook, Nicholas 38
Così fan tutte (Wolfgang Amadeus Mozart) 86
Couldry, Nick 150
crosstalk effect 64–65
culture as text 43, 50

Dahlhaus, Carl 71–72, 87, 88n11
Danuser, Hermann 29–31, 38
Da Ponte, Lorenzo 87
Decker, Willy 152
de la Motte-Haber, Helga 64–65
Deleuze, Gilles 157, 159
de Niese, Danielle 114
Der Ring des Nibelungen (Richard Wagner) 4
Dessay, Natalie 114, 158–159
Deutsche Oper Berlin 13, *91*, *97*, 100, *102*, *103*, 117, *118*, 132, *133*, 134, *136*, 143, *144*
DeVol, Luana 77, *78*, 96, 100, *101*
Dewey, John 139, 141
Die Entführung aus dem Serail (Wolfgang Amadeus Mozart) 1, *2*, 10–11, 21, 25–28, *26–28*, 39, 40, 71, 83–84, 89n35, 90
Die Fledermaus (Johann Strauss) 2–4, *3*, 14n10, *22–24*, 44, 48, 90
Die Meistersinger von Nürnberg (Richard Wagner) 8, 47, 90, 104–108, *105–107*, 108n10
Diener, Melanie 131, *132*
Die Walküre (Richard Wagner) 128–129, *129*
Diva (Jean-Jacques Beineix) 120, 158
Dohmen, Albert 101
Dolak, Gregor 153
Don Carlo/Don Carlos (Giuseppe Verdi) *81*, 81–82, 92, *92*, 114
Don Giovanni (Wolfgang Amadeus Mozart) 8, 25, *25*, 71, 86, 97–98, 119, 140, 143
Donizetti, Gaetano 12, 111, 116, 149, *151*, 158

dramaturgy *81*, 86, 88n11, *92*, 99, 138; film 136; musical 7–8, 10, 71, 131; opera 136; silent-film 136

Eggebrecht, Hans Heinrich 38
Elena da Feltre (Saverio Mercadante) 113
Elias, Norbert 126
Emrich, Hinderk 65
Engel, Johann Jakob 113
Engelke, Anke 151
eroticism 119–122, 123n21, 152
Evans, Anne 95
eventness of performance 9, 45, 50, 162–163
exclusivity 116–117

Fassbaender, Brigitte 3, 21
felt air temperature 125
Ferretti, Luigi 113
film dramaturgy 136
Fischer-Lichte, Erika 31–33, 40, 43, 50–54, 61
flash mobs 154–156, *156*
Flaubert, Gustave 116
Friedrich, Götz 5, 95
Frith, Simon 159

Gallese, Vittorio 62
Galou, Delphine *7*
gender performance 55
gender theory 54
Gerhard, Anselm 32–33
Gerhartz, Leo Karl 90
gestalt perception 66, 71; theory of 63
gestalt psychology 63, 143
gesture 6, 15n20, 38, 43, 55, 57, 76, 94–96, 101, 105, 107, 128, 136, 138, 141, 149; and vocal production, relationship between 110–115
Giulio Cesare (Georg Friedrich Händel) 114
Glyndebourne Festival 114
Goebbels, Heiner 139, 163
Götterdämmerung (Richard Wagner) 95–96
Gottschewski, Hermann 30
Gran Teatre del Liceu, Barcelona *76*, *78*, *101*, 150
Gruberová, Edita 13, 115–116, 122, 149–150, *150*, *151*
Gumbrecht, Hans Ulrich 47, 146n34, 162–163
Gürbaca, Tatjana 16n36
Guth, Claus 12, 72, *75*, 87

Index   185

Händel, Georg Friedrich 6, 7, 12, 114
Händel-Festspiele Karlsruhe 7
Harnoncourt, Nikolaus 72
Hartmann, Will 133, *136*
Hawkins, Gordon 101
Hawlata, Franz 104, *105–107*, 106
Hegel, Georg Wilhelm Friedrich 31
Heidenreich, Alexander 91, 93, 96, *97*
Helbling, Hanno 139
Hellekant, Charlotte 135–136
Hengelbrock, Thomas 79
Hepburn, Audrey 152
Heppner, Ben 47
Herheim, Stefan 16n36
Herrmann, Karl-Ernst 12, 117, *118*
Herrmann, Max 50, 61–62
Herrmann, Ursel 12, 117, *118*
Herz, Joachim 5
Hinrichsen, Hans-Joachim 31–32
Hintze, Werner 78, 98
Hofmann, Peter 95, 128, *129*
Holten, Kasper 12, 80, 100, 102, *103*
Homer 121
Hügel, Hans-Otto 154
Husserl, Edmund 60, 63, 126–127
Hutcheon, Linda 8
Hutcheon, Michael 8

Idomeneo (Wolfgang Amadeus Mozart) 143–144, *144*
Il trovatore (Giuseppe Verdi) *82*, 82–83, 90
incommunicability 121–122
intermodal integration 65–66, 71, 78, 105, 137, 142; theory of 63
intermodal qualities 64
interpretation 21–40; material 37–40; in musicology 28–32; opera in performance and concept of the work 32–34; opera in performance, as work on myth 34–36
intimacy 116, 148, 153
Iven, Christiane 141–142

Jackson, Michael 153
Jacobs, René 6, 98
Janáček, Leoš 12, 131–132, *135*
Jansen, Berit Barfred 7
Jenůfa (Leoš Janáček) 132–134, *133*, *136*
Jerusalem, Siegfried 128, *130*
Jones, Chris 159
jouissance 119

Kastón, Motti *81*, *92*
Katja Kabanowa (Leoš Janáček) 131, *132*, 134

Kaune, Michaela 132, *136*
Keller, Wilhelm 127–129, 134, 136
Kennedy, Jackie 152
Kerr, Alfred 125
Ketelsen, Hans-Joachim *75*
Kienberger, Jürg 85
Kierkegaard, Søren 157
Klangforum Wien 86
Koestenbaum, Wayne 61–62, 118–119, 121
Kolesch, Doris 123n11, 124n25, 124n35
Komische Oper Berlin 1, *2*, 13, *28*, 39, 88n3, 97, 109n28
König, Ekkehard 55–56
Konwitschny, Peter 8, 12, 33, 72–74, *75*, 76, *76*, 77, *78*, 95–101, *101*
Kovalik, Balázs 12, *82*, 83
Kowzan, Tadeusz 43
Krämer, Sybille 46, 57–58
Kravchuk, Alla 141
Kreuzer, Gundula 8
Kristeva, Julia 46
Kupfer, Harry 5, 95
Kuzmenko, Vladimir *81*

La Bohème (Giacomo Puccini) 153, 154, 157
La bohème im Hochhaus 154
Larmore, Jennifer 132–134, *133*, *136*
Larsen, Jens 1, *2*
La traviata (Giuseppe Verdi) 119, 131, 134, 152, *155*, 157
La Wally (Alfredo Catalani) 158
Lehmann, Hans-Thies 8, 45, 126
Le nozze di Figaro (Wolfgang Amadeus Mozart) 71, 72, *73–75*, *85*, 85–86, 87, 140
Les Ballets C de la B 86
Levin, David J. 8, 109n41
Lévi-Strauss, Claude 35
Lichtenthal, Pietro 112
liminal experience 39, 83, 121, 157
Lohengrin (Richard Wagner) 73–78, *75*, 76, *78*, 99–104, *101–103*
Loy, Christof 12, *133*, 134, *136*
Lucia di Lammermoor (Gaetano Donizetti) 111, 116, 158
Lucrezia Borgia (Gaetano Donizetti) 149–150, *150*, *151*

Macbeth (Giuseppe Verdi) 90–91
Madame Bovary (Gustave Flaubert) 116
Madonna 153–154, 160n24
Magee, Emily 76, *76*, *101*, 140, *140*, 141

186 *Index*

Marthaler, Christoph 6, 12, *85*
Marton, Eva *75*, 100
Massenet, Jules 12, 134
material, concept of 37–40
McGurk effect 65
McVicar, David 114
Médée (Luigi Cherubini) 117–118, *118*
Meier, Waltraud 128, *130*
Merbeth, Ricarda 102, *102*
Mercadante, Saverio 113
Mersch, Dieter 52
Metropolitan Opera, New York 47
Meyer, Leonard B. 63
Minkowski, Marc 2
Monadnock Music Festival 40n8, 88n1
Monroe, Marilyn 152, 160n24
Montero, José *25*, 141
Morabito, Sergio 12, 34, 81, *81*, *92*, 94–95, 114
Morris, Christopher 8, 157, 161n32
Mortier, Gérard 3, 6
Mösch, Stephan 8, 12, 96
Moser, Thomas *75*
Moss, David 3, *3*, 4, 13, 21, 37, 43–44, 46, 48, 90
Mozart, Wolfgang Amadeus 1, 5, 10–12, 21, 25, 39, 71, 72, *73*, 83, 85–87, 97, 119, 140, 143
Müller, Heiner 12, 113–114, 128, *130*, 146n13
Museum of Modern Art (MoMa) 161n27
musical dramaturgy 7–8, 71, 131
music as performance 9, 34, 38
musicology 8–9, 12, 34, 38; interpretation in 28–32
Mussbach, Peter 12, 64, 131, 134
myth 34–37, 42n44

Nabucco (Giuseppe Verdi) 91, *92*, 96–97, *97*
Naglestad, Catherine 114
National Socialism 106, 107
Netrebko, Anna 13, 150–154, 161n30
Neuenfels, Hans 1–2, *3*, 5, 10, 12, 14n10, 44, 48, 90–91, *91*, 93–94, 96, *97*, 143–144, *144*
Neves, Juliana 86
Neves, Susan 91, *91*, 96, *97*
Nielsen, Inga *75*
Nietzsche, Friedrich 46, 127, 137

Oberto (Giuseppe Verdi) 112, *112*, 113
objective time 126
Odyssey (Homer) 121

Opéra Bastille 158
opera dramaturgy 136
opera fan 148–149, 158–159, 159n3
opera in performance 54–58; and concept of the work 32–34; distribution of 148–159; mediated experience of 148–159; voice and body in 110–122; as work on myth 34–36
operatic performance practices 5–7
operatic repertoire 4, 10, 14n10, 33, 41n34
Oper Leipzig 99
Opernhaus Zürich 115, 157

Pannen, Stefan *150*
pantomimic intelligibility principle 72
Parodi, Giovanni Battista *112*
pasticcio 6
Paterson, Vincent 153
Pavis, Patrice 45, 141–142
PepsiCo Summerfare 40n8, 88n1
perceived time 125
perception theory 9, 60–66, 71, 105
performance: definition of 51, 60; distinguished from staging 52–53; as "drastic knowledge" 47–48; as event 9, 53; music as 9, 34, 38; opera in *see* opera in performance; representation and presence, interplay of 90–108; theory 9, 13, 30, 40, 50–54, 56–57, 60, 148
performative, theories of the 9, 13, 51, 54–58
Petrenko, Kirill 1
Phänomenologie des Theaters (Jens Roselt) 51–52, 60
Phelan, Peggy 148
phenomenology 9, 12, 52, 58, 60–63, 83, 115–116, 126, 138
Pier'Alli, Pierluigi 112, *112*
Platel, Alain 6, 86
Plato 137, 138
Pochat, Götz 63
Poizat, Michel 119, 161n39
Polaski, Deborah 95
Pöppel, Ernst 145n3, 145n9
popular listening 154
presence and representation in performance, interplay of 46–48, 90–108
protention 63, 83, 93, 114, 116, 120, 126–128, 130–132, 137–138, 146n34
"psychic time of presence" (*psychische Präsenzzeit*) 126
Puccini, Giacomo 12, 153–154

Index   187

Radamisto (Georg Friedrich Händel) 6, 7
Regietheater (director's theater) 4, 6–8, 10, 12, 14n11, 31, 71, 90, 94, 105
repetition 35, 37, 53–58, 92, 120, 142, 146n34, 157–159, 161n39, 162
representation and presence in performance, interplay of 46–48, 90–108
retention 63, 80, 116, 126–128, 130, 132, 134, 137–138, 146n34
rhythms of opera performance 9, 12, 25, 45, 60, 81–82, 86–87, 91–93, 137–145
Riefenstahl, Leni 106
Riemann, Hugo 32
Rienäcker, Gerd 8
Riethmüller, Albrecht 16n25, 16n37, 40n1
Rizzolatti, Giacomo 62
Rizzo, Pietro 93
Roselt, Jens 50–53, 60–61, 83
Rossini, Gioachino 62
Rubini, Giovanni Battista 62
Rügamer, Stephen *132*
Ruhrtriennale 6

Salzburg Festival 13, 72, 75, *85*, 152
Sandhovel, Roland 159
Sassu, Francesca *112*
Scaini, Francesca 25, 140, *140*
scenic concept 88n11
Schachtsiek, Mark 8
Schavernoch, Hans 95
Scheidegger, Hans-Peter 141
Schäfer, Christine 131
Schläder, Jürgen 8, 12, 41n12, 109n32
Schnaut, Gabriele 100
Schouten, Sabine 16n37, 147n37
Schrödl, Jenny 123n11
Seel, Martin 52–53
segmentation 43–44
Seidel, Wilhelm 146n24, 146n26, 146n29, 146n30, 146n32
Sellars, Peter 25, 71
semiotics 43–48
senses, entanglement of the 60–66
silent-film dramaturgy 136
Singer, Wolf 65
Smart, Mary Ann 8
Sollich, Robert 8, 104
Sontag, Susan 45–46
Spahn, Claus 85
speech acts 54, 56, 58n19
speechlessness 122
Spitzer, Manfred 146n31, 146n33, 147n41

Staatsoper Berlin Unter den Linden 13, 64, 131, *132*
Staatsoper Hamburg 13, 75
Staatsoper Hannover 13, 25, 84, 140, *140*
Staatsoper Stuttgart 13, *81*, 92
Staatstheater Karlsruhe 7
Staatstheater Nürnberg 13, 82, *82*
Stadttheater Bern 154
staging : definition of 52; distinguished from performance 52–53
Stahlhut, Marco 57–58
Strauss, Johann 2, 12, 14n10, 21, *22–24*
Strauss, Richard 115
Stravinsky, Igor 139
subjective time 125–126
subject–object dichotomy, dissolution of 60–61, 118–119, 122
Sulzer, Johann Georg 138
Sunset Boulevard (Billy Wilder) 118
Swanson, Gloria 118
symbioses 71–87
synchronization 65, 71, 78

Tamar, Iano 117–118, *118*
Tancredi (Gioachino Rossini) 62
Tannhäuser (Richard Wagner) 79, 79–81, *80*, 95, 119, 162
Tcherniakov, Dmitri 16n36
Teatro Verdi Busseto *112*
temporality 9, 12, 36, 54, 120, 126, 137, 145
text–performance relationship 9
Thalheimer, Michael 12, 131, *132*, 134
theater as laboratory 163
theater as museum 163–164
theater as text 45, 50
T'Hooft, Sigrid 6–7
time of opera performance: chronometric 125; compression 126, 128–130; dilation 126–127, 130; objective 126; "other" 125–137; perceived 125; signature 129, 137, 146n25, 147n36; subjective 125
Tomlinson, John 95
transgression 57, 121, 128
Tristan und Isolde (Richard Wagner) 114, 127–130, *130*

Ullrich, Wolfgang 31
Un ballo in maschera (Giuseppe Verdi) 94–95

Valayre, Sylvie 93, 109n27
van Lieshout, Joep 79, 162

Index

Vanmaeckelberghe, Kurt 86
Vaughn, Tichina 92, *92*
Verdi Festival, Parma/Busseto 112
Verdi, Giuseppe 5, 10–12, 39, 81–82, 90–94, 112, 114, 119, 131, 152, *155*
Vienna Festival 40n8, 88n1
vocal expression 46, 55, 115
vocal production and gestures, relationship between 110–115
Vogt, Klaus Florian 101–104, *103*
voice in opera performance 110–122
von Weber, Carl Maria 79

Wagner, Katharina 12, 104, *105–107*, 108n10
Wagner, Richard 5, 10, 12, 39, 73–74, 77, 79, 90, 95, 99–100, 104, 108, 108n10, 119, 127, 162
Wagner, Wieland 4, 95
Wagner, Wolfgang 95
Waldenfels, Bernhard 64, 115, 138, 157
Warns, Guntbert *2*, *28*
Weber, Horst 14n14, 108n9, 108n13
Weigle, Sebastian 104
Weisser, Johannes 97–98
Wellmer, Albrecht 32–33

Werktreue (faithfulness to a work) 6–7, 12, 32–33, 44
Werther (Jules Massenet) 134–136
Wiegand, Karsten 12
Wieler, Jossi 12, 34, 81, *81*, *92*, 94–95, 114
Wilder, Billy 118
Wilson, Robert 113
Wischmann, Claus *150*
Wolf oder wie Mozart auf den Hund kam (Alain Platel) 86
Wonder, Erich 128
Wördehoff, Thomas 123n13
work, concept of the 32–34
Workman, Charles 143, *144*
Wundt, Wilhelm 138

Yamamoto, Yohji 128
You, Haili 146n34

Zagrosek, Lothar 81–82
Zalasinski, Mikolaj *82*
Zamojska, Aleksandra 86
Zumthor, Paul 46, 56–57
Zwarg, Oliver 141–142

Printed in the United States
by Baker & Taylor Publisher Services